The Complete Book of Potatoes

The Complete Book of Potatoes

WHAT EVERY GROWER AND GARDENER NEEDS TO KNOW

Hielke De Jong
Joseph B. Sieczka
Walter De Jong

TIMBER PRESS
Portland · London

Published in 2011 by Timber Press, Inc.

The Haseltine Building
133 S.W. Second Avenue, Suite 450
Portland, Oregon 97204-3527
www.timberpress.com

2 The Quadrant
135 Salusbury Road
London NW6 6RJ
www.timberpress.co.uk

Printed in China

Library of Congress Cataloging-in-Publication Data

De Jong, Hielke, 1933–
   The complete book of potatoes: What every grower and
gardener needs to know/Hielke De Jong, Joseph B. Sieczka, and
Walter De Jong.—1st ed.
      p. cm.
   Includes bibliographical references and index.
   ISBN-13: 978-0-88192-999-7
   1. Potatoes. 2. Potatoes—North America. I. Sieczka, Joseph B.
II. De Jong, Walter. III. Title.
   SB211.P8D426 2011
   635'.21—dc22   2010034076

Contents

Color plates pages 33–48 and 145–176.

Acknowledgments

The writing of this book has been an exciting venture for us. The completion would not have been possible without the help of many colleagues and friends.

Most tuber samples were provided by the Cornell-Uihlein Farm, Lake Placid, New York. Additional tuber samples were provided by Agnes Murphy and Jane Percy of the Potato Research Centre, Fredericton, New Brunswick; Charles Brown, U.S. Department of Agriculture, Prosser, Washington; Eugenia Banks and Sam Squire, Ontario Ministry of Agriculture, Food and Rural Affairs; David Holm, Colorado State University; William Campbell, Alaska Plant Materials Center, Palmer, Alaska; Jim Gerritsen, Wood Prairie Farm, Bridgewater, Maine; and Craig Rockey, Ronniger Potato Farm, Austin, Colorado. A special thanks to Craig Rockey for arranging to hand dig our samples.

The lion's share of the photography was done by Kent Loeffler, Cornell University, who photographed all of the cultivar tubers. Other photographs were taken by the authors unless otherwise stated in the captions. Jeanne

Debons, Bend, Oregon, very generously prepared several drawings specifically for this book.

Invaluable library services were kindly provided by André Gionet, Potato Research Centre, Fredericton, New Brunswick, and Sheridan Alder, Southern Crop Protection and Research Centre, Vineland Station, Ontario.

Dave McManus kindly provided us with the appropriate addresses of the area offices of the Canadian Food Inspection Agency.

We are indebted to Carol MacNeil for her thorough and comprehensive review of the entire manuscript. In addition John Bamberg, Charles Brown, Margery Daughtrey, Richard Tarn, Ward Tingey, and Thomas Zitter provided us with many helpful suggestions on portions of the manuscript.

Thanks to the editorial and technical staff of Timber Press for their assistance.

Last, but not least, we thank our respective families for their understanding, encouragement, patience, and suggestions in the time-consuming (but very enjoyable) task of preparing this book.

Figure 1. Inca potato god, holding the power over the health of potatoes. In his/her right hand is a sick potato plant; in his/her left, a healthy plant. © International Potato Center.

Introduction

WELCOME TO THE WONDERFUL WORLD of the potato! It is truly amazing how this underground vegetable has had such a rich, profound impact on societies and how it has moved throughout the world. In this book we provide information about the plant, its origin, its versatility in food and nonfood uses, descriptions of popular cultivars (varieties), conventional and organic production techniques, pest management, and storage practices.

The potato was first domesticated in the area around Lake Titicaca, which is located 12,500 ft. (3800 m) above sea level at the border of modern-day Bolivia and Peru, in the Andes mountain range of South America. It was a major food source for various civilizations that preceded, and included, the Inca Empire. For these people potatoes provided sustenance throughout the year. Before refrigeration and long-distance transportation, Andean natives developed chuño, a freeze-dried product that allowed potatoes to be consumed long after harvest and in seasons when yields were poor.

Potatoes were so important to the survival of these early people, as well as to many other societies since, that they became part of the culture. Ancient pottery and tapestry demonstrate the influence that potatoes had on their lives. In the Andean highlands the potato even took on a spiritual significance (Figure 1). In today's societies many expressions of potato-people relationships can still be found, in monuments, songs, books, museums, postage stamps, and so forth.

European explorers came to the Americas to conquer new lands and send back riches. Perhaps the most remarkable treasure they brought home was the potato. It took some time before Europeans determined just how useful and nutritious potatoes could be, but once they did, potatoes rapidly became an important culinary staple. By the late eighteenth century potatoes were the mainstay of the Irish diet, so important that to this day they are referred to as "Irish potatoes." An unfortunate consequence of being dependent on a single crop is that if there is a shortage, people go hungry or starve. That is exactly what happened when late blight, caused by the fungal pathogen *Phytophthora infestans*, devastated potatoes in the mid-nineteenth century. The resulting Irish potato famine led many people to migrate to North America.

Within just a few hundred years of its discovery by Western explorers, the potato was being produced in almost every nation on earth, and increased adoption of potatoes continues to this very day (Figure 2). Until the early 1990s, most potatoes were grown and consumed in Europe, North America, and countries of the former Soviet Union. Since then, there has been a dramatic increase in potato production and demand in Asia, Africa, and Latin America. The output in these areas rose from less than 30 million tons in the early 1960s to more than 167 million tons in 2008, with China and India now accounting for almost a third of all potato production. Potato follows rice and wheat in world *food* crop production and is therefore a major component of the world's overall food supply.

One reason potatoes are so popular throughout the world is because they can be grown under a wide range of environmental conditions. While potato is considered a cool-season, short-day plant, cultivars have been developed that are well adapted to warm growing conditions and long days. The vast gene pool also provides potato breeders the resources to incorporate characteristics such as pest resistance, frost hardiness, high starch content, increased nutrients, and local adaptation into new cultivars. To accomplish this breeders use germplasm from a diverse array of wild and cultivated potato species distributed across South and North America. The process is a long one, taking approximately twelve years from the time a cross is made until a cultivar is available for commercial planting. To be a potato breeder one needs patience, a long-term perspective, and a great deal of optimism.

New potato cultivars are constantly being developed to meet the needs of different environments and uses of the crop. The primary use is consumption by humans but potato is also used as animal feed and in industrial applications. Potatoes are increasingly consumed as processed forms, such as frozen french fries, potato chips, and dehydrated products. Global consumption of processed potatoes is estimated to be greater than 50 percent of the annual harvest. Fresh (not processed when purchased) potatoes are used in a wide variety of ways, including stand-alone baked or boiled, as well as in casseroles, salads, and a large number of other dishes. Industrial applications include use of starch in producing adhesives, binders, and textural agents, and in manufacturing of biodegradable replacements for plastic products like disposable cutlery.

High nutritional value is another reason why potatoes are grown so widely. The potato is an excellent source of fiber, vitamin C, potassium, and numerous micronutrients. While the protein level on a fresh weight basis is relatively low, the protein quality is high. On a dry weight basis the protein level

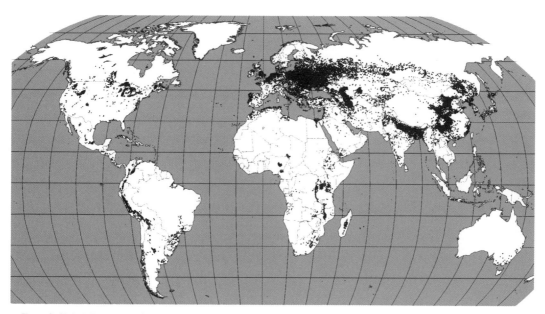

Figure 2. Global distribution of potato cultivation. © International Potato Center.

is similar to cereal grains. Potatoes are fat-free and cholesterol-free. It is no wonder, considering the potato's great versatility and nutritive value, that in history it has often become the "Bread of the Poor." Potatoes produce a large amount of food on relatively small areas of land. Small plots of potatoes sustained many Irish in the nineteenth century, and do the same for many families of the former Soviet Union today.

Potato tubers come in many shapes and colors. Common shapes include round, oval, oblong, long, and cylindrical. Cross-sectional shape varies from round to somewhat flattened. Common skin colors are white, russet, red, and yellow. Potatoes also can have purple skin and combinations of all the listed colors. Internal colors can be solid or mottled white, yellow, red, or purple. Culinary qualities vary from those that are suited for french fries or chips to those suited for cooking at home.

In this book we provide general guidelines about how to best grow potatoes, using either conventional or organic practices. This is a major challenge considering the geographic and climatic differences of the United States and Canada alone. Fortunately detailed recommendations for specific locations are available in various state and provincial extension publications. Extension offices are located in most counties in the United States and in each Canadian province. The role of extension is to provide research-based information to those living in their respective regions. County and provincial extension offices are typically affiliated with state or provincial agricultural universities. The information in this book is intended to provide a foundation for home gardeners and small-scale producers; local extension offices can help tailor it, if necessary.

 **CHAPTER 1**

Plant Structure and Function

A POTATO PLANT (Figure 3) consists of one or more stems that have grown from a seed tuber or seed piece. Tubers themselves are underground stems and are formed on stolons (rhizomes), not roots. After supplying the energy for the plant to emerge, the seed piece normally disintegrates. Since seed pieces usually have more than one eye, a potato plant can have several main stems, each of which arises from an eye on the main tuber. In addition, a potato plant generally has several lateral stems which develop from buds on the aboveground stems. A temperature between 68 and 77°F (20–25°C) is generally considered optimum for vine growth. The potato plant is susceptible to water stress; optimum yield requires a relatively constant supply of water. During periods of drought the stomates (pores) in the leaves close; this in turn reduces photosynthesis, and therefore yield.

Growth Type

Potato cultivars can differ considerably in plant type. Determinate types (plants that stop producing new growth after tuber initiation) tend to be rather short with fewer flower clusters and earlier maturity than indeterminate types, while indeterminate cultivars (plants that continue producing new growth indefinitely) require a longer growing season and therefore have the potential to produce a higher yield than determinate ones. The difference between the two types is not always clear-cut, and some cultivars fall into intermediate

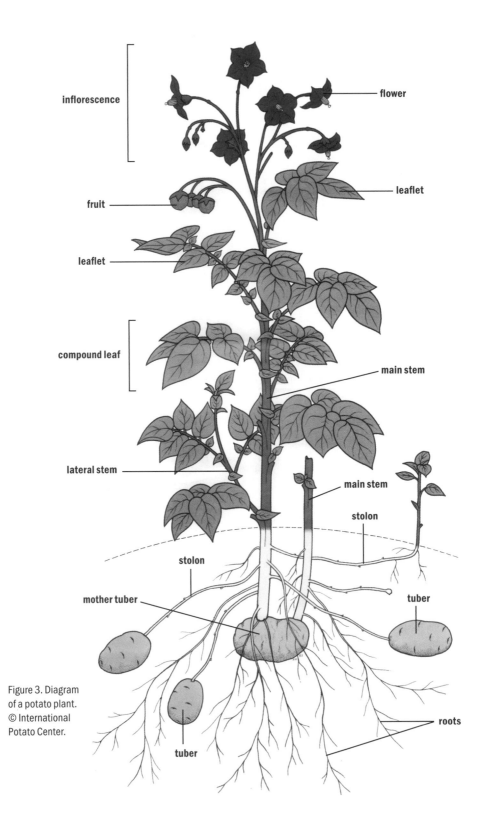

inflorescence

flower

fruit

leaflet

leaflet

compound leaf

main stem

lateral stem

main stem

stolon

stolon

mother tuber

tuber

roots

Figure 3. Diagram
of a potato plant.
© International
Potato Center.

tuber

categories. Examples of determinate cultivars are 'Caribe' and 'Norland'. 'Russet Burbank' is an example of an indeterminate cultivar.

Leaf

The potato leaf is compound (Figure 4) and consists of a petiole (the part of the midrib below the point of attachment of the lowest pair of primary leaflets), a midrib, a terminal leaflet, and several pairs of primary leaflets which are interspersed with secondary and sometimes tertiary leaflets. The silhouette of the leaves, the leaflets' size and shape, color, and hairiness, as well as the shape of the terminal leaflet are all useful in classifying potatoes and identifying cultivars. Like the eyes on a tuber, leaves are arranged in a spiral pattern on the stem. About 40 days after the leaves appear, their photosynthetic capacity declines considerably. This means that to get maximum growth of

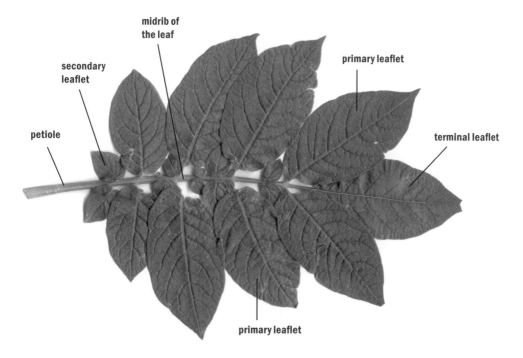

Figure 4. Compound potato leaf.

the plant older leaves have to be replaced by new ones. High temperatures, drought, and nutrient deficiencies accelerate leaf aging. This can be a serious problem in cultivars with a determinate growth habit; such cultivars often do not recover from exposure to severe stress.

Flower, Fruit, and Seeds

Potato flowers are bisexual: they have both female (pistil) and male (stamen) organs. The color of the corolla can be white, red, blue, or purple and can exhibit different color patterns (Plate 1). In nature potatoes are pollinated by insects, especially bumblebees. Since potato flowers generally do not produce nectar, the insects only visit them for their pollen. Male sterile cultivars do not produce pollen and are therefore avoided by pollinators.

Some potato cultivars will produce small green tomato-like fruits in addition to tubers (Plate 2). These fruits typically contain 25 to 200 seeds each. When mature, such fruits can be harvested, and their seed extracted. When stored in a dry cool place these seeds can maintain viability for ten years or more. In subsequent years such seeds can be used to grow potatoes from true seed (see chapter 8). However, such seeds will not result in the same cultivar from which they came. In genetic terms the potato is highly heterozygous which means that each such botanical ("true") seed is different, even if it was derived from the same fruit. The situation can be compared with human children; with the exception of identical twins, all brothers and sisters are different from each other.

Critical Day Length

After several centuries of selection (see chapter 12 for a detailed explanation) we now have cultivars that are able to produce tubers under the relatively long days of the Northern Hemisphere. In spite of this monumental achievement, there still remain differences in the effect of day length among North American and European cultivars. In general, short-day conditions favor early tuber formation. Under short days plants tend to remain relatively small, have relatively short stolons, and produce tubers rather early. Under long-day conditions potato plants grow taller and produce tubers later in the season.

The day length which determines whether or not a specific cultivar forms tubers is called the "critical day length." Different cultivars have different critical day lengths (CDL). Only when the day length is shorter than the CDL for a particular cultivar will that cultivar initiate and form tubers. The CDL of late-maturing cultivars is generally shorter than that of the early-maturing ones.

Differences in CDL also have implications for the international movement of potato germplasm. Cultivars that are late maturing in North America become early or medium maturing in regions closer to the equator and may therefore prove acceptable, while early maturing North American cultivars are generally not well adapted to short-day conditions of the tropics because they mature too early to produce much of a crop. Late-maturing cultivars from short-day regions are not suitable for use in areas with long days because they mature too late.

Contrary to some people's belief, tuber formation is not dependent upon flowering. Potato plants can form tubers without any flowers ever appearing on the vines. The misconception that tuber formation depends on flowering arose because unfavorable climatic growing conditions (such as hot and dry), which are normally unfavorable for flowering, also retard or even inhibit tuber formation. Because climatic conditions that favor flowering also favor tuber formation, it seems natural to make the mistake of associating flowering with high yields and poor flowering with low yields.

Tuber

Potato rhizomes (in most potato references, including this book, rhizomes are referred to as stolons) are underground stems that grow horizontally. Tubers are formed by the swelling of the terminal end of stolons (Plate 87). Not all stolons will form tubers. Stolon tips not covered by soil develop into vertical stems with normal foliage. Tuber formation is basically the result of translocation and storage of excess food and is dependent upon several genetic and environmental factors. We have already discussed the effect of day length. Temperature is another major factor.

A relatively cool night temperature between 55 and 65°F (13–18°C) is optimal for the translocation process. At higher night temperatures the carbohydrates produced in the leaves during the day tend to be used by the plant to support more vine growth rather than tuber growth. In well-adapted cultivars and under optimum growing conditions tuber initiation usually occurs when the plants are 6–8 in. (15–20 cm) high, or from five to seven weeks after planting. While the tubers are developing it is very important that adequate soil moisture levels are maintained. Severe moisture stress during the early stages of tuber formation may result in some previously initiated small tubers being reabsorbed by the stolons.

External Characteristics

Depending upon the cultivar, tuber shape can vary from very long fingerling types to round. All tubers, even round ones, have two ends: the heel, or stem end, where the tuber is attached to the stolon, and the apical, rose, or seed end. The eyes are located in the axils of scalelike leaves or "eyebrows." Morphologically the eyes correspond to the nodes of stems. Each eye contains several buds. Tuber lenticels correspond to the stomates of leaves and stems. It is through the lenticels that tubers "breathe." During prolonged wet periods the soil may become waterlogged. Under those conditions there is much less oxygen available. This in turn causes the lenticels to open and enlarge to the point where they become quite prominent.

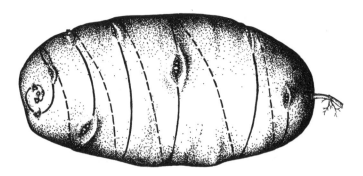

Figure 5. Spiral arrangement of the eyes. © Jeanne Debons.

Just like on aboveground stems, the eyes (buds) of the potato are arranged in a spiral fashion (Figure 5). They tend to be concentrated at the seed, or apical, end of the tuber. They are fewer in number and farther apart toward the stem end where the tuber is attached to the stolon.

The eyes of the seed (apical) end possess apical dominance and will normally sprout first, a condition characteristic of buds at or near the apex of stems in most plants. When the apical buds are removed, or die, other buds are stimulated to sprout in the same manner as lateral buds on a woody stem are stimulated to sprout when the leader is removed. The degree of apical dominance is a function of the physiological age of the tuber. As physiological age progresses, apical dominance is reduced and eventually eliminated.

The lower part of the sprout produces stolons and roots while the upper part develops into a stem (Plate 3). When sprouts are developed under certain conditions of light, temperature, and humidity, they display several cultivar-specific traits (Plate 4).

Internal Characteristics

In a cross section of a tuber (Figure 6) the following components can be seen, starting at the outside: skin (consisting of the epidermis and the periderm), cortex, vascular ring, and the medullar area (outer and inner medulla). The outer medulla, also called storage parenchyma, is the principal storage tissue

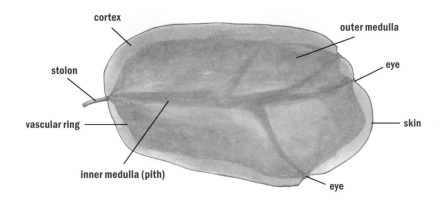

Figure 6. Internal view of the tuber. © Jeanne Debons.

of the tuber. It contains a relatively higher percentage of dry matter (primarily starch) than the pith. The inner medulla, or pith, extends toward each eye, forming a continuous tissue that connects all the eyes of the tuber. The epidermis, which is a single layer of cells, is usually colorless. Anthocyanin, the pigment that colors red and blue potatoes, if present, is in the periderm (several layers of corky cells immediately below the epidermis). 'Norland' is an example of a cultivar which has (red) pigment in the periderm. In some cultivars the pigment extends into the cortex and in extreme cases (such as 'Adirondack Blue' and 'Purple Majesty') the pigment extends throughout the entire tuber.

Dormancy

Immediately after harvest, potato tubers are in a rest period and are said to be dormant. Actually tuber buds are already in a rest period when the tubers are still growing. The length of the dormancy period (after harvest) depends on several factors, especially cultivar and storage temperature. The previous season's growing conditions also have an effect on the dormancy period but that is something over which growers have little or no control.

In chapter 12 we discuss the primitive cultivated species *Solanum phureja*, which has virtually no dormancy at all. Over the centuries this species has been selected for its ability to be planted immediately after harvest, thus allowing multiple crops per year. In the Northern Hemisphere where potatoes must be stored for several winter months, cultivars have been selected for a relatively long dormancy period. The length of the genetically controlled dormancy in North American cultivars can range from six weeks to more than three months. Most cultivars have a medium dormancy. Examples of short dormancy cultivars are 'Adirondack Blue' (very short), 'CalWhite', 'Irish Cobbler', and 'Superior'. Some long dormancy cultivars include 'Canela Russet', 'Island Sunshine', and 'Russet Burbank'.

The optimum temperature for storing seed potatoes is about 40°F (4°C). Storage at higher temperatures tends to shorten the dormancy period and speeds up the physiological aging process. For further discussion of physiological age see chapter 4.

 **CHAPTER 2**

Cultivar Descriptions A to Z

A CULTIVAR IS A CULTIVATED plant that has been selected and given a name because of its useful characteristics. The word is a contraction of the term *cultivated variety* and in a general sense it is synonymous with variety. Cultivars differ significantly from each other in many traits including adaptability, maturity, yielding ability, dormancy, pest resistance, appearance, tuber shape, skin and flesh color, and culinary qualities. The 2009–10 *World Catalogue of Potato Varieties* (Hils and Pieterse 2009) lists over forty-five hundred cultivars that are being grown in more than a hundred countries.

In this book we have included cultivars which we consider to be of most interest to North American home gardeners. This choice is by no means based on exact science; several compromises had to be made in the inclusion and exclusion of specific cultivars. The list and descriptions that follow include representative cultivars across the spectrum of many of the above-mentioned traits. Other factors considered include relative popularity in specific regions of North America as well as the availability of certified seed potatoes of specific cultivars.

White skin, white flesh

'Andover'	'Eramosa'	'Kennebec'	'Sebago'
'Atlantic'	'Green Mountain'	'King Harry'	'Shepody'
'Bake-King'	'Irish Cobbler'	'La Chipper'	'Superior'
'CalWhite'	'Katahdin'	'Reba'	'Warba'
'Catalina'			

Yellow to white skin, yellow flesh

'Banana'	'Island Sunshine'	'Rose Finn Apple'
'Bintje'	'Keuka Gold'	'Yellow Finn'
'Carola'	'La Ratte'	'Yukon Gold'
'German Butterball'	'Ozette'	

Red skin, white flesh

'Chieftain'	'Red Norland'	'Sangre'
'Red La Soda'	'Red Pontiac'	'Viking'

Red skin, yellow flesh

'Cecile'	'French Fingerling'
'Désirée'	'Romanze'

Red skin, red or pink flesh

'Adirondack Red'	'Mountain Rose'	'Red Thumb'
'All Red'	'Papa Cacho'	

Purple or blue skin, white flesh

'Caribe'	'Purple Viking'

Purple or blue skin, purple or blue flesh

'Adirondack Blue'	'Purple Majesty
'All Blue'	'Purple Peruvian'

Russet skin, white flesh

'Canela Russet'	'Ranger Russet'	'Russet Burbank'
'Goldrush'	'Rio Grande Russet'	'Russet Norkotah'

Fingerling

'Austrian Crescent'	'French Fingerling'	'Purple Peruvian'
'Banana'	'La Ratte'	'Red Thumb'
'Cecile'	'Papa Cacho'	'Rose Finn Apple'

Very early

'Eramosa'   'Warba'

Early

'Caribe'   'Red Norland'
'Irish Cobbler'   'Superior'

Long dormancy

'Canela Russet'   'Russet Burbank'
'Island Sunshine'

True Potato Seed (TPS)

'Catalina'

"Low carb"

'Chieftain'   'Red Norland'   'Russet Norkotah'
'Eramosa'   'Red Pontiac'   'Warba'
'Red La Soda'

The environment in which a cultivar is grown can have a considerable effect on some traits. For example, cultivars such as 'Atlantic' and 'Keuka Gold' do well in northeastern North America but often develop internal necrosis (unsightly brown tissue in tuber flesh) in the warmer soils of the South. The intensity of tuber skin and flesh color is also affected by environmental conditions. Some cultivars, including 'Russet Burbank' and 'Rose Finn Apple', are susceptible to second growth (knobbiness) when the environmental conditions are variable (this can occur if there are extremes in moisture and temperature).

Due to the variability in geographic adaptation of potato cultivars and personal preferences of growers, we suggest that beginning potato growers try several cultivars to determine the most suitable ones. Selecting cultivars with different maturities will provide early season and storage options. In the northern United States and Canada the growing season is considerably shorter than in more southern areas. Thus some late-maturing cultivars may not be suitable for the more northern areas. However, this does not necessarily mean that late-maturing cultivars are better suited for the southern United States. For example, in Florida late-maturing cultivars generally suffer from an increase in diseases and insects in the hot summer weather. Several provinces and states have issued extension publications with cultivar recommendations specific for their regions.

Each plant entry in this chapter begins with a brief description of the physical characteristics of the tuber, including shape and size, depth of eyes, and color and texture of skin and flesh. Other specific categories in which the cultivars differ from each other are as follows.

YIELD refers to a mature plant's potential to produce tubers and is ranked from low to high as follows:

Low yield	less than 1 lb. (0.5 kg) per plant
Medium yield	1–3 lbs. (0.5–1.4 kg) per plant
High yield	3–4 lbs. (1.4–1.8 kg) per plant

VINE MATURITY indicates when in the season mature tubers are ready for harvesting:

Very early	70–80 days from planting
Early	90 days from planting
Early main season	100–110 days from planting
Main season	120 days from planting
Late main season	130 days from planting
Late	140 days from planting
Very late	150 or more days from planting

DRY MATTER CONTENT is the amount of solid material (mostly starch) left in a tuber after the water content is removed:

Low dry matter	firm when boiled, moist when baked
Medium dry matter	moderately firm when boiled, moderately moist when baked

High dry matter   mealy and dry when baked, breaks apart when
                      boiled

TEXTURE AFTER COOKING, CULINARY CHARACTERISTICS, and
STORABILITY are self-explanatory, as is the **COMMENTS** category.

TUBER DORMANCY refers to the length of time during which harvested
tubers are at rest and therefore produce no sprouts even under favorable
conditions:

Short dormancy   4–6 weeks
Medium   6–8 weeks
Medium long   2–3 months
Long   3 months or longer

SEED AVAILABILITY indicates how hard or easy it is to find the named
cultivar.

Limited   not likely available from local garden centers,
                     available from mail-order sources and likely to be
                     sold out quickly
Home garden sources may be carried at local garden centers, available
                     from mail-order sources
Commercial   should be widely available at local garden centers
                     and from mail-order sources

'Adirondack Blue'

Plates 5 and 6

DESCRIPTION: Tubers are oblong with intermediate to shallow eyes, blue skin,
and blue flesh.

YIELD: Medium high.

VINE MATURITY: Main season.

DRY MATTER CONTENT: Low.

TEXTURE AFTER COOKING: Firm, moist.

CULINARY CHARACTERISTICS: Good for roasting, steaming, brightly colored salads, and blue chips (but not from cold storage). Moist when baked. Color may leach out during boiling but not if microwaved, baked, or fried.

COMMENTS: Developed in New York. High in antioxidants.

TUBER DORMANCY: Short.

STORABILITY: Moderate.

SEED AVAILABILITY: Very limited.

'Adirondack Red'

Plates 7 and 8

DESCRIPTION: Tubers are oblong with shallow eyes, red skin, and red flesh.

YIELD: Medium high.

VINE MATURITY: Main season.

DRY MATTER CONTENT: Low.

TEXTURE AFTER COOKING: Firm, moist.

CULINARY CHARACTERISTICS: Good for microwaving and frying. Moist when baked. Color may leach out during boiling, but not if microwaved, baked, roasted, or fried.

COMMENTS: Developed in New York. High in antioxidants.

TUBER DORMANCY: Medium.

STORABILITY: Good.

SEED AVAILABILITY: Very limited.

'All Blue'

Plates 9 and 10

DESCRIPTION: Tubers are medium-sized, oblong, and slightly irregularly shaped with moderately deep eyes, blue skin, and blue flesh.

YIELD: Medium.

VINE MATURITY: Late.

DRY MATTER CONTENT: Low to medium.

TEXTURE AFTER COOKING: Moderately mealy.

CULINARY CHARACTERISTICS: Excellent for microwaving, brightly colored salads, and blue chips. Moist when baked. Color may leach out during boiling, but not if microwaved, baked, roasted, or fried.

COMMENTS: Heirloom cultivar. High in antioxidants. This popular blue-fleshed cultivar has more synonyms than any other potato cultivar. Confirmed or purported synonyms include 'Black Russian', 'Blue Congo', 'Blue Marker', 'British Columbia Blue', 'Congo', 'Congo Blue', 'Davis Purple', 'Eureka Purple', 'Fenton Blue', 'Himalayan Black', 'McIntosh Black', 'Nova Scotia Blue', 'Purple Congo', 'Purple Mountain', 'River John Blue', 'Sharon's Blue', and 'Shaw #7'. Additional confusion is caused by the existence in Europe of two different cultivars with the name of "Congo" (homonyms).

TUBER DORMANCY: Medium long.

STORABILITY: Good.

SEED AVAILABILITY: Carried by many home garden seed potato sources.

'All Red'

Plates 11 and 12

DESCRIPTION: Tubers are round with red skin and pink flesh.

YIELD: Medium.

VINE MATURITY: Late main season.

DRY MATTER CONTENT: Low.

TEXTURE AFTER COOKING: Firm, moist.

CULINARY CHARACTERISTICS: Suitable for salads and sautéing. Color may leach out during boiling but not if microwaved, baked, or fried.

COMMENTS: Developed by Robert Lobitz of Paynesville, Minnesota. Released through Seed Savers Exchange in 1984. High in antioxidants. A popular cultivar with organic potato growers in the northeastern United States. Moderately resistant to common scab and drought. 'Cranberry Red' is a synonym.

TUBER DORMANCY: Medium.

STORABILITY: Good.

SEED AVAILABILITY: Carried by many home garden seed potato sources.

'Andover'

Plate 13

DESCRIPTION: Tubers are round with shallow eyes, a slightly flaky buff skin, and white flesh.

YIELD: Medium high.

VINE MATURITY: Early main season.

DRY MATTER CONTENT: Medium high.

TEXTURE AFTER COOKING: Mealy.

CULINARY CHARACTERISTICS: Good for boiling, baking, and chipping. Mealy when baked.

COMMENTS: Developed in New York as a dual purpose chip and table cultivar. It has a very rapid emergence and early tuber set. Favorite eating potato of the Cornell University potato breeding staff. Tolerant to common scab.

TUBER DORMANCY: Medium long.

STORABILITY: Good.

SEED AVAILABILITY: Commercial cultivar.

'Atlantic'

Plate 14

DESCRIPTION: Tubers are round with shallow lateral and deep apical eyes, a lightly netted to heavily scaled buff skin, and white flesh.

YIELD: Medium to high.

VINE MATURITY: Main season.

DRY MATTER CONTENT: Very high.

TEXTURE AFTER COOKING: Mealy.

CULINARY CHARACTERISTICS: Good for chips and baking. Tends to break apart (slough) when boiled.

COMMENTS: Developed as a chip cultivar by the U.S. Department of Agriculture in Beltsville, Maryland. Grows well in an unusually wide range of environments. Susceptible to internal heat necrosis, particularly when grown in sandy soils in warm, dry seasons. Tolerant to common scab.

TUBER DORMANCY: Medium.

STORABILITY: Good.

SEED AVAILABILITY: Commercial cultivar.

'Austrian Crescent'

Plates 15 and 16

DESCRIPTION: Fingerling type tubers are curved with yellow-tan skin and light yellow flesh.

YIELD: Medium.

VINE MATURITY: Late main season.

DRY MATTER CONTENT: Medium.

TEXTURE AFTER COOKING: Firm, waxy.

CULINARY CHARACTERISTICS: Suitable for boiling, steaming, roasting, and salads.

COMMENTS: Popular heirloom cultivar, possibly of European origin. May be synonymous with 'Kifli' and 'Kipfel' (European baking terms referring to crescent-type cookies). Moderately resistant to common scab.

TUBER DORMANCY: Medium.

STORABILITY: Good.

SEED AVAILABILITY: Carried by many home garden seed potato sources.

'Bake-King'

Plate 17

DESCRIPTION: Tubers are round to oblong with shallow eyes, white skin, and white flesh.

YIELD: Medium high.

VINE MATURITY: Main season.

DRY MATTER CONTENT: High.

TEXTURE AFTER COOKING: Very mealy.

CULINARY CHARACTERISTICS: Excellent for baking. Breaks apart (severe sloughing) after boiling. Not suitable for chips.

COMMENTS: Developed in New York. Susceptible to common scab and *Verticillium* wilt. 'Russet Bake-King' is a selection with the same culinary qualities but with a moderately russeted skin.

TUBER DORMANCY: Medium.

STORABILITY: Good.

SEED AVAILABILITY: Limited.

'Banana'

Plates 18 and 19

DESCRIPTION: Fingerling type tubers have light yellow skin and pale yellow flesh.

YIELD: Medium low.

VINE MATURITY: Late.

DRY MATTER CONTENT: Medium.

TEXTURE AFTER COOKING: Firm, semi-mealy.

CULINARY CHARACTERISTICS: Excellent for salads; can also be used for baking, boiling, and roasting. Holds well together when boiled.

COMMENTS: Heirloom cultivar. Probably the most popular fingerling cultivar. Has been grown in British Columbia for nearly a century where it may have been introduced to the early settlers by Russian fur traders. Produces many (12 to 20) small banana-shaped tubers per plant, so recommended in-row spacing is 12–16 in. (30–40 cm) apart. Moderately resistant to common scab. Very similar (and in at least some cases we have observed, identical) to 'La Ratte'. Synonyms include 'Banana Fingerling' and 'Russian Banana'.

TUBER DORMANCY: Medium.

STORABILITY: Good.

SEED AVAILABILITY: Carried by many home garden seed potato sources.

'Bintje'

Plates 20 and 21

DESCRIPTION: Tubers are long-oval with shallow eyes, yellow skin, and light yellow flesh.

YIELD: High.

VINE MATURITY: Late main season.

DRY MATTER CONTENT: Medium.

TEXTURE AFTER COOKING: Fairly firm to mealy.

CULINARY CHARACTERISTICS: Good for boiling, baking, and french fries.

COMMENTS: A Dutch cultivar released in 1910. The breeder was a school teacher who named his cultivars after students in his class. One of these students was a girl named "Bintje." Very well adapted to growing under different environmental conditions. One of the most widely grown cultivars around the world. Produces many tubers, so recommended in-row spacing is 16–18 in. (40–46 cm) apart. Susceptible to common scab.

TUBER DORMANCY: Medium.

STORABILITY: Good.

SEED AVAILABILITY: Commercial cultivar; also carried by several home garden seed potato sources.

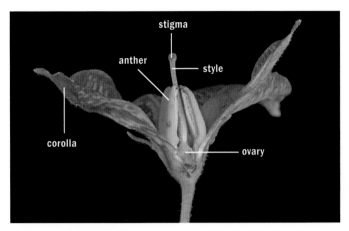

Plate 1. Dissected potato flower.

Plate 2. Potato fruits and seeds.

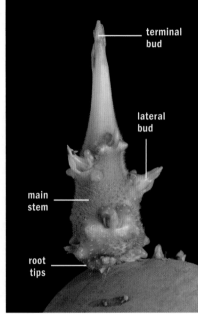

Plate 3. Potato sprout.

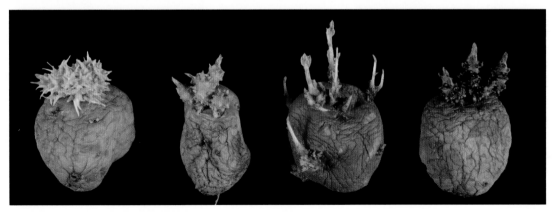

Plate 4. Sprout color and growth habit are important tools in cultivar identification.

Plate 5. 'Adirondack Blue'

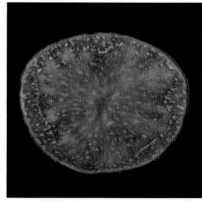

Plate 6. 'Adirondack Blue' flesh

Plate 7. 'Adirondack Red'

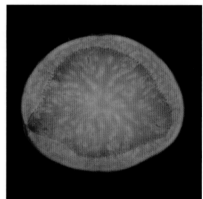

Plate 8. 'Adirondack Red' flesh

Plate 9. 'All Blue'

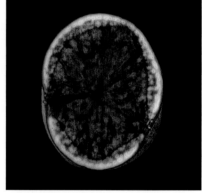

Plate 10. 'All Blue' flesh

Plate 11. 'All Red'

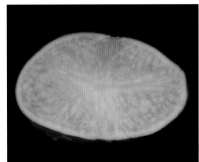

Plate 12. 'All Red' flesh

Plate 13. 'Andover'

Plate 14. 'Atlantic'

Plate 15. 'Austrian Crescent'

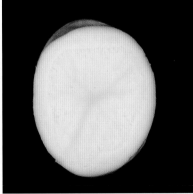

Plate 16. 'Austrian Crescent' flesh

Plate 17. 'Bake-King'

Plate 18. 'Banana'

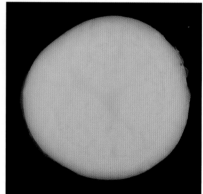

Plate 19. 'Banana' flesh

Plate 20. 'Bintje'

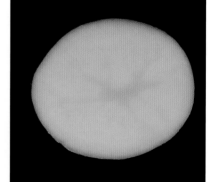

Plate 21. 'Bintje' flesh

Plate 22. 'CalWhite'

Plate 23. 'Canela Russet'

Plate 24. 'Caribe'

Plate 25. 'Carola'

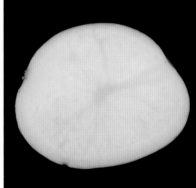

Plate 26. 'Carola' flesh

Plate 27. 'Catalina'

Plate 28. 'Cecile'

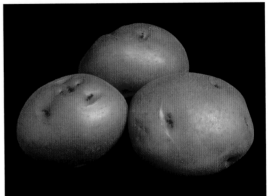

Plate 29. 'Chieftain'

Plate 30. 'Désirée'

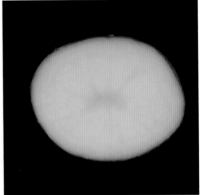

Plate 31. 'Désirée' flesh

Plate 32. 'Eramosa'

Plate 33. 'French Fingerling'

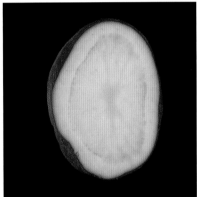

Plate 34. 'French Fingerling' flesh

Plate 35. 'German Butterball'

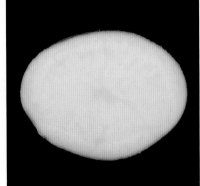

Plate 36. 'German Butterball' flesh

Plate 37. 'Goldrush'

Plate 38. 'Green Mountain'

Plate 39. 'Irish Cobbler'

Plate 40. 'Island Sunshine'

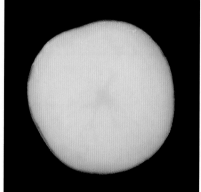

Plate 41. 'Island Sunshine' flesh

Plate 42. 'Katahdin'

Plate 43. 'Kennebec'

Plate 44. 'Keuka Gold'

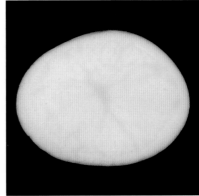

Plate 45. 'Keuka Gold' flesh

Plate 46. 'King Harry'

Plate 47. 'La Chipper'

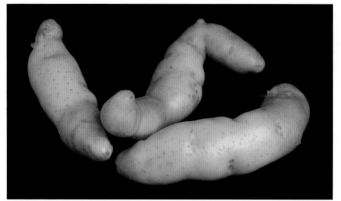

Plate 48. [Plate 52]. 'La Ratte'

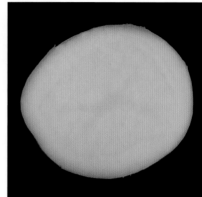

Plate 49. 'La Ratte' flesh

Plate 50. 'Mountain Rose'

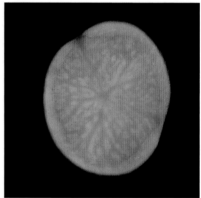

Plate 51. 'Mountain Rose' flesh

Plate 52. 'Ozette'

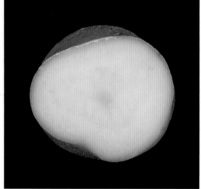

Plate 53. 'Ozette' flesh

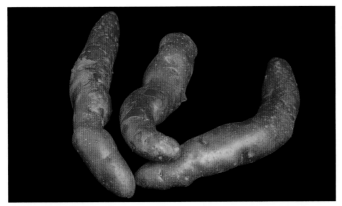

Plate 54. 'Papa Cacho'

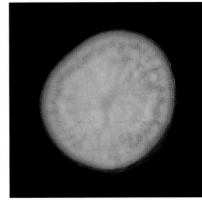

Plate 55. 'Papa Cacho' flesh

Plate 56. 'Purple Majesty

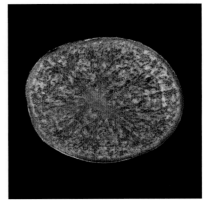

Plate 57. 'Purple Majesty' flesh

Plate 58. 'Purple Peruvian'

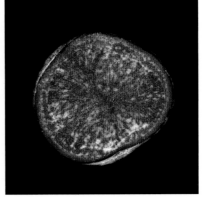

Plate 59. 'Purple Peruvian' flesh

Plate 60. 'Ranger Russet'

Plate 61. 'Reba'

Plate 62. 'Red La Soda'

Plate 63. 'Red Norland'

Plate 64. 'Dark Red Norland'

Plate 65. 'Red Pontiac'

44

Plate 66. 'Red Thumb'

Plate 67. 'Rio Grande Russet'

Plate 68. 'Romanze'

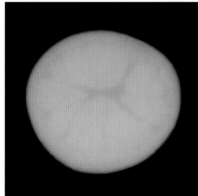

Plate 69. 'Romanze' flesh

Plate 70. 'Rose Finn Apple'

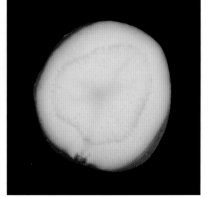

Plate 71. 'Rose Finn Apple' flesh

Plate 72. 'Russet Burbank'

Plate 73. 'Burbank's Seedling'

Plate 74. 'Russet Norkotah'

Plate 75. 'Sangre'

Plate 76. 'Sebago'

Plate 77. 'Shepody'

Plate 78. 'Superior'

Plate 79. 'Viking'

Plate 80. 'Purple Viking'

Plate 81. 'Warba'

Plate 82. 'Red Warba'

Plate 83. 'Yellow Finn'

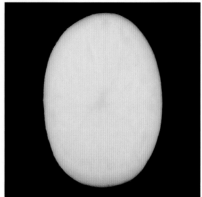

Plate 84. 'Yellow Finn' flesh

Plate 85. 'Yukon Gold'

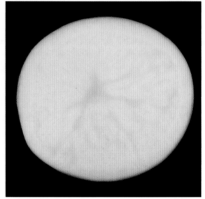

Plate 86. 'Yukon Gold' flesh

'CalWhite'

Plate 22

DESCRIPTION: Tubers are large with medium deep eyes, buff skin, and white flesh.

YIELD: High.

VINE MATURITY: Main season.

DRY MATTER CONTENT: Medium.

TEXTURE AFTER COOKING: Fairly firm to mealy.

CULINARY CHARACTERISTICS: Excellent for boiling, salads, soup, and french fries. Moderately moist when baked.

COMMENTS: Developed in California. Produces only a few tubers per plant, so in-row spacing should be close, no more than 6–9 in. (15–23 cm) apart, to avoid oversized tubers. Performs well in hot climates. Susceptible to common scab.

TUBER DORMANCY: Short.

STORABILITY: Good.

SEED AVAILABILITY: Commercial cultivar.

'Canela Russet'

Plate 23

DESCRIPTION: Tubers are large and oblong with russet skin and white flesh. Excellent appearance.

YIELD: High.

VINE MATURITY: Late main season.

DRY MATTER CONTENT: Medium high.

TEXTURE AFTER COOKING: Moderately mealy.

CULINARY CHARACTERISTICS: Good for boiling. Mealy when baked.

COMMENTS: Developed in Colorado.

TUBER DORMANCY: Long.

STORABILITY: Excellent.

SEED AVAILABILITY: Commercial cultivar.

'Caribe'

Plate 24

DESCRIPTION: Tubers are oblong with smooth, purple or blue skin and white flesh. Excellent type and appearance.

YIELD: Medium.

VINE MATURITY: Early.

DRY MATTER CONTENT: Medium.

TEXTURE AFTER COOKING: Firm, moderately mealy.

CULINARY CHARACTERISTICS: Excellent for boiling and chips. Does not break apart (slough) after boiling. Moderately moist when baked.

COMMENTS: Developed in New Brunswick, Canada. Widely adapted. Moderately resistant to common scab.

TUBER DORMANCY: Medium.

STORABILITY: Good.

SEED AVAILABILITY: Carried by many home garden seed potato sources.

'Carola'

Plates 25 and 26

DESCRIPTION: Tubers are oval with smooth, yellow skin and yellow flesh.

YIELD: Medium.

VINE MATURITY: Main season.

DRY MATTER CONTENT: Medium low.

TEXTURE AFTER COOKING: Firm, moist.

CULINARY CHARACTERISTICS: Good for boiling, mashing, and scallops. Moist when baked.

COMMENTS: German cultivar. A favorite with organic producers in the northeastern United States. Moderately resistant to common scab. Susceptible to *Fusarium* seed piece decay.

TUBER DORMANCY: Medium.

STORABILITY: Good.

SEED AVAILABILITY: Very limited.

'Catalina'

Plate 27

DESCRIPTION: Tubers are medium-sized and oval to oblong with shallow eyes, buff skin, and white flesh.

YIELD: Medium.

VINE MATURITY: Late main season.

DRY MATTER CONTENT: Medium.

TEXTURE AFTER COOKING: Firm, moist.

CULINARY CHARACTERISTICS: Good for boiling. Holds together well when boiled.

COMMENTS: Developed by Bejo Seed company. Grown from true potato seed (TPS). TUBER DORMANCY: Short.

STORABILITY: Good.

SEED AVAILABILITY: Not available as seed tubers. True potato seed is available from some mail-order seed companies in the United States.

'Cecile'

Plate 28

DESCRIPTION: Fingerling type tubers have shallow eyes, red skin, and yellow flesh. Very attractive.

YIELD: Medium.

VINE MATURITY: Late main season.

DRY MATTER CONTENT: Medium.

TEXTURE AFTER COOKING: Firm, waxy.

CULINARY CHARACTERISTICS: In Europe used as gourmet cultivar for boiling and salads.

COMMENTS: A newly developed fingerling cultivar from the Netherlands. Easier to grow and peel than some other (older) fingerling cultivars. Produces many tubers per plant. Good resistance to common scab.

TUBER DORMANCY: Short.

STORABILITY: Good.

SEED AVAILABILITY: Limited.

'Chieftain'

Plate 29

DESCRIPTION: Tubers are round to oblong with smooth, red skin and white flesh.

YIELD: High.

VINE MATURITY: Main season.

DRY MATTER CONTENT: Low.

TEXTURE AFTER COOKING: Firm, moist.

CULINARY CHARACTERISTICS: Good for boiling, after which it keeps its color. Moist when baked. Not suitable for chips.

COMMENTS: Widely adapted. Resistant to common scab.

TUBER DORMANCY: Medium.

STORABILITY: Good.

SEED AVAILABILITY: Commercial cultivar.

'Désirée'

Plates 30 and 31

DESCRIPTION: Tubers are oval to long with shallow eyes, smooth, light red skin, and pale yellow flesh.

YIELD: High.

VINE MATURITY: Late main season.

DRY MATTER CONTENT: Medium.

TEXTURE AFTER COOKING: Fairly firm to mealy.

CULINARY CHARACTERISTICS: Good for boiling; also suitable for frying and chips.

COMMENTS: Developed in the Netherlands. Widely adapted and grown in many countries. Susceptible to common scab.

TUBER DORMANCY: Short.

STORABILITY: Good.

SEED AVAILABILITY: Commercial cultivar; also carried by several home garden seed potato sources.

'Eramosa'

Plate 32

DESCRIPTION: Tubers are oval and semi-flattened with shallow eyes, smooth, white skin, and white flesh.

YIELD: Medium.

VINE MATURITY: Very early.

DRY MATTER CONTENT: Medium low.

TEXTURE AFTER COOKING: Firm, moist.

CULINARY CHARACTERISTICS: Excellent for boiling as a first early.

COMMENTS: Developed in Ontario, Canada. Harvest can be significantly advanced by green sprouting seed tubers before planting. Moderately resistant to common scab.

TUBER DORMANCY: Medium.

STORABILITY: Moderate.

SEED AVAILABILITY: Very limited.

'French Fingerling'

Plates 33 and 34

DESCRIPTION: Tubers have red skin and yellow flesh with streaks of red. Very attractive.

YIELD: Medium low.

VINE MATURITY: Late.

DRY MATTER CONTENT: Medium.

TEXTURE AFTER COOKING: Firm, waxy.

CULINARY CHARACTERISTICS: Excellent for salads, roasting, and sautéing.

COMMENTS: Heirloom cultivar. It has been said that this cultivar arrived in North America from Europe in a horse's feedbag! Resistant to common scab.

TUBER DORMANCY: Medium.

STORABILITY: Good.

SEED AVAILABILITY: Commercial cultivar; also carried by several home garden seed potato sources.

'German Butterball'

Plates 35 and 36

DESCRIPTION: Tubers are oval to oblong with shallow eyes, lightly netted golden skin, and deep yellow flesh.

YIELD: Medium.

VINE MATURITY: Late.

DRY MATTER CONTENT: Medium.

TEXTURE AFTER COOKING: Fairly firm.

CULINARY CHARACTERISTICS: Good for boiling.

COMMENTS: Heirloom cultivar. Produces many (12 to 18) relatively small tubers per plant, so recommended in-row spacing is 12–16 in. (30–40 cm) apart. Moderately resistant to common scab.

TUBER DORMANCY: Medium.

STORABILITY: Good.

SEED AVAILABILITY: Carried by several home garden seed potato sources.

'Goldrush'

Plate 37

DESCRIPTION: Tubers are oblong to long with shallow eyes, brown russeted skin, and very white flesh.

YIELD: High.

VINE MATURITY: Main season.

DRY MATTER CONTENT: Medium high.

TEXTURE AFTER COOKING: Fairly firm to mealy.

CULINARY CHARACTERISTICS: Good for boiling, baking, and frying.

COMMENTS: Developed in North Dakota. One of the top five most widely grown cultivars in Canada. Moderately resistant to common scab.

TUBER DORMANCY: Medium.

STORABILITY: Good.

SEED AVAILABILITY: Commercial cultivar.

'Green Mountain'

Plate 38

DESCRIPTION: Tubers are large, oblong, and irregularly shaped with buff skin and white flesh.

YIELD: Variable.

VINE MATURITY: Late season.

DRY MATTER CONTENT: High.

TEXTURE AFTER COOKING: Mealy.

CULINARY CHARACTERISTICS: May break apart (slough) when boiled. Dry and mealy when baked. Has a distinctive flavor.

COMMENTS: Heirloom cultivar. Released in 1885 in Vermont, named after the Green Mountains. Susceptible to most diseases, including common scab.

TUBER DORMANCY: Medium.

STORABILITY: Good.

SEED AVAILABILITY: Limited.

'Irish Cobbler'

Plate 39

DESCRIPTION: Tubers are round with deep stem and apical ends, deep eyes, creamy skin, and creamy white flesh.

YIELD: Medium.

VINE MATURITY: Very early.

DRY MATTER CONTENT: Medium high.

TEXTURE AFTER COOKING: Fairly firm.

CULINARY CHARACTERISTICS: Good for boiling. Relatively dry when baked.

COMMENTS: Heirloom cultivar. Reported to have been first grown by an Irish shoemaker in Massachusetts. The major strong point is its earliness. Widely adapted as a home garden cultivar. Susceptible to many potato diseases including common scab. 'Cobbler' is a synonym.

TUBER DORMANCY: Short.

STORABILITY: Moderate.

SEED AVAILABILITY: Limited.

'Island Sunshine'

Plates 40 and 41

DESCRIPTION: Tubers are round with rough, yellow skin and deep yellow flesh.

YIELD: Medium.

VINE MATURITY: Late.

DRY MATTER CONTENT: Medium high.

TEXTURE AFTER COOKING: Fairly firm.

CULINARY CHARACTERISTICS: Good for boiling. Slightly moist when baked.

COMMENTS: Developed in Prince Edward Island, Canada, by private breeders Gerrit and Evert Loo. Popular with organic producers in eastern Canada and the northeastern United States. Some resistance to late blight. Moderately resistant to common scab.

TUBER DORMANCY: Long.

STORABILITY: Good.

SEED AVAILABILITY: Limited.

'Katahdin'

Plate 42

DESCRIPTION: Tubers are round to oblong with smooth, buff skin and creamy white flesh.

YIELD: Medium high.

VINE MATURITY: Main season.

DRY MATTER CONTENT: Medium.

TEXTURE AFTER COOKING: Firm, moist.

CULINARY CHARACTERISTICS: Good for boiling.

COMMENTS: Named after Mount Katahdin in Maine. Widely adapted and was once grown throughout North America. Because of its abundance of flowers, fertile pollen, and general overall characteristics, this cultivar has been widely used as a parent in breeding programs and appears in the pedigrees of many North American cultivars. Susceptible to common scab.

TUBER DORMANCY: Medium.

STORABILITY: Good.

SEED AVAILABILITY: Commercial cultivar.

'Kennebec'

Plate 43

DESCRIPTION: Tubers are oval to oblong with thin, white skin and white flesh.

YIELD: High.

VINE MATURITY: Main season.

DRY MATTER CONTENT: Medium high.

TEXTURE AFTER COOKING: Firm, moderately mealy.

CULINARY CHARACTERISTICS: Good for boiling, chips, and french fries. Mealy when baked.

COMMENTS: Named after the Kennebec River in Maine. Widely adapted to many different growing conditions throughout the world. Because of its consistent performance this cultivar is frequently used as a standard for comparative purposes with new potential cultivars. Tends to produce sunburned tubers. Some resistance to late blight. Susceptible to common scab and *Verticillium* wilt.

TUBER DORMANCY: Medium.

STORABILITY: Good.

SEED AVAILABILITY: Commercial cultivar.

'Keuka Gold'

Plates 44 and 45

DESCRIPTION: Tubers are medium-sized and oval with shallow eyes, yellow skin, and pale yellow flesh.

YIELD: High.

VINE MATURITY: Late main season.

DRY MATTER CONTENT: Medium.

TEXTURE AFTER COOKING: Firm, medium moist.

CULINARY CHARACTERISTICS: Excellent for boiling but not for chips. Slightly moist when baked.

COMMENTS: Developed in New York. Well suited for growing under organic conditions in the northeastern United States. Resistant to common scab.

TUBER DORMANCY: Medium.

STORABILITY: Good.

SEED AVAILABILITY: Commercial cultivar.

'King Harry'

Plate 46

DESCRIPTION: Tubers are medium-sized and round with white skin and white flesh.

YIELD: Medium.

VINE MATURITY: Main season.

DRY MATTER CONTENT: Medium.

TEXTURE AFTER COOKING: Firm, moderately moist, waxy.

CULINARY CHARACTERISTICS: Good for boiling.

COMMENTS: Developed in New York. Resistant to flea beetles and leafhoppers, and suitable for organic gardens where these pests are a problem. Won a 2007 Green Thumb Award from the Mail-order Gardening Association.

TUBER DORMANCY: Medium.

STORABILITY: Good.

SEED AVAILABILITY: Very limited.

'La Chipper'

Plate 47

DESCRIPTION: Tubers are round-oval with deep eyes, white skin, and very white flesh.

YIELD: Medium.

VINE MATURITY: Main season.

DRY MATTER CONTENT: Medium.

TEXTURE AFTER COOKING: Fairly firm.

CULINARY CHARACTERISTICS: Excellent for boiling and chips. Moist when baked.

COMMENTS: Developed in Louisiana. Well adapted to growing in the southeastern United States. Some resistance to late blight. Moderately susceptible to common scab.

TUBER DORMANCY: Short.

STORABILITY: Moderate.

SEED AVAILABILITY: Commercial cultivar.

'La Ratte'

Plates 48 and 49

DESCRIPTION: Fingerling type tubers have yellow skin and deep yellow flesh.

YIELD: Medium low.

VINE MATURITY: Late.

DRY MATTER CONTENT: Medium.

TEXTURE AFTER COOKING: Firm, waxy.

CULINARY CHARACTERISTICS: Excellent for salads and roasting. A favorite with French chefs.

COMMENTS: Heirloom cultivar. Originated in Europe (probably France) in the late nineteenth century. Very similar to 'Banana'. Resistant to common scab. Synonyms include 'Asparges', 'LaRatte', 'La Ratte French Fingerling', 'Princess', 'Princess La Ratte', and 'Ratte'.

TUBER DORMANCY: Medium.

STORABILITY: Good.

SEED AVAILABILITY: Carried by several home garden seed potato sources.

'Mountain Rose'

Plates 50 and 51

DESCRIPTION: Tubers are oval to oblong with shallow eyes, red skin, and red flesh. Excellent appearance.

YIELD: Medium.

VINE MATURITY: Main season.

DRY MATTER CONTENT: Medium low.

TEXTURE AFTER COOKING: Firm and moist, but not waxy.

CULINARY CHARACTERISTICS: Good for boiling, salads, and red chips. Moist when baked.

COMMENTS: Promising cultivar from Colorado.

TUBER DORMANCY: Medium long.

STORABILITY: Good.

SEED AVAILABILITY: Commercial cultivar; also carried by some home garden seed potato sources.

'Ozette'

Plates 52 and 53

DESCRIPTION: Tubers are oblong to long with many evenly spaced deep eyes, yellow skin, and creamy yellow flesh.

YIELD: Medium low.

VINE MATURITY: Late.

DRY MATTER CONTENT: Medium.

TEXTURE AFTER COOKING: Waxy.

CULINARY CHARACTERISTICS: According to Ronniger's catalog, "one of the tastiest of all fingerlings. . . . The slightly earthy, nutty flavor comes through beautifully when lightly steamed or sautéed."

COMMENTS: Heirloom cultivar. Probably introduced directly from Chile or Mexico by Spanish explorers to the Makah nation at Neah Bay in Washington in the late eighteenth century (see chapter 13). The Slow Food Organization has elected 'Makah/Ozette' (the mutually agreed upon name between the Makah and Slow Food) to the U.S. Ark of Taste in 2006, a catalog of delicious foods in danger of extinction.

TUBER DORMANCY: Medium.

STORABILITY: Good.

SEED AVAILABILITY: Very limited.

'Papa Cacho'

Plates 54 and 55

DESCRIPTION: Fingerling type tubers are very long with shallow eyes, red skin, and pink flesh.

YIELD: Low.

VINE MATURITY: Very late.

DRY MATTER CONTENT: Low.

TEXTURE AFTER COOKING: Waxy.

CULINARY CHARACTERISTICS: Suitable for salads.

COMMENTS: Heirloom cultivar from southern Chile where it is considered a gourmet potato. In Spanish *cacho* means "horn."

TUBER DORMANCY: Medium long.

STORABILITY: Good.

SEED AVAILABILITY: Very limited.

'Purple Majesty'

Plates 56 and 57

DESCRIPTION: Tubers are oblong with shallow eyes, purple skin, and purple flesh.

YIELD: Medium.

VINE MATURITY: Main season.

DRY MATTER CONTENT: Medium.

TEXTURE AFTER COOKING: Firm, moist.

CULINARY CHARACTERISTICS: Good for roasting, microwaving, salads, and chips. Moderately moist when baked.

COMMENTS: Developed in Colorado. High in antioxidants. In 2007 and 2008 this was the most widely grown purple-fleshed cultivar in the United States. Moderately resistant to common scab.

TUBER DORMANCY: Short.

STORABILITY: Good.

SEED AVAILABILITY: Commercial cultivar.

'Purple Peruvian'

Plates 58 and 59

DESCRIPTION: Fingerling type tubers have many distinct deep eyes, purple skin, and deep purple flesh.

YIELD: Low.

VINE MATURITY: Late.

DRY MATTER CONTENT: Medium.

TEXTURE AFTER COOKING: Fairly firm, slightly mealy.

CULINARY CHARACTERISTICS: Good for baking, roasting, salads, and frying.

COMMENTS: Heirloom cultivar. Unique combination of fingerling and purple flesh traits. High in antioxidants. Resistant to common scab.

TUBER DORMANCY: Medium long.

STORABILITY: Good.

SEED AVAILABILITY: Very limited.

'Ranger Russet'

Plate 60

DESCRIPTION: Tubers are long with medium deep eyes, russet skin, and white flesh.

YIELD: High.

VINE MATURITY: Late main season.

DRY MATTER CONTENT: High.

TEXTURE AFTER COOKING: Mealy.

CULINARY CHARACTERISTICS: Excellent for baking and french fries.

COMMENTS: Developed in the western United States. The third most widely grown cultivar in the United States (after 'Russet Burbank' and 'Russet Norkotah').

TUBER DORMANCY: Short.

STORABILITY: Good.

SEED AVAILABILITY: Commercial cultivar.

'Reba'

Plate 61

DESCRIPTION: Tubers are oblong to round with bright white skin and white flesh.

YIELD: High.

VINE MATURITY: Late main season.

DRY MATTER CONTENT: Medium.

TEXTURE AFTER COOKING: Firm, moist.

CULINARY CHARACTERISTICS: Good for boiling (does not slough) and chips. Slightly moist when baked.

COMMENTS: Developed in New York. Very suitable for home gardens in the northeastern United States. Resistant to common scab and early blight.

TUBER DORMANCY: Medium long.

STORABILITY: Good.

SEED AVAILABILITY: Commercial cultivar.

'Red La Soda'

Plate 62

DESCRIPTION: Tubers are round to oblong with medium to deep eyes, red skin, and white flesh.

YIELD: High.

VINE MATURITY: Main season.

DRY MATTER CONTENT: Medium low.

TEXTURE AFTER COOKING: Firm, moist.

CULINARY CHARACTERISTICS: Good for boiling.

COMMENTS: Developed in Louisiana. A deep red mutant of 'La Soda'. Relatively wide adaptation; grows well in both northern and southern areas. In the southeastern United States it is commercially harvested in the winter months as a fresh market cultivar. Susceptible to common scab.

TUBER DORMANCY: Medium long.

STORABILITY: Good.

SEED AVAILABILITY: Commercial cultivar.

'Red Norland'

Plate 63

DESCRIPTION: Tubers are oblong with moderately shallow eyes, red skin, and white flesh.

YIELD: Medium.

VINE MATURITY: Early.

DRY MATTER CONTENT: Low.

TEXTURE AFTER COOKING: Firm, moist.

CULINARY CHARACTERISTICS: Very good for boiling. Moist when baked.

COMMENTS: Developed in North Dakota. Widely grown as a commercial cultivar. Resistant to common scab. Is a darker-skinned selection from the red-skinned 'Norland'. An even darker red-skinned selection, 'Dark Red Norland', is also available (Plate 64).

TUBER DORMANCY: Short.

STORABILITY: Good.

SEED AVAILABILITY: Commercial cultivar.

'Red Pontiac'

Plate 65

DESCRIPTION: Tubers are oblong to round with deep eyes, red skin, and white flesh.

YIELD: High.

VINE MATURITY: Late.

DRY MATTER CONTENT: Low.

TEXTURE AFTER COOKING: Firm, moist.

CULINARY CHARACTERISTICS: Good for boiling. Moist when baked.

COMMENTS: Developed in Michigan. Widely adapted. Grown in numerous countries. Is a deeper red color mutant of 'Pontiac'. Susceptible to most common potato diseases including common scab.

TUBER DORMANCY: Medium.

STORABILITY: Good.

SEED AVAILABILITY: Commercial cultivar.

'Red Thumb'

Plate 66

DESCRIPTION: Fingerling type tubers are small but uniform and thumblike in shape with shallow eyes, red skin, and pink flesh. Very attractive.

YIELD: Medium low.

VINE MATURITY: Main season.

DRY MATTER CONTENT: Medium.

TEXTURE AFTER COOKING: Fairly firm.

CULINARY CHARACTERISTICS: Good for roasting, frying, and other gourmet uses.

COMMENTS: Heirloom cultivar. Small to medium-sized plants. Moderate resistance to common scab.

TUBER DORMANCY: Medium.

STORABILITY: Good.

SEED AVAILABILITY: Carried by several home garden seed potato sources.

'Rio Grande Russet'

Plate 67

DESCRIPTION: Tubers are oblong to long with russet skin and white flesh. Very attractive. Uniform in size and shape.

YIELD: High.

VINE MATURITY: Late main season.

DRY MATTER CONTENT: Medium.

TEXTURE AFTER COOKING: Fairly firm.

CULINARY CHARACTERISTICS: Good for boiling. Slightly moist when baked.

COMMENTS: Developed in Colorado. Well adapted to the western United States.

TUBER DORMANCY: Medium long.

STORABILITY: Good.

SEED AVAILABILITY: Commercial cultivar.

'Romanze'

Plates 68 and 69

DESCRIPTION: Tubers are long-oval with shallow eyes, red skin, and yellow flesh. Excellent appearance.

YIELD: Medium.

VINE MATURITY: Late main season.

DRY MATTER CONTENT: Low.

TEXTURE AFTER COOKING: Fairly firm.

CULINARY CHARACTERISTICS: Good for boiling and salads.

COMMENTS: German cultivar. Moderate resistance to common scab.

TUBER DORMANCY: Medium.

STORABILITY: Good.

SEED AVAILABILITY: Carried by several home garden seed potato sources.

'Rose Finn Apple'

Plates 70 and 71

DESCRIPTION: Fingerling type tubers have rose-yellow skin and yellow flesh (with occasional red streaks).

YIELD: Low.

VINE MATURITY: Late.

DRY MATTER CONTENT: Medium low.

TEXTURE AFTER COOKING: Firm, waxy.

CULINARY CHARACTERISTICS: Specialty cultivar known for its flavor. Good for boiling, grilling, roasting, and sautéing.

COMMENTS: Heirloom cultivar. Not as easy to grow as some other fingerlings such as 'Banana'. May develop secondary growth (knobs) when moisture supply is uneven. Synonyms include 'Pink Fir Apple', 'Rose Fir Apple', and 'Ruby Crescent'.

TUBER DORMANCY: Medium.

STORABILITY: Good.

SEED AVAILABILITY: Carried by many home garden seed potato sources.

'Russet Burbank'

Plate 72

DESCRIPTION: Tubers are long with shallow eyes, russet skin, and white flesh.

YIELD: High.

VINE MATURITY: Late.

DRY MATTER CONTENT: High.

TEXTURE AFTER COOKING: Mealy.

CULINARY CHARACTERISTICS: The most popular cultivar for making french fries. Tends to break apart (slough) after boiling. Dry and mealy when baked.

COMMENTS: The most widely grown cultivar in the United States and Canada. Development of this cultivar was initiated by the famous plant breeder Luther Burbank after he found a single fruit on a plant of 'Early Rose' growing in his garden in 1872. Burbank (1914) described in detail how he found this fruit, then lost it, and eventually found it again. The fruit contained 23 seeds. By 1874 Burbank had selected one of the seedlings from this fruit which he subsequently sold to J. H. Gregory of Marblehead, Massachusetts, for $150. Gregory decided to name this new cultivar 'Burbank's Seedling' in honor of the originator and allowed Burbank to keep 10 tubers. With the proceeds of this sale Burbank moved to Santa Rosa, California, where he promoted his new potato cultivar and set up his now-famous plant breeding enterprise.

The original 'Burbank's Seedling' was smooth-skinned (Plate 73). In 1914 Lou Sweet, a farmer in Colorado, discovered a mutation with a russeted skin and named it 'Russet Burbank'. Apparently Burbank was not impressed with this new cultivar; he is reported to have stated, "These Burbank potatoes raised by Lou Sweet of Denver, Colorado, have modified their coat in a way that does not add to their attractiveness" (Davis 1992). Burbank's negative opinion notwithstanding, 'Russet Burbank' quickly replaced 'Burbank's Seedling'. Synonyms include 'California Russet', 'Golden Russet', and 'Netted Gem'. It is also known by the trade names of Idaho Baker and Idaho Russet.

Well-adapted to growing conditions in western United States but less so in the east. The cultivar tends to produce knobby tubers if water supply is irregular. Produces a relatively high number of tubers, so recommended in-row spacing is 14–18 in. (36–46 cm) apart. Resistant to common scab.

TUBER DORMANCY: Long.

STORABILITY: Excellent.

SEED AVAILABILITY: Commercial cultivar.

'Russet Norkotah'

Plate 74

DESCRIPTION: Tubers are long to oblong with shallow eyes, russet skin, and white flesh. Excellent appearance.

YIELD: High.

VINE MATURITY: Early main season.

DRY MATTER CONTENT: Medium to low.

TEXTURE AFTER COOKING: Fairly firm.

CULINARY CHARACTERISTICS: Moderate boiling quality. Moist when baked. Under certain conditions may have after-cooking discoloration. Not suitable for chips or french fries.

COMMENTS: Developed in North Dakota. Widely adapted to growing in the western United States. In 2008 this was the second most widely grown cultivar in the United States (after 'Russet Burbank'). Several selections have been made in Colorado and Texas and are also widely grown. These selections differ from the original primarily in plant type and maturity. Resistant to common scab.

TUBER DORMANCY: Medium.

STORABILITY: Moderate.

SEED AVAILABILITY: Commercial cultivar.

'Sangre'

Plate 75

DESCRIPTION: Tubers are oval to oblong with shallow eyes, red skin, and white flesh. Good appearance.

YIELD: Medium.

VINE MATURITY: Main season.

DRY MATTER CONTENT: Low.

TEXTURE AFTER COOKING: Firm, moist.

CULINARY CHARACTERISTICS: Good for boiling and baking.

COMMENTS: Developed in Colorado.

TUBER DORMANCY: Medium.

STORABILITY: Good.

SEED AVAILABILITY: Commercial cultivar.

'Sebago'

Plate 76

DESCRIPTION: Tubers are round-oval with white skin and white flesh.

YIELD: High.

VINE MATURITY: Late.

DRY MATTER CONTENT: Medium.

TEXTURE AFTER COOKING: Firm, moist.

CULINARY CHARACTERISTICS: Good for boiling and chips. Slightly moist when baked.

COMMENTS: Old cultivar, selected in Maine in the early 1930s. Formerly a major commercial cultivar but still popular with home gardeners in the southeastern United States. Some resistance to common scab, late and early blight.

TUBER DORMANCY: Short.

STORABILITY: Good.

SEED AVAILABILITY: Very limited.

'Shepody'

Plate 77

DESCRIPTION: Tubers are long with medium deep eyes, smooth white skin, and white flesh.

YIELD: High.

VINE MATURITY: Main season. Depending on location, 'Shepody' matures up to three weeks earlier than 'Russet Burbank'.

DRY MATTER CONTENT: High.

TEXTURE AFTER COOKING: Moderately mealy.

CULINARY CHARACTERISTICS: Excellent for boiling and french fries. Because of long shape not suitable for chips. Mealy when baked.

COMMENTS: Developed in New Brunswick, Canada. Among the top five most widely grown cultivars in both Canada and the United States. Widely used around the world by the french fry industry. Susceptible to common scab.

TUBER DORMANCY: Medium.

STORABILITY: Good.

SEED AVAILABILITY: Commercial cultivar.

'Superior'

Plate 78

DESCRIPTION: Tubers are round to oblong with medium to deep eyes, flaky white skin, and white flesh.

YIELD: Medium.

VINE MATURITY: Early.

DRY MATTER CONTENT: Medium.

TEXTURE AFTER COOKING: Fairly firm.

CULINARY CHARACTERISTICS: Good for boiling and chips. Moderately dry when baked.

COMMENTS: Developed in Wisconsin. Widely adapted to growing as a medium early cultivar. One of the top five most widely grown cultivars in Canada. Resistant to common scab.

TUBER DORMANCY: Short.

STORABILITY: Moderate.

SEED AVAILABILITY: Commercial cultivar.

'Viking'

Plate 79

DESCRIPTION: Tubers are round to oblong with red skin and very white flesh.

YIELD: High.

VINE MATURITY: Main season.

DRY MATTER CONTENT: Medium.

TEXTURE AFTER COOKING: Fairly firm.

CULINARY CHARACTERISTICS: Excellent for boiling. No after-cooking darkening. Slightly moist when baked. Not suitable for chips.

COMMENTS: Developed in North Dakota. Produces relatively few tubers per plant, so tubers are large. Cultural practices such as relatively close spacing must be used. A purple-skinned mutant, 'Purple Viking' (Plate 80), is also available. Other than the different skin color the traits for both 'Viking' and 'Purple Viking' are the same.

TUBER DORMANCY: Medium.

STORABILITY: Good.

SEED AVAILABILITY: Commercial cultivar.

'Warba'

Plate 81

DESCRIPTION: Tubers are round with very deep eyes, white skin often with reddish areas around the eyes, and with white flesh.

YIELD: Medium.

VINE MATURITY: Very early.

DRY MATTER CONTENT: Low.

TEXTURE AFTER COOKING: Firm, moist.

CULINARY CHARACTERISTICS: Good for boiling and baking.

COMMENTS: Heirloom cultivar. Developed in Minnesota in the late 1920s. A red-skinned mutant, 'Red Warba' (Plate 82), is also available. Susceptible to most diseases, including common scab.

TUBER DORMANCY: Short.

STORABILITY: Moderate.

SEED AVAILABILITY: Very limited.

'Yellow Finn'

Plates 83 and 84

DESCRIPTION: Tubers are round, sometimes flat, with medium deep eyes, yellow skin, and yellow flesh. Produced on long stolons.

YIELD: Medium low.

VINE MATURITY: Late.

DRY MATTER CONTENT: Medium.

TEXTURE AFTER COOKING: Firm, waxy.

CULINARY CHARACTERISTICS: Good for boiling, baking, french fries, and salads.

COMMENTS: Heirloom cultivar. Reportedly of European origin. Resistant to common scab.

TUBER DORMANCY: Medium long.

STORABILITY: Good.

SEED AVAILABILITY: Carried by many home garden seed potato sources.

'Yukon Gold'

Plates 85 and 86

DESCRIPTION: Tubers are round with shallow eyes and distinct pink buds, yellow skin, and yellow flesh.

YIELD: Medium high.

VINE MATURITY: Early main season.

DRY MATTER CONTENT: Medium.

TEXTURE AFTER COOKING: Fairly firm.

CULINARY CHARACTERISTICS: Excellent for boiling. Moderately moist when baked. Can also be used for french fries.

COMMENTS: Developed in Ontario, Canada. Widely adapted and currently by far the most popular yellow-fleshed cultivar in North America. It is among the top five most widely grown cultivars in Canada and among the top ten in the United States. Some dealers have used the name "Yukon Gold" to sell other yellow-fleshed cultivars. Susceptible to common scab and hollow heart.

TUBER DORMANCY: Medium long.

STORABILITY: Good.

SEED AVAILABILITY: Commercial cultivar; also carried by most home garden seed potato sources.

CHAPTER 3

Soils and Fertility

THE TYPE OF SOIL, how it is prepared, and the levels of plant nutrients it contains have a great impact on potato yield and quality. Potatoes are adapted to many soil types but proper adjustments in preparation and fertility are often required to get the most from the soil resource. Knowledge of the physical characteristics and the native fertility level is the starting point in developing a successful approach.

Soils

Soils are reservoirs of nutrients, water, and oxygen, all necessary for plant growth. The right combination of physical and chemical properties is critical to getting a good crop of potatoes. That said, potatoes can be and are grown in many different soil types. They are grown commercially on a wide range of mineral soils, from the clays of the Canadian prairies and the Red River Valley of North Dakota and Minnesota to the sands of Florida. They also are grown on organic muck or peat soils. Regardless of the soil types, the main concern is to make the proper adjustments in providing a well-drained environment for the plant's root system. Sandy loam to loam soils are ideal for potatoes.

The water-holding capacity of soils is critical in areas where irrigation is not available or used. It is less important when irrigation is provided. However, in soils with high water-holding capacities, such as clays and organic soils, the root zone should not get waterlogged. Waterlogged soils starve roots of the oxygen they need and create an environment for pathogens to enter potato tubers. In areas where internal drainage is poor it is critical to raise rows to provide surface drainage. There is less potential for waterlogging in sandy soils but there is greater need to maintain adequate moisture.

Organic matter in mineral soils improves soil structure and aids in providing moisture and nutrients to the crop. Rotations with soil-building crops such as grasses and legumes also help to improve soil structure. Often home gardeners don't have the luxury to rotate with sod crops, so another option is to plant oats, rye, or other cover crops at the end of the growing season. The organic matter and the root development of the sod crop improve the friability (open pore spaces) of the soil.

Additions of well-rotted manure benefit all soil types. In clay soils organic matter improves soil structure and thereby provides better aeration and water drainage. In sandy soils the added organic matter binds the soil particles together and increases water-holding capacity and improves nutrient availability. Ideally the addition of well-rotted manure should be made prior to the potato crop year to minimize the potential of scabby potato tubers. Fresh manure should not be applied in the potato year, as this practice could increase potato scab and the potential for microbial contamination of the tubers.

Soil pH

Soil pH, a measure of the soil's acidity or alkalinity, is important in plant nutrition and in managing potato scab. A pH level of 7.0 is considered neutral. In areas where the soils are acidic, maintaining pH levels below 5.2 has been a common practice to reduce (not eliminate) the potential of potato scab. Growing potatoes at this pH level nevertheless presents problems with nutrient availability and in growing rotational crops that have higher pH requirements. Where the native pH is 6.0 or higher it is impractical to lower pH to a level to control scab. Generally pH levels above 7.0 are not conducive to the development of scab.

In addition to the effect on scab, pH is an important factor in plant nutrition. Potatoes can be grown over a wide range of soil pH levels—with some adjustments. Nutritionally a slightly acid soil is desirable. At pH levels near 6.0, soil nitrogen, phosphorus, potassium, calcium, magnesium, and other important elements are all readily available. When pH levels are at or below 5.5, macronutrients are less available and levels of iron, aluminum, and manganese may be toxic to the plants. At soil pH levels of 7.0 and above, phosphorus is tied up by calcium and the availability of zinc and manganese is reduced. When pH levels are at either extreme it may be necessary to apply appropriate nutrients: magnesium at pH levels below 5.5, zinc or manganese at pH levels of 7.0 and above.

Fertilization

Potatoes remove substantial quantities of nitrogen and potassium, and a lesser amount of phosphorus from the soil. Small quantities of other essential elements are extracted but these are important nevertheless. In most cases only nitrogen, phosphorus, and potassium need to be applied. Soil pH and fertility are closely linked. When pH levels are lower than desired (below 5.5 or the pH level that is appropriate for rotational crops), calcium and magnesium can be added by applying limestone. It is desirable to apply lime to crops preceding potatoes to reduce the potential for potato scab.

Knowing soil pH is the first step in having a successful fertilizer program. Kits for measuring soil pH are available at garden supply stores and through local extension offices. Soil pH and complete soil tests may also be done through extension offices. Complete soil tests report levels of elemental nitrogen (N) or nitrate nitrogen (NO_3), phosphorus (P), and potassium (K). This is different than how fertilizer labels describe content; these report nitrogen, available phosphate (P_2O_5), and available potash (K_2O). When soil nutrient levels are too low, fertilizer should be applied, either in an inorganic fertilizer or an organic form (see Plate 88).

Application rates of lime vary with soil type; more is required on clay soils and less on sandy soils. In the western United States soils often have pH levels above 7.0 and may require applications of zinc and manganese. Soil pH levels between 5.5 and 7.0 are conducive to the development of scab. If potatoes are grown in this range, which is likely since many other vegetables grown in rotation require pH levels near 6.0, scab-resistant cultivars should be selected. Consult local agricultural extension offices to determine rates of lime for soil types in your area.

Inorganic Fertilizers

Usually in conventional (not organic) production an application of a complete fertilizer is adequate for good yields of quality potatoes. Fertilizers come in various formulations, 10–10–10 or 10–20–20 are common. The first number stands for the percentage of nitrogen, the second for available phosphate (P_2O_5), and the last for available potash (K_2O). In some fertilizers there may be an additional number that represents another nutrient, such as magnesium. Be sure the fertilizer used doesn't include herbicides, as many lawn fertilizers do.

A reasonable amount of a 10–X–X fertilizer to apply in most situations is 3 pounds per 30 feet of row (or 1.5 kg per 10 m) or 3.5 pounds per 100 square feet (or 1.7 kg per 10 sq m). The rate should be adjusted downward if well-rotted manure was previously applied or if a legume was incorporated into the soil the year potatoes are grown. A good stand of red clover can conservatively provide about half of the nitrogen needs. Excess fertilizer can be detrimental to the crop. Applying too much nitrogen promotes vigorous vine growth and delays tuberization and maturity. Immature tubers do not store well and are susceptible to tuber decay. Too much potassium results in an uptake of more potassium than the plant needs, often referred to as "luxury consumption." Excess potassium reduces tuber dry matter.

Inorganic fertilizer can be applied several ways. An easy way is to spread the fertilizer uniformly over the soil surface and incorporate with a rototiller, spade, or rake. All or part of the fertilizer can be applied prior to planting. If split applications are made the second application should be made when plants are 4–6 in. (10–15 cm) tall. In sandy soils or after heavy rains when fertilizer is leached from the root zone, additional nitrogen may be justified. However, applications after plants are 10 in. (25 cm) tall may delay maturity.

Another approach that is closer to commercial application is to band the fertilizer on one or both sides of the seed furrow (Plates 89 to 91). The bands should be 2–4 in. (5–10 cm) to the side and 2 in. (5 cm) deeper than the seed pieces. Care should be taken so that the fertilizer doesn't come in contact with the seed pieces, which can result in fertilizer burn of the developing sprouts and roots. The same would apply if the fertilizer is placed immediately below the seed pieces and covered with soil. (Do not apply banded fertilizer directly below seed pieces.) Either all or part of the fertilizer can be applied in the band(s). Applying only part of the fertilizer at planting may be more efficient from the standpoint of plant nutrition, especially when plants are grown in areas where frequent early rains result in nutrient leaching.

Organic Fertilizers

Organic production of potatoes requires a different approach to fertilization. Manures, organic fertilizers, and legumes can be used alone or in combination to provide needed nutrients. Well-decomposed manure applied at a rate of 50 pounds per 100 square feet (24 kg per 10 sq m) will provide a base amount of nutrients in most circumstances and is a reasonable starting point. The manure should be incorporated with a rototiller or spade.

The amount of nitrogen supplied by the manure will vary by source of the manure, amount of straw or wood shavings present, and age. For example, poultry manure contains more nitrogen than cattle manure. Improperly aged or applied manure can increase the potential for microbial contamination of the crop. Therefore it is important to compost manure and apply at least 120 days prior to harvest. Granulated forms of various manures are available and can be used in the manner described in the conventional fertilizer section.

The utilization of legumes, such as red clover and alfalfa, in the preceding year can in some cases provide most or all the needed nitrogen for good yields. Red clover is somewhat tolerant of low pH and can be grown at pH levels around 5.5 whereas alfalfa requires pH levels above 6.0.

Applications of wood ash will provide potassium and can increase soil pH. Care should be given to apply only nominal amounts. Phosphorus can be applied by banded applications of bone meal. Banding is important since phosphorus is an immobile element and is readily tied up in the soil.

Specific recommendations will vary by location and soils. Local agricultural extension offices can provide more detailed information.

 CHAPTER 4

Seed Potatoes

THE SELECTION OF GOOD quality seed is one of the most important decisions in growing potatoes. Good quality extends beyond the physical appearance of tubers and their ability to produce sprouts. Potato plants are often found growing from potato peels and discarded portions of potatoes in compost heaps. This leads many people to believe that all potatoes can be used for seed. While some potato tubers purchased in supermarkets will produce viable sprouts, many will not. Potatoes purchased at stores have often been treated with sprout inhibitors, which prevent or significantly reduce sprout formation. These obviously are poor choices for seed.

Even tubers that produce sprouts may not be good choices for seed. Potatoes that are not specifically grown for seed are grown for optimal yield and may harbor plant disease organisms that affect the growth of the subsequent crop. While the diseases don't affect the nutritional quality of the potatoes, they do affect emergence, vigor, tuber quality, and yield.

With the exception of the relatively small portion of potatoes produced from true seed (see chapter 8), potatoes are vegetatively propagated. This presents a major challenge when it comes to producing high-quality seed and maintaining varietal purity. Many diseases that infect field-grown plants are transmitted through the tubers to the developing sprouts. These plant diseases often do not produce visible symptoms and therefore can't be eliminated just by looking at the tubers.

Seed Potato Certification

Potato seed certification agencies in the United States and Canada were established in the early twentieth century to address the need for seed lots to be of the same cultivar and to certify the quality of the seed tubers. Prior to the establishment of such agencies, growers were subject to mislabeled cultivars or mixtures of cultivars. Also, growers observed the "running out" of their crops. The "running out" was due to the presence of virus diseases that were transmitted to growing plants by aphids or mechanical injury. As seed tubers were saved from year to year the disease frequency increased and yields became progressively lower.

Seed certification agencies are responsible for the production of disease-free basic seed stock (referred to as nuclear seed) and the inspection of field-grown plants and harvested tubers. In addition to being inspected at the site of production, seed tubers from commercial seed farms are tested in fields in southern states, greenhouses, or laboratories during the winter. Certain diseases have a zero tolerance, which means an entire field is rejected if such a disease is detected. These diseases include bacterial ring rot and potato spindle tuber (caused by a viroid). Descriptions of potato diseases are included in chapter 6.

There are fifteen state certification agencies in the United States. All provinces in Canada have certification activities through one governmental agency. Appendix 2 has contact information for each certification agency. The agencies can provide directories of seed producers in their respective areas.

Production of Certified Seed Potatoes

Seed is generally produced in cool growing areas that have few problems with aphids, which transmit some viruses. Basic seed stock is produced by a process called meristem tissue culture. This approach takes very small growing points, the size of black pepper flakes, from developing sprouts and places them on a sterile growing medium in test tubes. Plantlets are developed by adjustments in the medium and growing temperature. As the plantlets grow, cuttings are taken to increase the number of plant units. Eventually the plant-lets are placed in a soilless plant mix in greenhouses where mini tubers are produced.

Depending on individual state programs, the mini tubers are grown in field soil on agency farms or are distributed to seed growers for further increase. The tubers produced are then distributed to commercial seed producers and begin a limited generation program. Depending on state regulations, the progeny of a specific seed stock can only be grown for seed for a prescribed number of years. Generally, the quality of seed closest to the first generation of seed is best. The generation designation by various certification agencies varies and it is best to review information provided by the agency where the seed is produced. Foundation seed precedes certified seed in the sequence regardless of the other categories the agencies list.

Certain seed companies cater to the needs of home gardeners, as do local garden stores. A list of some suppliers of small amounts of seed is also provided in appendix 1. However the seed is purchased, it is important to verify it has passed certification standards. The take-home message is to only use foundation or certified potato seed!

Getting the Most from Foundation and Certified Seed

The use of foundation or certified seed cannot be overemphasized. In addition to the use of good-quality seed tubers a number of factors determine the productivity of the seed planted. These include physiological age, type of seed (whole or cut), size, curing of cut surfaces, spacing, planting depth, and physical condition. Whole seed or seed pieces are the energy source for developing plants for at least the first three weeks after emergence, therefore the size and the integrity of the seed units is critical for optimum production.

Physiological Age

The age of seed tubers is a function of the chronological age (basically the time from harvest to planting) and the temperature at which the tubers are stored. Little can be done about the chronological age but subsequent storage temperatures have a major effect on the physiological age. Typically long-term storage of seed is at 40°F (4°C). If the seed is subjected to higher temperatures the aging process is accelerated and sprouts form. The higher the temperatures or the longer the tubers are held at warm temperatures, the greater the impact on physiological age.

The age of seed has an impact on earliness, tuber size and number, and overall productivity (Plates 92 to 95). Young seed is characterized by tubers that are firm and sprout-free. When temperatures are conducive to sprouting, young seed tubers develop single dominant sprouts at the apical eyes. In older seed, sprouts are also formed at lateral eyes and as the seed gets older multiple sprouts are formed at many eyes. At a certain point seed can be too old to use. Tubers that are shriveled and have multiple branched sprouts at eyes may not emerge after planting. This type of seed should be avoided.

In areas with long growing seasons, young seed is more desirable since it has a high-yield potential and tends to produce large tubers. However, in short-growing regions or when early harvest or small tubers are desired, slightly older seed is more desirable. Warming seed prior to planting initiates sprout formation. Having sprouts between ⅛ and ¼ in. (3–6 mm) in length at planting hastens emergence and is generally desirable.

Seed Potato Size and Type

Seed size should average about 2 oz. (57 g) and range from 1½ to 2½ oz. (43–71 g) (see Plate 96). In areas where frost may be expected after sprouts emerge, slightly higher weights are desirable to regenerate sprouts after tops have been frosted. Whole seed will produce more sprouts and more tubers per hill than cut seed of the same size. Whole seed is more resistant to decay under wet conditions than cut seed.

Because it is often difficult to find small seed tubers, large tubers need to be cut to appropriate size. Commercial seed producers store tubers at 40°F (4°C). Prior to cutting, tubers should be warmed to 50–60°F (10–16°C) for a day or so. Cut seed should be as blocky as possible to minimize exposure to decay organisms in the soil. Minimally each seed piece must have one eye, and ideally two or more viable eyes. Tubers of some cultivars have eyes evenly distributed while tubers of other cultivars have uneven distribution of eyes, so care must be taken to cut tubers properly.

Cutting tubers through the apical (bud) end stimulates lateral eyes to develop. The stem and apical ends of tubers are opposite each other. The stem end of any tuber can be located by following the positioning of eyebrows; the high point of each eyebrow always points toward the stem end. Cutting through the apical end of long tubers isn't always practical. Such cuts result in sliver-shaped seed pieces with large cut surfaces. So, cutting long seed tubers may be best done by cutting them in cross-section. Figure 7 shows several ways to cut variously sized and shaped seed tubers.

Curing Cut Seed

While many gardeners think it is important to "dry" the cut surface of seed pieces, this should never be done. Drying cut surfaces results in desiccated dead tissue at the cut surfaces and facilitates subsequent entry of disease organisms. Cut seed should instead be cured to allow the cut surfaces to "heal." Wound healing produces layers of cells that create a barrier against water loss and soil-inhabiting diseases.

Optimal conditions for curing cut surfaces are a temperature between 50 and 60°F (10–16°C), high relative humidity, and adequate oxygen. In many cases, these conditions are best provided by planting freshly cut seed in warm, moist (not wet) soil. However, if it is more convenient or desirable to cut seed before planting, the seed should be stored at 50–60°F (10–16°C) at 90 percent relative humidity with ample air circulation for three to four days.

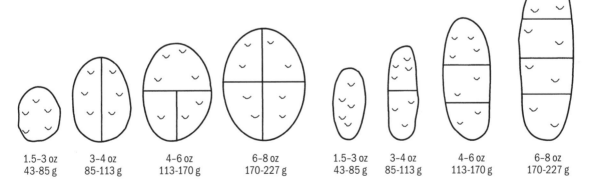

| 1.5-3 oz | 3-4 oz | 4-6 oz | 6-8 oz | 1.5-3 oz | 3-4 oz | 4-6 oz | 6-8 oz |
| 43-85 g | 85-113 g | 113-170 g | 170-227 g | 43-85 g | 85-113 g | 113-170 g | 170-227 g |

Figure 7. The goal of seed cutting should be to produce blocky seed pieces that weigh between 1½ and 2½ ounces (43–71g).

Maintaining 90 percent relative humidity may be a challenge for gardeners. One means of increasing relative humidity is to put cut seed tubers in a small room or closed-off area and place moist burlap bags (or other material) on the floor to add moisture into the environment. If planting is delayed, the temperatures should be subsequently reduced to 40–45°F (4–7°C) to prevent excess sprout growth.

A variation of this procedure is to green sprout (chit) seed before planting. This can be achieved by placing whole or cut seed in single layers in the manner outlined in the preceding paragraph and adding light exposure. The warm temperatures provide the sprouting stimulus and the light causes the stem length between the nodes to shorten, creating short stubby sprouts. These sprouts are less prone to damage while planting and under favorable conditions emerge from the soil rapidly. Depending on soil temperatures plant emergence can occur 10 to 14 days earlier with green-sprouted seed than with seed that doesn't have visible sprouts at planting (Plate 97).

Spacing

When planting seed potatoes in the garden, an appropriate distance between rows is 28–36 in. (71–91 cm). The distance between seed pieces within rows is a function of the genetics of cultivars (some produce many small tubers and others produce few large tubers) and the personal preferences for tuber size. Generally 9- to 12-in. (23- to 30-cm) spacing is suggested, but this range can be adjusted to increase or decrease tuber size. Seed size and type will also affect tuber size and number. Large seed pieces produce more sprouts and ultimately more tubers than smaller seed pieces. Similarly, whole seed tubers the same size as cut seed tend to do the same. Adjustments in seed size, type, and spacing should be done to achieve desirable yield and tuber size.

Depth of Planting

The depth of planting has an effect on how quickly sprouts emerge. The longer the time between planting and emergence, the greater the potential for seed decay or diseases, such as *Rhizoctonia*, to attack the developing sprouts. Therefore it is important to place seed pieces at depths that are conducive to hastening emergence and minimizing tuber decay. Soil types and tendency for wet or dry conditions determine the ideal planting depth.

In well-drained soils, which are not subject to extremes of moisture, the depth of planting should be 3–4 in. (8–10 cm) below the soil surface. This is accomplished by making a V-shaped furrow with a hoe or garden implement and placing seed pieces at the desired spacing. If fertilizer has already been incorporated in the soil the seed pieces should just be covered. For band application of fertilizer refer to chapter 3 for details.

In very dry regions seed pieces should be planted deeper to be in a good moisture zone. In poorly drained soils or in areas where standing water is possible, seed pieces should be placed in hills that will shed water.

Physical Condition

The physical status of seed pieces is an obvious predictor of emergence and therefore yield potential. Seed pieces that have areas of decay or have many multiple sprouts are indicators of poor emergence. Decaying seed pieces may break down before emergence. Old seed with many branched sprouts often develop small tubers before sprouts emerge. Seed pieces with attached small tubers should never be planted.

CHAPTER 5

Establishing and Maintaining Plants

MANY FACTORS ARE INVOLVED in growing a good crop of potatoes. The importance of good soil, adequate fertility, and virus-free seed has been discussed in previous chapters. Soil preparation, time of planting, cultivation and hilling, and water management are other factors that affect both yield and quality of the harvest.

Soil Preparation

Generally, soil is prepared at or near the time of planting. Soil should be spaded or tilled to a loose but not pulverized condition. Unlike true seed of many plants, seed potatoes do not need a fine seed bed. Overworking the soil breaks down the structure and can create a sealing effect that reduces needed air exchange to seed pieces and to developing tubers later in the growing season. The soil should be turned over when it is dry enough to work. Tilling wet soil compacts it and creates a poor physical condition that lasts throughout the growing season. Air infiltration, water penetration, and drainage are negatively impacted when soils are compacted.

Clay soils are the most difficult to prepare for planting. There is a fine line between clay soil that has ideal soil moisture and one that is too wet. Developing good soil structure by adding organic matter and rotating with sod crops will improve crop growth in these soils. In northern humid areas, heavy clay soils may need to be turned over in the fall to benefit from the freezing and thawing during the winter and spring to "open" pore spaces. Prior to planting, these soils should again be loosened by spading or tilling when soils are dry enough to work. It is important in poorly drained soils to develop rows that have troughs or valleys on each side to provide surface drainage away from the seed.

In arid areas it may be necessary to irrigate the soil prior to tilling it and planting. As in humid areas, care should be taken not to work soils while they are excessively wet. That also applies to any practice during the growing season.

Time of Planting

Date of planting varies with geographic location and the desired harvest time. In the northern tier of the United States and the southern Canadian provinces planting usually is between April and June. In the mid-Atlantic area this period is mostly between March and April, and in the southern states it is between November and February.

Planting generally begins approximately two weeks prior to the average last frost date. Emerging sprouts can tolerate temperatures between 28 and 32°F (–2 and 0°C). Soil temperatures at time of planting should be at least 45°F (7°C) but not above 70°F (21°C). In general early planting results in high yields of good quality tubers.

Dates of planting may need to be adjusted to maximize the best environmental conditions. For example, late planting in areas where high temperatures are experienced late in the growing season may result in tubers with internal necrosis (brown spots in tubers) or increase the potential of tuber decay.

When a very early harvest is desired, early planting of green-sprouted seed pieces coupled with plastic tunnels (hoops covered with vented clear plastic) or woven row covers hastens crop development. Plastic tunnels require adequate ventilation especially as temperatures increase. Plastic should be slit and removed as temperatures approach 80°F (27°C) to prevent plant damage.

Cultivating and Hilling

Tilling the soil after planting is critical to control weeds, improve soil aeration, break up clods, and shape hills to prevent greening of tubers. The most
effective time to control weeds is when annual weed seeds are beginning
to germinate or when perennial weeds are beginning to sprout. Cultivation
doesn't need to be deep to be effective. Usually a scratching of the surface,
not more than 1–2 in. (2.5–5 cm) deep, is adequate shortly after planting.

Annual weeds are more easily controlled than perennial ones. Quackgrass
(*Elytrigia repens*) and nutsedge (*Cyperus* spp.) and other perennial weeds
require very aggressive cultivation to keep them from materially reducing
yield. Quackgrass and nutsedge rhizomes are particularly obnoxious because
they can penetrate tubers (Plate 98). If at all possible do not plant in areas
infested with these weeds.

Certain nonselective herbicides can be used in the fall prior to planting to
control perennial weeds. Note that nonselective herbicides will kill or injure
most plants (crops and weeds alike), so use with care. Cultivars that rapidly
develop a dense plant canopy are also quite helpful in controlling weeds.

Shaping the soil into broad "hills" provides room for tubers and helps prevent sunlight from coming in contact with them. The development of hills
should be a gradual process beginning when plants are 6–8 in. (15–20 cm)
tall (Plate 99). Exposure to direct sunlight causes the affected portion of the
tubers to turn green and develop alkaloids that impart a bitter flavor. To be
effective the hills should cover developing tubers. While many gardeners consider a high hill to be best, a wide, not pointed, hill will keep tubers protected
from the sun (Plate 100). Hilling should be finished by the time the plants
are blooming, approximately 30 to 40 days after emergence. Cultivation and
hilling should never be done when the soil is wet.

Water

Proper soil moisture is important throughout the season for good productivity and quality. In humid regions it is critical to have good surface or internal drainage. Excess water near seed pieces early in the season increases the

potential for seed piece decay and complete crop loss. Wet cool conditions early in the season may increase *Rhizoctonia* stem canker, which can reduce or delay emergence and in extreme cases lead to formation of tubers without forming plants above ground.

Too much water during the growing season and at harvest can result in oxygen deficiency, enlarged lenticels (breathing pores), and tuber decay (see Plate 101). Moisture on foliage for extended periods of time provides conditions favorable to late blight, the disease responsible for the Irish potato famine in the nineteenth century. Conversely, too little moisture results in low yields, small tubers, and increased risk of internal necrosis and heat sprouts. Consistent moisture is also important as fluctuation between wet and dry conditions increases the possibility of knobs, growth cracks, and hollow heart.

Amount and Frequency of Water

Decisions on the amount of water to apply will depend on stage of growth, water-holding capacity and infiltration rate of the soil, weather conditions, and moisture status of the soil. Water needs of plants are relatively low shortly after planting when the root system is sparse. Water demand increases as the plants develop, with demand leveling off about two weeks after maximum canopy development. Unless soils are very dry it is unlikely that supplemental watering will be needed for the first month or so after planting. The aim of irrigation should be to keep the soil moist but not overly wet. Potatoes are heavy consumers of water but their root systems are relatively shallow. While roots may extend to 2 ft. (60 cm), much of the water uptake is in the top 12 in. (30 cm). The soil profile should be moist to a depth of 12–18 in. (30–46 cm).

The exact amount of water and the timing needed to achieve that goal depend on humidity and soil type. The frequency of irrigation is higher in arid areas than in humid zones. Sandy or gravelly soils require more frequent irrigations than loams or clay soils. The rate of irrigation, however, should not exceed the infiltration rate of the soil. Applying more water than the soil can absorb causes run off or the formation of puddles ("puddling") in both light-textured and heavy soils.

Some sandy soils have fine sand particles that reduce infiltration rates. Excess applications of water to sandy and well-drained soils result in leaching of nutrients. Since the water-holding capacity of these soils is relatively low, applying large amounts of water at one time will not extend time between irrigations. Soils with greater water-holding capacity have more water reserve. This gives them a bit of a buffer between irrigations but care should be taken not to let them dry too much.

Excess water in heavy soils will lead to poor growth, oxygen deficiency, and tuber decay. Peak demand for water is during the active growth and tuberization periods. Water requirements diminish as plants begin to mature and lower leaves start to yellow.

Methods of Applying Water

There are various methods of applying water. The most common is the overhead sprinkler. Care should be taken to have uniform application. One approach to determine how well the water is being applied is to place cans at the height of the canopy at several locations and collect the water for a set period of time. When the soil is dry enough to collect the cans, measure the level in each can and adjust the distance between nozzles or change nozzle size to maximize uniformity.

Furrow irrigation and subsurface irrigation are other approaches used in some areas in North America. These specialized methods are not covered in this book.

Another approach to applying water is trickle irrigation. This can be quite helpful in conserving water and may be convenient in many gardens. Water is distributed at low pressure through drip tape with emitters spaced 6–12 in. (15–30 cm) apart in the case of potatoes. Periodic determination of the adequacy of irrigation is advisable. A major advantage to trickle irrigation is that water is placed at the soil level and foliage doesn't get wet. This technique reduces the threat from diseases such as late blight, which requires moist foliage to invade. While trickle irrigation is most often used in conjunction with plastic mulch, it can also be utilized with bare ground culture. The use of straw mulch (see chapter 8) helps to conserve moisture.

 **CHAPTER 6**

Pests and Other Problems

NONVERTEBRATE PESTS come in three major categories: diseases, insects, and weeds. Within these groupings are many individual pests that attack potatoes. Some reduce yield, others reduce quality, and still others make harvesting difficult. Physiological disorders usually result from a combination of cultivar vulnerability and adverse environment. Examples of physiological disorders include internal defects in tubers and air pollution effects on foliage. Vertebrate pests include deer and rodents. The following sections provide a brief description of the major pests and physiological disorders that affect potato production; a comprehensive listing would require a book of its own.

Pest control is a term often used but *pest management* is a better term because it is hard, and in most cases impossible, to have total control. An integrated approach to pest management employs cultural, biological, and chemical strategies. A basic knowledge of the biology of the pests is important in making use of these approaches for maximum effect. It is critical to know how the environment affects the growth and the progression of the pests that affect potatoes. Cultural strategies include date of planting and tillage practices. Biological approaches include making use of resistant cultivars and the use of predators and parasites.

The use of chemicals should be based on specific pest threshold levels or damage. Specific chemical recommendations will not be listed here since there are regional differences in availability of materials labeled for small-scale use and regulations vary with time. Some materials are available for use in organic production; local organic production organizations determine which products are acceptable. An excellent resource for information about allowable pesticides, either organic or conventional, is the local county or provincial extension office.

Diseases and Physiological Disorders

Diseases are caused by pathogens—fungi, bacteria, viruses, and nematodes—while physiological disorders are primarily caused by environmental factors. The following is a breakdown of some of the major diseases by microbe group:

FUNGI	BACTERIA,	VIRUSES	NEMATODES
Late blight	including	Calico	Root lesion
Early blight	phytoplasmas	Leafroll	nematode
Fusarium wilt	Common scab	Potato viruses A,	Root knot
Verticillium wilt	Ring rot	S, X, and Y	nematode
Rhizoctonia	Black leg		Potato cyst
Powdery scab	Soft rot		nematodes
Pythium leak	Potato purple top		(golden and
Black dot			pale)

The brief descriptions of the diseases and disorders that follow are grouped by symptoms and include information on conditions that favor the disease or disorder, and management strategies.

Poor Emergence

Various diseases or physiological disorders can cause poor emergence. Above- and below-ground symptoms include decaying seed pieces, sprouts with burned tips or brown lesions, small tubers forming on seed pieces, and the absence of sprouts.

Brown Decay in Seed Pieces

DESCRIPTION: Seed pieces are in various stages of decay (Plate 102). The decay is categorized by brown discoloration.

CAUSE: Probably *Fusarium* spp. Bacterial soft rot (*Pectobacterium carotovorum*) often follows *Fusarium* infection. The organisms are present in most soils and can invade cut seed pieces, especially in wet conditions.

MANAGEMENT OPTIONS: Plant when soil conditions favor quick emergence and cure cut seed prior to planting, especially when wet soil conditions are expected.

Burned Tips of Sprouts or Brown Lesions

DESCRIPTION: Sprouts have "burned" tips or brown lesions (Plate 103). In severe cases eyes have multiple sprouts and seed pieces may have small tubers without top growth. Seed pieces may be sound.

CAUSE: *Rhizoctonia solani*. The disease is favored by cool wet conditions.

MANAGEMENT OPTIONS: Avoid planting seed tubers that have the black scurf stage (resting stage) of the disease. Plant in well-drained soils when temperatures are favorable for growth and cover seed pieces with no more than 2–4 in. (5–10 cm) of soil.

Seed Pieces with Small Tubers

DESCRIPTION: Small tubers are formed on seed pieces.

CAUSE: Physiologically old seed.

MANAGEMENT OPTIONS: Do not plant seed that has been exposed to temperatures above 50°F (10°C) for long periods of time or has multiple sprouts at many eyes.

Eyes Without Sprouts

DESCRIPTION: No sprouts on eyes.

CAUSE: Tubers were treated with a chemical sprout inhibitor.

MANAGEMENT OPTIONS: Plant only certified or foundation seed tubers.

Foliar and/or Stem Lesions

Leaf and stem lesion color and shape help identify the disease or physiological disorder responsible for the symptoms.

Round to Irregular Green Spots with Lighter Green Halo Areas

DESCRIPTION: Round to irregularly shaped, light to dark green water-soaked spots are initial symptoms. Lesions are bordered by a halo of light green tissue (Plate 104), and under moist conditions white sporulation forms in the halo areas especially on the underside of leaves (Plate 105). Stems and tubers may also be infected (Plate 106).

CAUSE: Late blight (*Phytophthora infestans*). This devastating disease caused the potato famine in Ireland and is still the most important threat to potato production today. Foliar destruction can limit yields but the more serious aspect of the disease is tuber rot. The pathogen causing late blight requires host tissue to survive. It overwinters in stored and discarded tubers (often referred to as cull piles). Conditions favoring disease development are high humidity and moderate temperatures of 60–80°F (16–27°C). Under these conditions the disease can spread rapidly.

MANAGEMENT OPTIONS: Use disease-free seed, eliminate cull piles, and apply approved conventional or organic fungicides. In humid regions fungicides should be applied at 5- to 10-day intervals, depending on environmental conditions, beginning when plants are about 8 in. (20 cm) high. Infected plants should be killed or removed. Delay harvest for at least two weeks after plants are dead or removed to minimize late blight tuber rot.

Brown Lesions on Older Leaves or on Stressed Plants

DESCRIPTION: Circular to angular small brown lesions located primarily on oldest leaves or on stressed plants. Lesions have concentric rings (Plate 107) and are bordered by leaf veins. As the disease progresses upper portions of plants are also affected. Dark brown lesions may be present on stems.

CAUSE: Early blight (*Alternaria solani*). This disease is especially troublesome in western production areas but is observed in all regions. The pathogen overwinters in tubers and other tissue of plants in the potato family. Symptoms first appear on the oldest leaves or on plants that are stressed by low nutrition, especially nitrogen, or by diseases such as *Verticillium* or *Fusarium* wilts. Early maturing cultivars are more susceptible than late maturing ones. Immature and bruised tubers are susceptible to infection.

MANAGEMENT OPTIONS: Minimize stress by adequate crop rotation, fertilization, and irrigation. Appropriate fungicides can reduce damage but should not be applied until early symptoms arise. Plant debris should be incorporated into the soil shortly after harvest. Harvest should be two weeks after vines die so that tubers develop firm skin. Minimize bruising tubers as bruises are entry points for the pathogen.

Purplish Speckled Leaflets

DESCRIPTION: Upper portions of leaflets are speckled and purplish, lower portions have a bronzed to glassy appearance.

CAUSE: Air pollution. Natural and man-made air pollutants affect plants in various ways. Often the damage observed is at the stomata, the breathing pores of plants on the undersides of leaflets. Some pollutants cause a color change, usually a red to purple cast to the tissue. The common culprits are ozone and engine exhaust coupled with environmental conditions such as fog and cloudy, hazy days that concentrate pollutants in low-lying areas. Cultivars differ in susceptibility. 'Norland' is susceptible to air pollution. Symptoms often occur when plants are senescing (turning yellow) or are not fertilized well.

MANAGEMENT OPTIONS: Adequate fertilization and selecting resistant cultivars.

Grayish Lesions on Leaflets and Stem Rot

DESCRIPTION: Various size lesions with grayish fuzz on leaflets or stem rot.

CAUSE: Gray mold, botrytis vine rot (*Botrytis cinerea*). The lesion symptoms can be confused with late blight. The difference in symptoms is the color and the location of the sporulation. Botrytis has a gray mass of spores over the affected tissue whereas late blight sporulation is limited to the halo area around the lesions and is white. Botrytis is a weak pathogen and invades dead tissue, such as tip burn areas due to moisture stress and where blossoms have dropped on leaflets. The stem rot occurs when plants develop dense canopies that inhibit air circulation.

MANAGEMENT OPTIONS: Do not overfertilize, especially with nitrogen.

Foliar Distortions

Leaf distortion is another diagnostic symptom that provides clues to the cause of abnormal growth. Included here are curled and crinkly leaves, bright yellow areas on otherwise green leaves, and cupped, reddish leaves.

Curled, Leathery Leaflets

DESCRIPTION: Young plants are stunted with curled, stiff "leathery" leaflets and pale color. Older plants have curled, leathery leaflets in the upper portion of the plant. Some pink to red color may be present at the margins of leaflets.

CAUSE: Potato leafroll virus (PLRV). The symptoms on young plants are due to planting tubers infected with the virus, often a problem when non-certified seed is planted. The symptoms on older plants are due to current season infection of otherwise healthy plants. The use of infected seed results in severe yield reduction. Late-season infection does not necessarily cause major crop loss; however, in susceptible cultivars, such as 'Russet Burbank' and 'Bake-King', net necrosis may develop in tubers. Net necrosis is a discoloration of the phloem tissue. It appears as brown flecks mostly at the stem end of tubers but may extend deeper. These symptoms can be confused with vascular discoloration due to wilt diseases (*Fusarium* or *Verticillium*) or rapid death of the vines. Current season infection is the result of transmission of the virus from infected plants to noninfected plants by aphids. The most effective transmitter is the green peach aphid (*Myzus persicae*). Once this aphid species is infected with the virus it can transmit it for the remainder of its life.

MANAGEMENT OPTIONS: Plant certified or foundation seed, eliminate cull piles and volunteer potato plants, and control aphids.

Mottled, Crinkly Leaflets

DESCRIPTION: Leaflets have a mottled coloration, crinkly appearance (Plate 108) or veins have brown to black specks. Plants may be stunted.

CAUSE: One or more potato viruses A, S, X, Y (PVA, PVS, PVX, PVY). When more than one virus is present symptoms may be intensified. Viruses may not show symptoms if infection takes place late in the season; however, tuber infection will likely have occurred. Except for certain strains of PVY, infected tubers do not have external symptoms. Transmission of viruses can occur by mechanical means, but is most often by aphids, especially for PVA, PVS, and PVY.

MANAGEMENT OPTIONS: Plant only certified or foundation seed potatoes, minimize mechanical damage when cultivating, disinfect cutting knives with 1 part 5.25-percent chlorine bleach and 200 parts water.

Yellow-spotted Leaflets

DESCRIPTION: Some plants have bright yellow portions.

CAUSE: Calico or alfalfa mosaic virus. The virus is transmitted from alfalfa plants to potatoes by aphids. While the symptoms are quite dramatic the disease typically doesn't cause major reductions in yield or tuber quality.

MANAGEMENT OPTIONS: Plant certified or foundation seed.

Cupped, Reddish Leaflets and Stunted Plants

DESCRIPTION: Plants are stunted, leaflets are cupped and reddish at the upper portions of plants, and small tubers are formed above ground. Excessive numbers of shoots and/or bushy plants.

CAUSE: Various phytoplasmas, which are bacteria that lack cell walls, are transmitted to potatoes by leafhoppers. The phytoplasmas most commonly found associated with disease symptoms on potatoes are potato purple top or aster yellows, beet leafhopper transmitted virescence, and potato witches broom. Symptoms associated with these diseases may be confused with those of potato leafroll virus and blackleg. Leafhoppers infect potatoes after first feeding on infected host plants, which typically include weeds.

MANAGEMENT OPTIONS: Plant certified or foundation seed and control leafhoppers.

Wilts

Various wilts can affect plants at any time in the growing season, from early to late, and can appear at the top or the base of the plant.

Premature, One-sided Wilt

DESCRIPTION: Plants begin to wilt prematurely. Wilting begins in the lower portion of plants and may be more pronounced on one side of leaves or plants (Plate 109). Brown discoloration is present at the base of the stem when cut diagonally (Plate 110).

CAUSE: *Verticillium* wilt (*V. dahliae* or *V. albo-atrum*). Similar symptoms with the exception of one-sided wilting can be attributed to *Fusarium* spp. Both diseases cause yield reductions and can cause vascular discoloration in tubers. *Fusarium* can cause decay at the stem end of tubers. *Verticillium* and *Fusarium* wilts affect other members of the potato family (tomatoes, eggplant, and peppers) and strawberries; potatoes should not be rotated with these crops. Corn and other grasses tend to be resistant to *Verticillium*. High populations of root lesion nematodes (*Pratylenchus* spp.) facilitate infection of *Verticillium* by creating entry points on roots.

MANAGEMENT OPTIONS: Rotate with corn, incorporate debris from crops in the mustard family (broccoli, cabbage, cauliflower) the season before potato planting (as these decay they create a natural biofumigant), and fertilize and water adequately.

Mid- to Late-season Wilt

DESCRIPTION: Plants wilt rapidly at mid- to late-season. Symptoms are similar to *Verticillium* wilt but the one-sided wilting associated with *Verticillium* is absent. Roots tend to decay and small black dots are present on stems and tubers.

CAUSE: Black dot (*Colletotrichum coccodes*). The disease often infects plants that are weakened by other wilt-causing diseases and accelerates early dying of plants. Conditions favoring the disease include moisture stress from too much or too little moisture, too much or too little nitrogen fertilization, and high temperatures.

MANAGEMENT OPTIONS: Rotate with grass crops, do not rotate tomatoes, eggplant, or other members of the potato family, plant certified or foundation seed, fertilize adequately, and avoid excessive irrigation.

Wilted Plants and Black Decaying Stems

DESCRIPTION: Plants wilt, leaflets in the upper portions of plants are cupped (Plate 111) and may have a reddish cast, stems have black and slimy portions (Plate 112).

CAUSE: Blackleg (*Pectobacterium carotovorum*). Seed tubers infected with this bacterium may also be the cause of poor emergence. When older plants are infected, the black discoloration at the base of plants is very descriptive of the name blackleg. When these symptoms occur further up the stem the disease is referred to as aerial blackleg. The disease can extend into the tubers and cause a soft rot that is delineated from healthy tissue by dark brown to black margins. The decay can start at stem ends, lenticels, or wounds. The disease progresses rapidly in wet conditions.

MANAGEMENT OPTIONS: Plant certified or foundation seed, cure seed properly, plant in well-drained soil, or provide for adequate drainage away from seed pieces.

Wilted Plants and Black Scurf on Tubers

DESCRIPTION: Plants wilt, leaflets in the upper portions of plants are cupped and may have a reddish cast, below-ground stems have brown lesions that may girdle the stems, and aerial tubers may be present at the base of leaves (Plate 113).

CAUSE: *Rhizoctonia* stem and stolon canker (*R. solani.*) The symptoms described above are due to mid- to late-season infection of the same fungus that reduces plant stands. Cool wet conditions favor disease development. The fungus overwinters on plant debris or as black resting bodies (sclerotia) on tubers. Severe infection can reduce yield by decreasing tuber size. Quality is impacted by skin cracking, growth cracks, and "black scurf" on tuber surfaces. The black scurf does not affect eating quality but is considered a defect.

MANAGEMENT OPTIONS: Avoid planting seed pieces with sclerotia, rotate with grass crops.

Tuber Rots

Some diseases or physiological disorders cause tuber rots. Such diseases often enter through bruised areas.

Odorless Soft Decay

DESCRIPTION: Rot begins as an odorless soft decay with margins bordered by healthy tissue. Rots are initially associated with bruises, lenticels (breathing pores), or stem ends (Plate 114).

CAUSE: Bacterial soft rot (*Pectobacterium carotovorum*). Infection in the field occurs during wet conditions through lenticels and stem ends. Bruises, especially of immature tubers, provide entry points for the bacterium. Warm, moist conditions after infection favor other soft rotting bacteria. Cool dry conditions may keep the rot from spreading.

MANAGEMENT OPTIONS: Minimize wet conditions, harvest mature tubers, minimize bruising, and cure harvested tubers at 50–55°F (10–13°C) for 7 to 10 days before reducing temperatures for long-term storage.

Gray-black Soft Decay

DESCRIPTION: Rot has a distinctive border between gray to black soft tissue and healthy tissue. When cut tubers are squeezed, clear liquid is released.

CAUSE: *Pythium* leak (*Pythium* spp.). This fungus enters the tubers through wounds at harvest, especially during hot weather, and in excessively wet field conditions.

MANAGEMENT OPTIONS: Do not harvest in hot weather and minimize wet field conditions.

Cream to Brown Soft Decay

DESCRIPTION: Rot begins with a cream to brown vascular ring discoloration. When tubers are squeezed a creamy exudate is forced out of the vascular tissue.

CAUSE: Bacterial ring rot (*Clavibacter michiganensis* subsp. *sepedonicus*). This is a serious disease because it is persistent and causes yield reduction and decay. There is zero tolerance for this disease in seed certification programs.

MANAGEMENT OPTIONS: Plant only certified or foundation seed, clean and disinfect equipment (for example, knives, containers), eliminate cull piles and volunteer (plants that emerge from tubers of the previous planting) potatoes.

Brown Granular Decay

DESCRIPTION: Tan to brown granular discoloration extends from the surface of tubers (Plate 115). Some tubers are completely decayed.

CAUSE: Late blight (*Phytophthora infestans*). Tuber infection takes place when water washes spores from infected foliage into soil. See late blight description in foliar disease section.

MANAGEMENT OPTIONS: Kill or remove diseased plants as soon as disease is diagnosed, delay harvest for at least two weeks after vine death or removal.

Soft Stem End

DESCRIPTION: Stem end of elongated tubers is soft or is filled with a jelly-like substance.

CAUSE: Low moisture levels. This disorder is especially troublesome in cultivars that produce long, or elongated, tubers. In its initial stages the disorder is called translucent end or sugar end. Under moisture stress starch is moved from the region near the stem of tubers to other portions of plants. The stem end of affected tubers is high in sugar and becomes dark when fried. In later stages the jelly portion may slough off leaving normal tissue below the affected area.

MANAGEMENT OPTIONS: Maintain good moisture conditions.

External Tuber Defects

The appearance of tubers can be marred by various types of lesions, growth cracks, knobbiness, green and pink discolorations, and freckled and blotchy spots in a range of colors.

Corky Tissue

Descriptions: Tubers have corky tissue that may be superficial or pitted (Plate 116). The affected areas may be limited to one spot or may affect entire tubers.

CAUSE: Common scab (*Streptomyces scabies*, *S. acidiscabies*). This disease is favored by dry conditions during tuber initiation. Soil pH has an effect on the development of scab-causing organisms. Favorable pH levels for *S. scabies* range from 5.5 to 7.5 and are below 5.5 for *S. acidiscabies*. Cultivars vary in their susceptibility to common scab.

MANAGEMENT OPTIONS: Grow resistant cultivars, control pH, do not plant seed pieces with scab lesions, and maintain optimum moisture levels at tuber initiation.

Cracked Areas

DESCRIPTION: Tubers have slight to deep cracks (Plate 117).

CAUSE: Irregular moisture conditions during rapid tuber expansion. Moisture extremes from dry to wet are often the cause of this physiological disorder. Cultivars vary in their tendency to develop growth cracks.

MANAGEMENT OPTIONS: Maintain uniform moisture conditions throughout the growing season, grow resistant cultivars.

Knobby or Misshaped Tubers

DESCRIPTION: Tubers are misshapen (Plate 118) or knobby (Plate 119).

CAUSE: Irregular moisture conditions similar to the ones described for growth cracks. Cultivars that produce long tubers are more vulnerable to knobs than cultivars that produce round tubers.

MANAGEMENT OPTIONS: Maintain uniform moisture conditions throughout growing season, grow resistant cultivars.

Greenish Tubers

DESCRIPTION: Tubers have green portions (Plate 120).

CAUSE: Chlorophyll is produced in areas exposed to light. Dark green areas are due to direct exposure to sunlight. In addition to chlorophyll, alkaloid substances are present in the green tissue. *Alkaloids cause bitter taste and green portions should not be eaten* (see chapter 10). Cultivars vary in their tendency to produce "sunburned" tubers. Cultivars that develop tubers high in the hills or on long stolons tend to have more sunburned tubers than those that produce tubers deep in the hills.

MANAGEMENT OPTIONS: Plant seed pieces deep and develop broad hills.

Freckled Tubers

DESCRIPTION: Tubers have pronounced "freckled" spots (Plate 121). Some may be raised and others may be sunken.

CAUSE: Enlarged breathing pores (lenticels). Under wet conditions the area near the pores swell, resulting in white "bumps." These spots shrink when tubers dry, creating brown "freckles." When tubers remain wet the enlarged lenticels are entry points for decay-causing organisms. Under these conditions rot can became severe.

MANAGEMENT OPTIONS: Plant in well-drained soils or provide for adequate drainage in poorly drained soils, do not over irrigate.

Blotchy, Shiny Skin

DESCRIPTION: Tuber skin has blotchy areas that exhibit a sheen when moist (Plate 122).

CAUSE: Silver scurf (*Helminthosporium solani*). This disease is limited to tuber skin. Symptoms are most pronounced on red- and purple-skinned cultivars where the affected areas appear bleached. The disease progresses with time in the field after vine death. The affected tissue is subject to moisture loss in storage.

MANAGEMENT OPTIONS: Plant seed without silver scurf, harvest as soon as tubers are mature after vine death, prevent condensation on tuber surface during storage. Few varieties have meaningful resistance.

Blotchy, Black-dotted Skin

DESCRIPTION: Tuber skin has blotchy areas with many small black dots.

CAUSE: Black dot (*Colletotrichum coccodes*). Symptoms are similar to silver scurf with the addition of black resting bodies of the fungus in the affected areas. Early death of the vines due to the disease may warn of tuber symptoms. Tubers may have both silver scurf and black dot, but not in the same affected areas.

MANAGEMENT OPTIONS: Rotate with grass crops, do not rotate with tomatoes, eggplant, or other members of the potato family, plant certified or foundation seed, fertilize adequately, and avoid over irrigation.

Purplish-brown Lesions

DESCRIPTION: Tuber skin has small purplish-brown raised lesions to brown lesions with powdery appearance to coalesced lesions that are similar to common scab. Roots may have white to dark brown galls.

CAUSE: Powdery scab (*Spongospora subterranea*). The disease infects roots, tubers, and stolons and is favored by cool, wet soils. The fungus is spread by planting infected seed and using contaminated cattle manure. Once introduced the organism is persistent for as many as six years. The fungus is a vector of mop top virus.

MANAGEMENT OPTIONS: Plant disease-free seed, maintain optimum moisture level, do not use manure from animals that have eaten infected tubers.

Pink Discoloration

DESCRIPTION: Pink discoloration that may be moist on the surface of tubers near eyes or lenticels (Plate 123).

CAUSE: Pinkeye. This defect is currently considered a physiological disorder associated with moisture stress. Often, affected tubers have vascular discoloration and there has been an association between pinkeye and *Verticillium* wilt. Under moist conditions soft rot may invade damaged tissue. The pink discoloration may turn tan to brown in dry storage conditions. Cultivars susceptible to *Verticillium* wilt tend to be more vulnerable to this disorder.

MANAGEMENT OPTIONS: Rotate with crops not susceptible to *Verticillium* wilt and avoid growing susceptible cultivars, such as 'Superior' or 'Kennebec'.

Internal Tuber Defects

Internal defects are as important as those visible on tuber surfaces. Among such defects are discolorations and cavities. Cutting open a tuber is the only way to detect these symptoms.

Hollow Heart

DESCRIPTION: Hollow area near the center of the tuber (Plate 124).

CAUSE: This disorder occurs when tubers enlarge rapidly and is most often observed in large tubers. Cultivars vary in their susceptibility to hollow heart.

MANAGEMENT OPTIONS: Use recommended seed piece spacing, maintain uniform moisture conditions during growing season, and avoid planting susceptible cultivars.

Brown Center

DESCRIPTION: Brown firm discoloration near the center of the tuber (Plate 125).

CAUSE: This disorder is associated with cool temperatures at or shortly after tuber initiation. Cultivars vary in susceptibility.

MANAGEMENT OPTIONS: Delay planting to avoid cool temperatures at tuber initiation, plant resistant cultivars.

Black Heart

DESCRIPTION: Black discoloration near center of tubers.

CAUSE: Lack of oxygen. Conditions favoring black heart are waterlogged soils, high storage temperatures, and poor air movement. The discolored tissue may be solid or may surround a cavity.

MANAGEMENT OPTIONS: Employ good drainage practices, provide adequate ventilation in storage, and maintain proper storage temperatures.

Brown Flecks

DESCRIPTION: Scattered brown flecks sometimes concentrated at the bud end of tubers but can be located in other portions (Plate 126).

CAUSE: Internal necrosis or internal brown spot. Both disorders are the result of susceptible cultivars exposed to high soil temperatures, low soil moisture and low tuber calcium levels. 'Atlantic' is especially susceptible.

MANAGEMENT OPTIONS: Select planting dates so that tubers are mature by the time high temperatures are expected (especially in southern regions), maintain adequate soil moisture, use mulch, add calcium to low-calcium soils, grow resistant cultivars.

Nematodes

Nematodes are very small round worms that are present in soil, water, and plant tissue. Plant parasitic nematodes cause damage by feeding on roots and tubers or by providing entry points for other disease organisms.

Root Knot Nematodes

DESCRIPTION: Root knot nematodes (*Meloidogyne* spp.) cause swellings or bumps on tubers and roots. Tuber symptoms are more easily seen. The Columbia root knot nematode (*M. chitwoodi*), which primarily occurs in the western United States, and the northern root knot nematode (*M. hapla*) are more active at cool temperatures than the southern root knot nematode (*M.*

incognita). These pests have a wide host range and can persist for two years in the absence of host plants.

MANAGEMENT OPTIONS: Where northern root knot nematode is present a two-year rotation with corn or other grasses is effective. Since grasses are hosts of the other two species listed, a rotation with grass crops is not effective. Incorporation of green manures of sudangrass or members of the mustard family can reduce nematode populations. Green manures of sudangrass or members of the mustard family should be thoroughly incorporated into the soil so that the plant material can decompose and release toxic compounds (biofumigants) that can reduce nematode populations. Another technique to reduce nematodes is to leave the soil free of plants (including weeds) for a season, a practice called fallow cultivation. Early harvest will reduce nematode damage.

Root Lesion Nematodes

DESCRIPTION: Root lesion nematodes (*Pratylenchus* spp.) feed on roots and tubers and can cause serious yield losses directly or by providing entry points for *Verticillium* or *Fusarium* wilts. In the absence of these two organisms, *P. penetrans* can reduce yield whereas *P. negelectus* does not. When populations of *P. penetrans* are high, feeding on tuber surfaces can result in rough-textured skin. Root lesion nematodes have a wide host range.

MANAGEMENT OPTIONS: Incorporation of green manures (see management options for root knot nematodes) and fallow cultivation are approaches suitable for small-scale plantings.

Potato Cyst Nematodes

DESCRIPTION: Potato cyst nematodes (*Globodera* spp.) are quarantine pests. Although they are not widespread in North America, they have the potential to cause significant yield reductions and can remain viable in the soil for decades. For these reasons government agencies have strict regulations on how or if potatoes can be grown in areas where these pests, which feed and reproduce on roots of members of the potato family, are known to occur. Females develop eggs while attached to roots and eventually develop into light colored cysts containing as many as 200 eggs. The cysts of the golden nematode (*G. rostochiensis*) turn golden brown as they mature whereas the cysts of the pale cyst nematode (*G. pallida*) maintain the light color (Plate 127).

MANAGEMENT OPTIONS: If either potato cyst nematode is suspected, agricultural authorities should be contacted.

Insects

Insect pests reduce yield directly by feeding on plants or by injecting plant pathogens or toxins into plants. Some insects feed on tubers and thereby reduce marketability and storability. Regular observation of plants is important to determine if insects are present and at what levels. Weekly observations (scouting) of upper and lower leaves, brushing of plants to notice flying insects, and placing yellow sticky cards to trap aphids and other insects are techniques that help make that determination.

Not all insects present on and around potato plants are injurious. Many are innocuous transients and others are beneficial, feeding on the pests that cause plant damage. Proper identification of insects is necessary before applying insecticides so that appropriate management practices are employed and that beneficial insects aren't sacrificed in the process. The following symptoms will help provide identification of problem insects. Brief descriptions of beneficial insects are presented in chapter 7.

Leaf Holes or Defoliation

Missing leaves or parts thereof and leaves with holes are symptoms of insect damage.

Numerous Small Holes

DESCRIPTION: Large number of small holes in leaflets giving a shot hole appearance (Plate 128).

CAUSE: Flea beetles (*Epitrix cucumeris*, *Systena frontalis*, and other species). Adults are small (1/16 in. [1.6 mm]), shiny black, with large back legs. Beetles tend to jump when disturbed. Larvae are slender white worms that feed on roots and tubers. Tuber damage appears as pitting and narrow tunnels. Foliar damage is often seen shortly after plants emerge and unless very severe is usually not problematic from a yield standpoint.

MANAGEMENT OPTIONS: Floating row covers and trap crops of mustard family members could reduce early season damage. In severe cases, approved insecticides may be necessary.

Partially or Entirely Consumed Leaflets

DESCRIPTION: Portions or entire leaflets consumed, in severe cases plants are totally defoliated (Plate 129).

CAUSE: Colorado potato beetle (*Leptinotarsa decemlineata*). Adults overwinter in soil, emerging shortly after potatoes emerge. They walk to the plants since their wing muscles are not yet capable of flight. There they lay clusters of yellow-orange eggs (Plate 130), usually on the underside of leaflets. Larvae hatch in four to nine days, depending on temperature, and rapidly defoliate plants as they progress through four stages. When larvae mature they enter the soil and pupate. Five to nine days later they emerge and the cycle begins anew.

Adults have alternate black and yellow-orange stripes that run lengthwise on the wing covers (Plate 131). There are 10 dark stripes in total, hence "*decemlineata*" in the scientific name. Larvae are hump-backed with reddish orange bodies that have two rows of black dots on each side (Plate 132).

MANAGEMENT OPTIONS: In small plantings the best option may be to pick off adults and larvae. Covering plants with floating row covers (spunbond fabric that allows sunlight, water, and air exchange but pores are small enough to exclude insects) protects young plants. Digging a 12-in. (30-cm) deep trench around where potatoes are planted and lining the trench with black plastic is effective at intercepting overwintering adults—after beetles fall into the trench, they are unable to climb back out. While this insect is resistant to many commonly applied insecticides, some conventional and organic materials may be effective. Check with local extension staff for specific information. There are also some naturally occurring organisms that help suppress populations (see chapter 7).

Holes in Leaflets, Stems, or Branches

DESCRIPTION: Holes in leaflets, in some cases stems or branches are cut.

CAUSE: Various cutworms. The larval stage of night-flying moths causes the damage. Some species feed on lower portions of plants often cutting stems at the soil line. Others climb and feed on the upper portions of plants. Damage may be most severe in wet, weedy areas. Feeding takes place at night. During the day the insects are found under soil clods or plant debris, or deep in the plant canopy. When disturbed the caterpillars curl into a C shape.

MANAGEMENT OPTIONS: Control weeds, provide adequate drainage, apply appropriate insecticide or bait.

Older Leaflets with Holes

DESCRIPTION: Holes mostly in older leaflets.

CAUSE: Loopers (*Trichoplusia ni, Autographa californica*). Symptoms of looper feeding on leaflets are similar to damage caused by cutworms. The distinguishing factor is that the loopers are present during daylight whereas cutworms avoid sunlight. The larvae are primarily green with several narrow pale green stripes along the sides and back. They arch their backs when moving, giving a looping motion. Loopers are not considered major pests of potato. They are subject to attack by naturally occurring predators and parasites.

MANAGEMENT OPTIONS: Generally no action is necessary. Some organic insecticides are effective.

Wilting, Leaflet Curling, or Stunting

Insect damage to potatoes includes wilted stems and branches, curled leaves, and stunted plants.

Curled, Sticky Leaflets

DESCRIPTION: Leaflets curled, plants stunted, shiny sticky substance on leaflet surfaces.

CAUSE: Various aphid species. Predominant aphids attacking potatoes are green peach (*Myzus persicae*), potato (*Macrosiphum euphorbiae*) (Plate 133), buckthorn (*Aphis nasturii*), and foxglove (*Aulacorthum solani*), although other species may also feed on potato plants. Of the listed species, the green peach aphid is the most significant. It not only causes injury directly by feeding, but also is the most effective vector of potato viruses. In general, aphids are small, round to pear-shaped insects that range in color from yellow to pink to various shades of green. They feed by piercing leaves and stems, and sucking plant fluids. In the process, they can transmit viruses to healthy plants if the aphids have fed on infected plants. In cold climates aphids overwinter on fruit trees as eggs. In warm climates aphids reproduce with no egg stage. When large colonies develop, severe stunting can result. In addition to seeing the insects, another indication of their presence is seeing a sticky substance, called honeydew, on leaf surfaces.

MANAGEMENT OPTIONS: Minimize use of pesticides that may kill predators, use certified or foundation seed to minimize virus spread, apply dormant sprays to nearby fruit trees, monitor plants and physically crush colonies, apply appropriate insecticides.

Yellow to Brown Leaflet Margins and Tips

DESCRIPTION: Leaflet margins and tips are yellow to brown and are curled upward. In severe cases outer edges of leaflets have a scorched appearance.

CAUSE: Potato leafhopper (*Empoasca fabae*). These pests do not overwinter in the northern United States and Canada, but migrate to these areas from southern locations. Adult leafhoppers are tiny, pale green, and wedge-shaped. They are very quick and fly when plants are disturbed. Young leafhoppers, referred to as nymphs (Plate 134), move rapidly sideways. Adults and nymphs are usually found on undersides of leaflets. Both forms feed by sucking sap from leaves and stems and in the process inject a toxin. *Hopperburn* is the term used to describe severely affected plants (Plate 135). Potato leafhoppers can cause severe yield reduction. Careful observation of the undersides of leaves and sweeping with an insect net will determine if leafhoppers are a concern. Leafhoppers move from cut hay fields or grain fields as they mature.

MANAGEMENT OPTIONS: Monitor plants especially as hay is cut, apply appropriate insecticides, and grow resistant cultivars such as 'Elba', 'King Harry', or 'Prince Hairy'.

Pink to Purple Curled Leaflet Tips and Margins

DESCRIPTION: Leaflet margins and tips are curled upward, and have pink to purple coloration in the upper portions of plants.

CAUSE: Aster leafhopper transmission of aster yellows phytoplasma (see under "Diseases and Physiological Disorders" in this chapter). The insect is similar to potato leafhopper in shape but is larger and has six black spots on the front of the head.

MANAGEMENT OPTIONS: Plant certified or foundation seed and control leafhoppers.

Wilted Stems and Branches

DESCRIPTION: Main stems or branches wilt and then collapse.

CAUSE: Potato stem borer (*Hydracea micacea*) or European corn borer (*Ostrinia nubilalis*). The larvae of both species are found in the inner core of stems. The potato stem borer is primarily found at the base of plants, whereas the European corn borer larvae can be found in stems in other portions of plants. European corn borer pressure is increased when potatoes follow corn and the debris is not chopped to destroy overwintering larvae.

MANAGEMENT OPTIONS: Once the borers are inside plants there is no practical management strategy.

Yellow, Curled Leaflets and Stunted Plants

DESCRIPTION: Plants are stunted, leaflets curled and yellow.

CAUSE: Potato psyllid (*Bactericera cockerelli*). This insect problem is greater in the southern United States than in northern regions. However, as temperatures increase the insect migrates northward. Adults are very small and resemble cicadas. The adults do not cause much damage to plants but the nymphs inject a toxin that causes psyllid yellows. Adults range in color from light yellow to brown and finally to gray or black with white markings. Eggs are football-shaped, yellow to orange, borne on fine stalks, and are located on leaf margins. Nymphs are flattened and scalelike, and are located in the lower portion of plants. The nymphs move readily when disturbed and secrete a white granulated substance. Psyllids are associated with a disorder described as zebra chip. Affected tubers have discolored zones in the flesh that produce potato chips with light and dark areas.

MANAGEMENT OPTIONS: There are some naturally occurring enemies of psyllids. Some insecticides may kill beneficial insects but have no effect on this pest.

Blotchy, Brown Areas on Leaves

DESCRIPTION: Leaves have brown to bronze areas that may be blotchy or affect the entire leaf surface. Fine webbing may be seen on leaves.

CAUSE: Two-spotted spider mite (*Tetranychus urticae*). Injury is associated with hot dusty conditions and cultivars with hairy leaf surfaces, such as 'Prince Hairy' and 'King Harry'. Mites are very small creatures that can hardly be seen with the naked eye. The use of a 10X magnifying hand lens is helpful in observing them. Adults are yellowish brown with eight legs and two red eye spots near the head and two dark spots on the body. The insects feed by puncturing the leaf surface. Photosynthesis is reduced in severe cases.

MANAGEMENT OPTIONS: Minimize dusty conditions near plantings, grow cultivars with nonhairy leaf surfaces.

Tuber Injury

Holes of any size in a tuber are other symptoms of insect damage.

Small Holes in Tubers or Seed Pieces

DESCRIPTION: Pencil-point-sized holes in harvested tubers or in seed pieces.

CAUSE: Wireworms (*Limonius* spp.) or flea beetles (the latter were discussed previously in this chapter under "Leaf Holes or Defoliation"). Wireworms are soil-inhabiting larvae of click beetles. Adults are hard-shelled black to dark brown beetles. When placed on their backs they can right themselves, making a clicking sound in the process. The larvae are long, thin, and nearly cylindrical. They are yellow to light brown and have a smooth hard skin. The life cycle of most wireworms begins in sod crops or weedy areas and lasts for three to five years depending on species. When present at planting wireworms feed on sprouts as well as tubers and can cause stand reduction.

MANAGEMENT OPTIONS: Avoid planting potatoes directly after incorporation of sod. Monitor soil for wireworms prior to planting by placing carrot or potato pieces 6–10 in. (15–25 cm) deep and count wireworms after about three days. If wireworms are detected, consider planting potatoes in another location.

Large Cavities in Tubers

DESCRIPTION: Large external cavities in mature tubers.

CAUSE: White grubs of June beetles (*Phyllophaga* spp.). Larvae of other beetles, including Colorado potato beetle, also feed on tubers. June beetle larvae are white, relatively thick-bodied, with brown heads and legs. When exposed they curl into a C shape. The life cycle of June beetles begins in sod areas and lasts several years. Sandy areas are preferred sites for the beetles. Damage is most severe when tubers stay in the soil for long periods of time.

MANAGEMENT OPTIONS: Harvest tubers in a timely manner.

Weeds

There are major regional differences in which weeds are the most prevalent and problematic. The broad categories, however, are broad-leaved annuals, annual grasses, and perennials. Annual weeds are more easily managed than are perennial weeds. So whenever possible potatoes should be planted in areas not infested with perennial weeds. If that is not possible, fall tillage may be desirable to weaken the perennial weeds. During the growing season aggressive cultivation or hoeing and hand weeding will be required to control perennial weeds. In nonorganic production a labeled (registered), systemic, nonselective herbicide with short residual activity may be applied in the fall or when crops are not present.

Some brief definitions: *labeled* (registered) refers to the legality of the chemical; *systemic* means that the herbicide moves within the plant to kill or injure it; *nonselective* means the chemical affects all plants it comes in contact with—weeds and crops alike; and *short residual* means it does not last long after application. To be effective these materials need to be applied at specified rates to actively growing weeds. In using this approach it is critical to follow label instructions. Since there are many specifics about this approach, it should be the one of last resort.

Hoeing or other mechanical cultivation and hilling will help control annual and perennial weeds (Figure 8). Cultivation should begin just as weeds begin to emerge, sometimes referred to as the white thread stage because germinating annual weeds resemble white threads before they emerge (Plate 136). Cultivars with vigorous early growth aid in the management of all weed types. One approach that is suitable for small weeds is the use of a propane flamer (Figure 9). The flamer approach is more appropriate for the control of annual weeds than perennial weeds.

Broad-leaved Annuals

Typically broad-leaved annual weeds are the first to emerge and are the easiest to manage. The most effective time to cultivate or hoe is when these weeds are beginning to sprout. This may need to be done several times to address different times of germination. The most common broad-leaved weeds are lambs quarters (*Chenopodium album*), red root pigweed (*Amaranthus retroflexus*), ragweed (*Ambrosia artemisiifolia*), and smartweed (*Polygonum*

Figure 8. Finger weeders are effective in killing small emerging annual weeds and may be practical for small scale farmers. Finger weeders are primarily used as potatoes begin to emerge. Some models have teeth that may be adjusted to keep from injuring larger plants.

Figure 9. A propane flamer can be used to burn weeds, Colorado potato beetles (on young plants) and vines (to aid skin set prior to harvest).

pennsylvanicum). In western areas kochia (*Kochia scoparia*) can be a major problem. Black nightshade (*Solanum nigrum*) is one of the more-difficult-to-control annual broad-leaved weeds.

Annual Grasses

Generally annual grasses germinate later than broad-leaved weeds. The best time to manage these types of weeds is the same as for broad-leaved weeds, at or near the time of germination. Light cultivation or hoeing can be effective, especially if vigorously growing potato plants shade the soil surface. The most common annual grasses are barnyard grass (*Echinochloa crus-galli*), fall panicum (*Panicum dichotomiflorum*), and foxtails (*Setaria* spp.). Left unchecked these weeds develop dense growth that makes harvesting difficult.

Perennials

Perennials are the most difficult weeds to control. They are persistent and extremely competitive. Yields and quality are compromised when perennial weeds take over. The rhizomes of quackgrass (*Elytrigia repens*), nutsedges (*Cyperus* spp.), and Bermuda grass (*Cynodon dactylon*) can penetrate potato tubers (Plate 98). In addition the root mass these weeds develop makes harvest extremely difficult (Plates 137 and 138). Hedge bindweed (*Calystegia sepium*) is a broad-leaved perennial that develops a dense canopy above ground and extensive distribution of rhizomes below ground. While these rhizomes don't penetrate tubers, this weed species can greatly reduce tuber size and yield.

The best advice is not to plant potatoes in areas that contain any of the above perennial weeds. If you can't avoid planting in such areas, reduce the problem by tilling either in the fall or when the area is not cropped. Appropriate herbicides can be useful in these circumstances but they should be applied with care. Consult your local extension office for specific information.

 CHAPTER 7

Growing Potatoes the Organic Way

THE ORGANIC PRODUCTION of any crop relies on approaches that utilize natural processes and naturally occurring materials. Synthetic materials are not permitted. The use of crop rotations, cultural practices, beneficial organisms, and approved fertilizer and pesticide materials forms the basis of organic production. The philosophy of organic production is to produce crops by increasing soil productivity and thereby improve plant health to combat pest pressures, and to employ beneficial organisms and naturally occurring materials to control pests.

The challenges of organic production vary by geographical region. Late blight is potentially a major problem in humid areas. In arid locations where moisture is controlled by applying irrigation, late blight can be managed more easily. The effect of geographic location also applies to some insect problems. At high elevations and relatively short growing seasons, aphids are seldom a problem, whereas in areas with warm growing seasons, aphids can cause yield reductions by direct feeding and by transmitting virus diseases. Adjustments to production practices need to be made dependent on field realities.

Approved organic pesticides are used to control various pests but these are from naturally occurring sources or are formulated from such sources. Approved pesticides and fertilizer materials vary by region. National and local organic organizations can provide a list of approved materials.

Organic Enrichment of Soils

Adequate amounts of essential nutrients in the soil are necessary for good yields regardless of whether the crop is grown conventionally or organically. The organic approach relies on crop rotations; composted manures; fertilizers made from animal manures, fish, or plant materials; and mined minerals. Most organic fertilizers are released slowly, so the approach to using them needs to be thought through well in advance of planting.

Incorporating plant residues from previous crops adds to the available nutrients in the soil. The root action of rotational sod and certain row crops opens pore spaces in the soil, improving aeration and drainage. In addition to adding organic matter and nutrients to soils, crop rotations are often helpful in minimizing disease problems.

The availability of minerals in soil is to a large extent affected by soil pH. Low pH levels reduce the availability of essential nutrients and increase toxicity levels of others. At high pH levels the availability of phosphorus, manganese, zinc, and iron is reduced. Knowledge of soil pH levels is the first step in developing a meaningful fertility program.

Minerals needed for plant growth are most available at pH levels between 6.0 and 7.0. Unfortunately this range in pH is ideal for the organism that causes common scab. In naturally alkaline soils (greater than 7.0) scab is typically not a problem and it is not realistic to lower pH. In soils with a naturally low pH and where common scab is a problem, pH levels may need to be maintained at or below 5.5. Scab-resistant cultivars are recommended under these conditions. Refer to chapter 2 for scab-resistant cultivars and chapter 3 for more information on pH.

Crop Rotations

Legumes such as alfalfa, various clovers, vetches, and others provide significant amounts of nitrogen. These plants fix atmospheric nitrogen for their own benefit, but when residues of these plants are incorporated they can provide all or most of the needed nitrogen for optimal yields. The percentage of legumes in a plant stand is a critical factor in the amount of nitrogen released to the subsequent crop. Legume stands of 50 percent or less are not likely to provide the required amount of nitrogen that a potato crop needs for optimal yield.

Nonlegume crops can also provide some nitrogen but their contribution is relatively small compared to legumes. Cover crop grasses, such as rye, wheat, or oats grown after a crop is harvested, can take up some of the residual nitrogen in the soil. The nitrogen and other elements in the cover crop will be available to the next crop after incorporation in the spring. When used as cover crops these grasses should be incorporated before the stems get old and fibrous. The microbial decomposition of straw residue immobilizes nitrogen initially and delays its availability until the microbes die. The older the tissue is, the longer it takes to decompose.

Utilizing sod crops in potato production also has a downside. The sod can be a source of soil-inhabiting insects, such as wireworms and white grubs, which can reduce plant stand and increase tuber defects.

Manures and Composts

In addition to incorporating crop residue, another method of supplying minerals for plant nutrition is to use manures and compost. Manures vary in mineral content by the source (animal) and the amount of bedding included in the manure. Generally, chicken manures are higher in nitrogen content when compared to cattle or horse manure. Horse manure often has a high percentage of wood shavings or straw and may not supply as much nitrogen as other manures.

Manures provide organic matter that improves soil structure and increases microbial activity. The latter can be both good and bad for growing potatoes. Some microbes release minerals and in some cases compete with disease-causing microbes. Other microbes, such as *Escherichia coli*, can be a health hazard to humans. Manure should be applied at least 120 days prior to crop harvest to minimize microbial contamination.

One other concern with using manures is the potential for introducing weed seeds. Certain seeds will remain viable after passing through the digestive tract of animals. Fertilizers made from manure that has been composted can be used as conventional fertilizer. The nitrogen, phosphorous, and potassium content of organic fertilizers is considerably lower than conventional fertilizers and therefore more needs to be applied to get the same amount of nutrients.

Mined Minerals and Other Natural Substances

In addition to manure-based fertilizer, mined rock dusts and meals of plants and animal parts can be used to fertilize crops. Acceptable organic fertilizers include but are not limited to calcitic lime (calcium), dolomitic lime (calcium and magnesium), gypsum (calcium and sulfur), rock phosphates (slowly available phosphate), bone meal (phosphate), blood meal (nitrogen), sul-po-mag or langbenite (potash, magnesium, and sulfur), and fish meal (nitrogen).

Organic Insect Pest Management

Effective management of insect pests utilizes biological and mechanical approaches as well as approved organic insecticides. The first step in managing insect pests is to determine the insect population on the crop. Not all insects are injurious. In fact many are beneficial in reducing the number of problem insects. Therefore careful and timely observation is critical in managing insect pests.

Chapter 6 contains insect pest descriptions. Following are some approaches to help manage insect problems. The approaches include simple mechanical techniques and a list of beneficial insects and other biological organisms that have an impact on insect pests of potatoes.

Mechanical Approaches

By far the simplest effective means of managing insect pests is to physically crush eggs, larvae, and adults present on plants. This approach is a bit tedious and messy, but it works. Adult and larval stages of Colorado potato beetles, caterpillars, and other large insects can be removed and placed in a container of soapy water. The addition of soap to the water breaks the surface tension and insects then sink to bottom. Some insects, such as aphids and Colorado potato beetle larvae, can be knocked off plants by heavy rains or streams of water from a garden hose.

The use of floating row covers can reduce early season invasion of Colorado potato beetle adults and other insects. The row cover will also hasten early season growth in cool growing areas.

A trench barrier approach is described in the Colorado potato beetle section of chapter 6 and is another pesticide-free method to reduce the number of overwintering adults that can attack the plants.

Using a flamer (normally used to burn weeds) (see Figure 9) between the time of emergence and when plants are 4–6 in. (10–15 cm) tall and when Colorado potato beetle adults are present can be effective in killing the pests without materially affecting yield. The speed and the height at which the flame passes over the plants need to be such that the insects are killed or injured and the plants are only slightly singed. Flaming is most effective when temperatures are warm and the air is calm.

Beneficial Insects

Beneficial insects are available commercially but for the home gardener or small-scale producer it may be more realistic to manage naturally occurring populations than to introduce them. One way of accomplishing that is by planting strips of nectar- and pollen-producing plants nearby. These plants help harbor some beneficials by providing food when prey is absent.

Lady Beetles

Various species of lady beetles are helpful in reducing populations of aphids and Colorado potato beetles. Adults are oval, dome-shaped and have short legs. Colors range from reddish orange to yellow to black (Plates 139 and 140). Many species have spots, but not all. Yellow oval eggs are laid in clusters of 10 to 20 and resemble small Colorado potato beetle eggs. Larvae are elongated, slightly flattened and spiny, giving them the appearance of minute alligators (Plate 141). Colors of larvae vary from black to bluish gray with red, orange, or yellow markings. Both adults and larvae have voracious appetites and feed on aphids and other soft-bodied insects and Colorado potato beetle eggs.

Green Lacewings

Adult green lacewings (*Chrysopa* spp. and *Chrysoperla* spp.) are long slender insects with bright green color. As the name implies the wings are delicate; they are also transparent and fold over the body when the insect is resting.

Eggs of some species are borne singularly on long threadlike stalks. Larval shape is elongated, flattened, and tapered at each end. The larvae have long curved mandibles (mouthparts) that grasp and draw body fluids from their prey. Color is mottled gray to yellow-gray. The larvae feed on insect eggs and soft-bodied insects including aphids, Colorado potato beetles, leafhoppers, small caterpillars, and psyllids. Because of their insatiable appetites green lacewings are sometimes referred to as aphid lions.

Stink Bugs

The two-spotted stink bug (*Perillus bioculatus*) and the spined soldier stink bug (*Podisus maculiventris*) are the primary stink bugs that attack insects feeding on potatoes, mainly Colorado potato beetle larvae, cutworms, and armyworms. Adults have a shieldlike body and are about ½ in. (12 mm) long. The two-spotted stink bug adults are red to yellow with a black Y on their backs (Plate 142). Spined soldier stink bugs are tan to pale brown with spurs at the shoulders. Stink bugs get their name from the unpleasant odor they release when disturbed. Gray to gold barrel-shaped eggs are laid in clusters of 20 to 30 on leaves and stems. Young nymphs are red and black and round in shape. As they get older they develop patches and bands of yellow-orange, black, and cream colors. Both adults and nymphs use their beaks to pierce larvae of Colorado potato beetles and caterpillars.

Bigeyed Bugs

Adult bigeyed bugs (*Geocoris* spp.) are about 3/16 in. (5 mm) long and are tan to gray. Nymphs are similar in shape to adults but lack wings and are smaller. Nymph colors vary from gray to blue. Both adults and nymphs are predators of aphids, leafhoppers, and spider mites. They feed on nectar, which is an alternate food source when vulnerable insects are not available.

Damsel Bugs

Damsel bug (*Nabis* spp.) adults are tan to gray, winged, and have slender bodies ¼–½ in. (6–12 mm) long (Plate 143). They have enlarged front legs for grasping prey and piercing-sucking mouthparts. Larvae are similar in appearance except are smaller and lack wings. Both adults and larvae feed on aphids, leafhoppers, Colorado potato beetle larvae, psyllids, and spider mites.

Minute Pirate Bugs

Adult minute pirate bugs (*Orius* spp. and *Anthocoris* spp.) are about ⅛ in. (3 mm) long, black with white markings and a triangular head. Nymphs are smaller, pear shaped, yellow to amber, and have red eyes. Adults and nymphs feed on mites, insect eggs, aphids, and small caterpillars.

Predacious Ground Beetles

Predacious ground beetles are members of the family Carabidae that live on or in soil. They feed on larvae and pupae of soil-inhabiting insects including Colorado potato beetles. Adults are fast-moving shiny black to dark red beetles with long legs. Bodies of larvae are elongated, somewhat flattened, and taper toward the rear. The larvae have large heads and prominent mouthparts. Both larvae and adults feed on insects that spend part of their life cycle in soil.

Aphid Parasites

Aphidius colemani and other parasitic wasps are very small insects that parasitize adult and larval stages of aphids. Female wasps lay one egg per aphid. After the egg hatches the wasp larva develops in the body of the aphid. The aphid body swells and becomes leathery and "mummifies" (Plate 144). Adult wasps emerge shortly after the mummification begins.

Pathogens and Biological Pesticides

The fungus *Beauveria bassiana* and the bacterium *Bacillus thuringiensis* (*Bt*) are two naturally occurring microbes that have an effect on Colorado potato beetles. Various stages of Colorado potato beetle infected by *Beauveria bassiana* develop a white growth as the organism consumes the insect (Plate 145). *Bt* strains need to be consumed by Colorado potato beetle larvae while they are young to be effective. Late instars of the larvae are somewhat resistant to this organism. Some commercial *Bt* products are available but not all are certified for organic production. Other organic insecticides made from extracts of plants or fermentation of microorganisms may also be available. Contact local organic organizations or extension offices to find which materials are approved for use.

Organic Disease Management

Potatoes are susceptible to many diseases; however, with a bit of forethought, observation, and timely response the diseases may be satisfactorily addressed. The most important disease management strategy is prevention. Use of certified or foundation seed and planting disease-free seed pieces will go a long way in reducing the incidence of viruses and seed-borne disease.

Factors such as crop rotations (including biofumigant cover crops), use of resistant cultivars, proper fertilization, adequate moisture, planting and harvest dates, and sanitation play important roles in addressing potato disease problems. The nonchemical management options listed in chapter 6 are applicable and should be used in an organic production approach. Organic management options for late blight and early blight are presented below.

Late Blight

Late blight is a more significant problem in humid areas than in arid regions. The need for a humid environment for the germination of spores reduces the potential in areas where irrigation is needed to produce crops. In these areas late blight can still be a problem if sprinkler irrigation is used and the foliage remains moist for an extended period at favorable temperatures.

Planting certified or foundation seed and eliminating heaps of discarded potatoes (cull piles) and potato plants that are produced from tubers that over-wintered from the previous crop (volunteer potato plants) reduce the potential for inoculation. Since spores can be wind blown from distant sites, plants can still become infected, even if all reasonable precautions are taken.

Many extension offices in potato-producing areas have late blight forecasts and reports that provide information about the potential for infection. Certified organic fungicides can be applied from the time plants are 4–6 in. (10–15 cm) tall. There may be a limit on how many applications are allowed, depending on the fungicide used. Some cultivars have varying degrees of foliar resistance.

Even when a cultivar is advertised as resistant to blight, the resistance may not hold for all races of the fungus. Observe plants often. If suspect symptoms appear, contact local extension staff for confirmation. Destroy or remove infected plants so that they do not become a source of further infection and do not harvest tubers for at least two weeks after plants have been destroyed or removed. Inspect tubers prior to storage and discard those with late blight tuber rot symptoms.

Early Blight

Early blight is problematic on early maturing cultivars and on plants that are prematurely dying because of poor fertility, disease, or water stress. Reduce inoculum by rotating with crops not related to potatoes and incorporating potato debris after harvest. Careful attention to providing adequate fertility levels, especially in the initial stages of organic production, is required to hold this disease in check.

Organic Weed Management

Crop rotations and applications of manure or compost are typical practices used to enrich soils and improve crop growth. Both methods, however, have potential downsides when it comes to weeds. Rotations with sod crops increase the possibility for perennial weed problems and the use of manures can introduce weed seeds. These potential problems need to be recognized and appropriate management strategies should be taken to get the full benefit from these approaches.

Effect of Cover Crops and Manure

Perennial weeds are weakened by tilling and cultivation. Tilling a sod crop the season preceding potato planting is advisable to disrupt the plants. After tilling, a cover crop should be planted to protect the soil from erosion and to capture nutrients from the sod. Cover crops that are often used include rye (*Secale cereale*) or oats (*Avena sativa*). Oats will winter-kill in areas where temperatures drop below 18°F (−8°C) and should be planted in late summer to early fall in Canada and the northern United States. Rye is winter hardy and will grow vigorously in the spring. The advantage of oats is that the early growth competes with weeds but the winter-killed foliage is easy to till in the spring. Rye produces more biomass than oats but must be incorporated early in the spring to keep from getting too rank and fibrous. In warm locations oats may overwinter.

Composted manure greatly reduces the potential for bringing in weed seeds with the manure. Proper composting generates temperatures that kill weed seeds. If raw manure is used, plans should be in place to hoe and cultivate frequently to manage an increased population of weeds. To insure that the crop is safe to eat, raw manures should not be applied any sooner than 120 days prior to harvest. Discussion of manure is included in chapter 3.

Cover crops can be used to compete with weeds in the off-season. As mentioned previously, oats and rye are effective in the late summer and fall in the northern United States and Canada. In warm-season regions and during the summer in cool-season areas, crops that are effective competitors include buckwheat (*Fagopyrum esculentum*) (Plate 146), sorghum-sudangrass (*Sorghum bicolor*) (Plate 147), and Japanese millet (*Echinochloa frumentacea*). Buckwheat should be incorporated into the soil before its seeds mature otherwise it will become a weed to the succeeding crop.

Methods of Control

Cultivation, hoeing, and hand weeding remain the primary weed management options. The best time to control annual weeds is shortly after germination. The term that best describes this time is when the weeds are in the *white thread stage*. Cultivating and hoeing at this time, especially when it is sunny and dry, will eliminate a high percentage of the germinating weeds. Shallow cultivation and hoeing is preferable to deep disturbance of soil to conserve soil moisture and to minimize root pruning. Avoid any weed management practice when soils are wet. This increases soil compaction and reduces the effectiveness of the cultivation because the weeds have an opportunity to recover in the moist soil.

Some contact organic herbicides are available for use. These include materials containing vinegar, citric acid, and herbicidal soaps. Another contact option is flaming the weeds. To be effective, either approach should be used on small weeds. While these options may be available, they may not be any better than the more traditional way of dealing with weeds; that is, to hoe, cultivate, or pull them.

 CHAPTER 8

Special Techniques for Growing Potatoes

THE POTATO IS A REMARKABLY versatile plant. As such it can be grown in many nonconventional ways, several of which are described below. They offer opportunities to try something new.

Growing Potatoes in Mulch

Mulching is a practice which can be applied to many different vegetable crops. Advantages of mulching include reduced weed growth, more uniform moisture conditions, and moderation of soil temperature. There are many types of mulching, both with organic as well as with inorganic materials. In all cases there is no substitute for proper soil preparation and fertilizer application (see chapter 3).

Straw Mulch

An example of organic mulch for potatoes is straw. In the spring dig a furrow about 4 in. (10 cm) deep and 12 in. (30 cm) wide. Place the seed tubers in the center of the trench and cover the trench with 6 in. (15 cm) of clean straw. The straw should be weed-free to reduce the chances of weeds establishing in the mulch and because mice are attracted to weed seeds. When mice run out of seeds they will start munching on the potatoes. Rodents find straw mulch a comfortable place to reside so be aware of that at harvest time.

As the potato plants emerge, add another 4–6 in. (10–15 cm) of straw. The straw acts to keep the sunlight off the tubers and also keeps the soil moist. By late summer, you can begin harvesting clean, soil-free "new potatoes." Simply pull back the straw, take what you need, and carefully replace the mulch. After the vines die back, the main potato crop is ready for harvest (Healy 2009). Straw can also be used to simply cover the soil after the potatoes have emerged to conserve moisture (Plate 148).

Plastic Mulch

Potatoes can be grown successfully on raised plastic mulch beds similar to the way other vegetables are grown (Plate 149). The finished raised beds should be 3–5 in. (7.5–13 cm) high and 36 in. (91 cm) wide. Since the plastic is usually 4 ft. (1.2 m) wide this leaves 6 in. (15 cm) of plastic on both sides of the bed which can be secured by burying it along the edges.

There are several types of plastic mulch, including black, clear, and red. Black plastic provides excellent weed control and therefore is the material of choice for potatoes. Clear plastic will warm soil more than black plastic but provides a great environment for weeds. Since plastic mulches warm up the soil, this method can be used to speed up the growth of the potato crop early in the season and thus advance the harvest by seven to ten days.

If the use of plastic mulch is combined with planting green sprouted (chitted) potatoes (see chapter 4), then the harvest can be advanced even more. After the beds have been properly prepared and fertilized, spread and secure the plastic at the edges with a small amount of soil. Plant two rows of potatoes in the bed, with the rows 18–22 in. (46–55 cm) apart and the potatoes 10 in. (25 cm) apart within each row. You can use a bulb setter to punch a hole in the plastic. Plant the potatoes 4–5 in. (10–13 cm) deep and cover them with soil to the level of the plastic.

Particular attention must be paid to the watering of plants growing in plastic mulch as rainfall and surface irrigation will be shed off the plastic layer. An easy way to do this is by means of drip irrigation tubes under the plastic. The equipment is usually available at local garden centers. Another way is careful watering by hand.

Growing Potatoes in Containers

Container gardening is increasing in popularity. It is a good solution for those who only have a small yard or no yard at all. There is an almost endless list of containers which can be used to grow potatoes.

The container should be large enough to accommodate a large potato plant—about 5 gallons (19 liters). Make sure that the container has one or more drainage holes in the bottom. Potatoes growing in containers must be monitored very carefully for water stress. Try to avoid constant direct sunshine on the container, especially on hot afternoons.

Various types of containers and suitable growing mixes can be purchased at local garden centers. Appropriate fertilizer for container gardening should also be available at the local garden center.

Some container gardeners grow potatoes in bushel baskets. Potatoes can also be grown inside old tires. As the plants grow you can add more tires and more soil. Some gardeners even grow potatoes on their compost pile (Plate 150)! Detailed descriptions about different types of containers and how to grow potatoes in them can be found in McGee and Stuckey's (2002) *The Bountiful Container.*

Growing Potatoes from True Potato Seed

The use of true potato seed (TPS) for growing potatoes is probably as old as the cultivation of the potato. Many potato cultivars in the area where potato was domesticated flower profusely and produce a lot of fruit. So it is only natural that the ancient people in the Andean highlands used TPS both to produce a crop for consumption as well as to develop better-adapted cultivars. As discussed in chapter 11, the use of TPS is still routine in the development of new potato cultivars.

Advantages of True Potato Seed

Since the latter part of the twentieth century the International Potato Center in Lima, Peru, has promoted the use of TPS in growing potatoes for consumption in developing countries. In this case TPS is used as an alternative to seed potato tubers. Developing countries which do not have a strong infrastructure to produce their own high-quality seed potatoes must import seed potatoes from abroad. This can become very expensive, especially if these seed potatoes have to be shipped over long distances. Unlike seed tubers, TPS is generally free from viruses, easy to transport, and can be stored for several years without losing its ability to germinate. A disadvantage of TPS compared with seed potato tubers is that it is more labor intensive and requires a longer growing season.

Because TPS is the result of sexual reproduction, the crop is not genetically uniform (see chapter 11). It was precisely because of this genetic diversity that a century or more ago gardeners exhibited potatoes raised from TPS at county fairs. This was often done in the hope of being able to sell seed tubers of their new "cultivars" to which various exotic names such as 'Mortgage Lifter', 'Rot Proof', and 'Money Maker' were applied. In other words, these gardeners were forerunners of modern potato breeders.

Breeding efforts in the past few decades have resulted in new TPS cultivars with greater genetic uniformity. Although these new cultivars will never have the same genetic uniformity as traditional cultivars grown from seed tubers (which are clones), they are a big improvement over previously available TPS cultivars. On commercial potato farms in most developed countries the disadvantages of TPS outweigh the advantages. Commercial potato fields in North America are invariably planted with seed tubers.

In recent decades the seed industry has made progress in pelleting seeds. This involves coating seeds with a thin layer of clay or other inert substances which results in a product with uniform size and shape. Pelleted seeds are easier to handle; this is especially the case for potato where the (uncoated) seeds are small and tend to stick together. Fortunately for home gardeners, true potato seeds are now available commercially in pelleted form (Plate 151).

Germinating Seeds and Raising Seedlings

The best way to grow potatoes from TPS is to treat them the same way you would treat tomatoes when growing them from seeds. Plant the seed indoors in a flower pot or a seedling flat about four weeks before the last expected frost in your area (Plate 152). The major difference in the requirements for TPS and tomatoes is that TPS requires a cooler temperature for germination than tomatoes. The optimum temperature for germinating TPS is 60–65°F (16–18°C); at temperatures above 70°F (21°C) the rate of germination decreases rapidly. The seeds should germinate in about two weeks.

When the seedlings are about 1 in. (2.5 cm) tall they should be transplanted to small pots (Plate 153). The pots should remain indoors in a well-lighted cool location having a maximum temperature of 65°F (18°C). After the plants are well-rooted they can be transplanted to the garden just like you would transplant tomatoes or other vegetable crops (Plate 154).

In contrast to potato plants growing from a tuber, potato plants from TPS have only one stem. Care must be taken that this stem does not break or get damaged by wind or frost. Some gardeners place potato plants from TPS in groups of two or three every 12 in. (30 cm) in a previously made furrow. If the plants are rather tall and stretched then they should be laid in the bottom of the furrow with only the top 3 or 4 in. (7.5–10 cm) of the plant uncovered.

Sometimes local garden centers sell potato plants which are grown from TPS along with other vegetable transplants and ornamental bedding plants. Two currently popular TPS cultivars, produced by the Bejo Seed Company, are 'Catalina' and 'Zolushka'. There are several retail outlets in the United States which sell TPS (see appendix 1). In contrast to seed potato tubers, TPS can be imported into Canada through the regular mail.

Harvesting Seeds

Home gardeners may want to experiment with harvesting TPS from their garden. Remember that you will not get the same cultivar back that produced the seeds. For example, true seeds from a red-skinned cultivar may give (some) white-skinned progeny and vice versa. Cultivars differ considerably in their ability to produce fruits; growing a cultivar which produces at least some fruits is an obvious prerequisite. Do not harvest the fruits until the plants are mature. Even then some of the fruits may still be somewhat immature but in a few weeks they should soften up. After cutting the fruits open squeeze the seeds out onto a piece of blotting paper and allow to dry. After about a week the seeds should be thoroughly dry. Scrape the seeds from the blotting paper and store in a small envelope. Fresh potato seeds usually have a dormancy period of up to a year so it is best to wait that long before sowing them. If they are stored in a cool, dry place the seeds will keep their viability for ten years or longer.

Potato-Tomato Grafting

Grafting is a common practice in many horticultural crops. Potatoes and tomatoes can be grafted together because they are closely related. This involves grafting the top of a tomato plant (scion) onto the stem of a potato plant (rootstock), thus (at least theoretically) enabling the combination to produce both tomatoes and potatoes (Plate 155). This is not a new procedure. Nearly a century ago Luther Burbank (1914) described "The tomato and an interesting experiment—a plant which bore potatoes below and tomatoes above."

Some companies which sell potato-tomato grafting kits display misleading drawings which show an abundance of both tomatoes and potatoes on the same plant. The grafting process itself is relatively simple, and the resulting plants can bear a good crop of tomatoes (Plate 156), but the tubers tend to be small and immature (Plate 157) even when the plant is past maturity and the foliage starts turning yellow. The reason for the low yield of potatoes from such graft hybrids is twofold: (1) in the competition for photosynthetic product the tomatoes usually win out and (2) tomato vines do not provide the tuberization stimulus to the stolons in the way that potato vines do. Nevertheless, for some home gardeners it may be fun to do some experimenting with this technique and thus demonstrate the close relationship between potatoes and tomatoes.

Occasionally the potato rootstock may produce one or more sideshoots. These should be removed. If they are inadvertently left on the plant then care should be taken to only eat fruit produced by the tomato portion of grafted plants. Potato fruits, regardless of whether they are produced on "normal" (ungrafted) or sideshoots of potato rootstock contain glycoalkaloids (see chapter 10) and should not be eaten.

Preparing the Rootstock and the Scion

It is important to synchronize the development of the tomato scion with the potato rootstock. If you are starting the tomatoes from seeds then they should be planted about two weeks before the first potatoes are planted. A few successive plantings at one-week intervals of both tomato seeds and seed potatoes is recommended to ensure that you will have suitable plants of each at the right stage.

Plant the seed potato in a pot 4–5 in. (10–12.5 cm) in diameter. Eventually the grafted plants can be repotted into larger containers or planted in the garden. After the potato plant is 4–6 in. (10–15 cm) tall, the grafting can take place.

Grafting Techniques

There are several grafting techniques; the cleft and wedge technique works well in this case. Using a sharp, single-edged razor blade, remove all secondary stems of the potato plant, all the leaves, and all above-ground potato stems growing from any stolons. Remove and discard the top of the potato plant. Make a vertical cut in the potato stem, creating a cleft of 1 in. (2.5 cm). Now cut off the top 3 in. (7.5 cm) of the tomato plant as a wedge (in the shape of a flat-headed screw driver) to fit in the cleft in the potato. Leave only a minimal amount of leaves on the tomato scion.

Ideally the potato rootstock and the tomato scion should be about the same thickness. If the tomato scion is thinner than the potato rootstock the scion should be placed at the edge of the potato stem so that at least one side of the tomato scion completely contacts one side of the potato rootstock. Wrap the graft with grafting tape. Place the pot with the grafted plant in a shady location and, to avoid excessive evaporation, keep a slightly vented clear plastic bag over the grafted plant for about 10 days.

 **CHAPTER 9**

Harvesting and Storing

POTATO TUBERS ARE THE STORAGE ORGANS of potato plants and while they appear inert and show little evidence of being living organisms except when sprouts appear, they are in fact alive. As living organisms they require oxygen to survive and certain environmental conditions to minimize deterioration. Factors at the time of harvest and subsequent storage practices greatly affect how tubers can be used and how long and how well they will store. This chapter covers harvest and storage techniques that maximize the benefits of growing potatoes.

Harvesting Early (Immature) Tubers

The rules for harvesting potatoes for maximum yield and long-term storage do not apply to potatoes harvested in early summer. If only a few tubers are needed they can be stripped individually from plants by scraping away some of the soil in the hill and finding desirably sized tubers. This should be done in a way to minimize damage to the plants. After tubers are removed soil should be replaced so that plants can continue producing. This approach is difficult to accomplish.

An easier way is to carefully fork individual plants to get the needed quantity of potato tubers, trying not to disturb adjacent plants. Typically, a spading fork is used. The spading should begin at the edge of the hill to minimize piercing or otherwise damaging tubers. With some cultivars it is possible to loosen the soil on both sides of the hill and then pull plants up with attached tubers. Additional spading will retrieve tubers left in the soil.

Handling and Storing New Potatoes

Early harvested tubers are considerably different than tubers harvested when they are mature. "New potatoes," as they are commonly referred to, have thin skins and a bright appearance. There is a certain appeal to new potatoes when compared to storage potatoes, which have typically lost some of their "good looks" after many months in storage. The difference extends beyond appearance.

Immature potatoes have lower dry matter than mature ones of the same cultivar making them better suited for cooking whole or for use in salads. Early harvested potatoes should be eaten soon after harvest. There are several reasons for their short shelf life, including increased susceptibility to rot. In addition to thin skin, immature tubers have high respiration rates. The combination of these two factors results in an increase in weight loss.

Respiration in tubers is needed, as it is in humans, to maintain life. It uses carbon compounds in tubers and oxygen to generate energy and releases carbon dioxide, water, and heat. To a limited extent it is the reverse of photosynthesis where carbon dioxide, water, and the sun's energy produce sugars that, in the case of potato tubers, ultimately get converted into starch. The thin skins of immature tubers are less resistant to water loss by transpiration (evaporation). The loss of starch and water results in tubers that shrivel.

Early harvested tubers should also be handled carefully because of the tendency to skin and bruise. Skinned or bruised areas are entry points for decay organisms, which thrive in warm temperatures. Immature tubers can be stored for very short periods by placing them in a cool, dark, humid (but not wet) environment with adequate air movement. A temperature between 50 and 60°F (10–16°C) is about right.

Harvesting Mature Tubers

Potatoes for long-term storage should be mature at harvest. Unless potatoes are overfertilized or an extremely late cultivar is grown, potato foliage begins to yellow and dry by the end of the season (Plate 158). The process begins at the lower leaves and progresses upward. Leaves and stems of early and mid-season plants are usually dry by the end of the growing season.

To get the best skin set and therefore minimize bruising and weight loss, potatoes should be harvested no sooner than two weeks after plants have died. Plants that are still green and vigorous two weeks before freezing temperatures are anticipated should be defoliated so that skin set can begin.

Mechanical Defoliation

The simplest method of mechanical defoliation is to use a weed trimmer to shred leaves and stems (Plate 159). The process should be done so that vine death is gradual. Rapid vine death by any means including freezing can result in discoloration of the vascular ring of the tubers. The discoloration will be most noticeable at stem ends of affected tubers. It may extend only a short distance or may be more extensive. The discoloration can result in darkening of cooked tubers. Selection of appropriate cultivars for the growing region and proper fertilization will reduce the need for artificial defoliation.

If late blight symptoms are present on the foliage the vines should be cut and removed at least two weeks before harvest. In addition to helping develop thicker skins the two-week period reduces the potential for late blight spores to come in contact with potatoes. This time frame allows tubers to develop symptoms and possibly disintegrate before harvest if tubers were already infected.

Tubers from infected plants should be thoroughly inspected for late blight tuber rot (Plate 115). Infected tubers should not be stored since they will decay in storage. Suspect tubers should not be placed back in the field or in a cull pile.

Digging by Hand or Machine

Hand harvest for gardeners is generally done with a spading fork (Plate 160), shovel, or potato (silage) hook (Plate 161). Small-scale producers often use one- or two-row potato diggers (Plate 162). These machines dig under the potatoes and place tubers and soil onto a set of moving chains that separate tubers from soil and place the tubers on top of the soil to be picked up by hand. A single bottom plow may also be used to "lift" the tubers. This approach works reasonably well if the soil is light and friable and weeds are absent. Barring those conditions, finding the tubers can be a challenge.

Harvesting by hand requires a good sense of where the tubers are located so that minimal damage is done to the tubers and physical effort is also minimized. Regardless of approach, tubers should be handled carefully from the time they are lifted to the time they are placed in storage. Excess soil, stones, and plant (potato and weed) debris should be left in the field. Dug tubers should not be left in bright sun and hot temperatures. Ideal harvest temperatures range between 55 and 65°F (13–18°C). Harvesting potatoes at temperatures below 45°F (7°C) increases bruising. Digging when temperatures are above 80°F (27°C) and exposing tubers to bright sun increases the potential for sunscald and soft rot. Avoid dropping tubers on sharp edges of containers or better yet use smooth-sided containers with rounded tops. When transferring to storage containers (crates or boxes) keep drop distances as short as possible and have the potatoes "roll" onto each other to minimize bruising.

Successful Storage

Storing potatoes extends the enjoyment of the growing experience beyond the growing season. Depending on physical facilities of the storage and physical condition of tubers going into storage, tubers can be reasonably stored for three to six months in noncommercial storage. The use of sprout inhibitors and refrigeration in commercial storages extends the marketability considerably longer.

Successful storage starts with mature tubers in good physical condition. The best result of storage is to maintain the product; storage seldom improves quality. The one possible exception is that of frying color of tubers that have been chilled in the field. The effect of temperature on fry color is covered in chapter 10. Factors affecting keeping quality in storage include cultivar, maturity, physical condition, and environmental conditions in the storage.

Cultivar Sprout Development

One aspect of keeping quality is sprout development. Cultivars differ in how soon sprouting occurs, even when conditions are favorable. This is the genetic component of dormancy. Tubers of early sprouting cultivars are best suited for short-term storage. 'Canela Russet', 'Island Sunshine', and 'Russet Burbank' produce sprouts late in storage. The genetic control of sprouting is an important consideration in selecting which cultivars to store. The process of sprouting is associated with an increase in respiration and with it an increase in water loss and shriveling.

Maturity and Physical Condition

As tubers mature the depth of cells forming the periderm (skin) increases providing a barrier to water loss. While it may seem logical that russet-skinned tubers would therefore have an advantage over smooth-skinned tubers this is not the case. Whether tubers are smooth- or russet-skinned, the depth of the underlying cells is the key to minimizing water loss from tuber surfaces. Producing mature tubers is best accomplished by proper fertilization and by harvesting no sooner than two weeks after vines are dead. Respiration rate is another main factor in weight loss. Immature tubers respire at a greater rate than mature ones.

Maturity affects the ability of tubers to withstand skinning and bruising during harvest and handling. Thin skins of immature tubers are easily scrubbed off in harvesting, and during subsequent transfers from one container to another. Immature tubers also bruise more easily than mature ones. The exposed flesh of skinned or damaged tubers is a direct site of water loss. These sites are also entry points for decay-causing organisms. Fungi, such as *Fusarium* and soft rot bacteria, can be the most significant causes of weight loss in storage. Minimizing damage during harvest is a major step in having good quality in storage, but no matter how careful the harvest or handling operation is there will inevitably be some damage. Under the proper conditions potatoes have the ability to "heal" damaged areas.

Curing (Wound Healing)

Skinned and bruised areas of tubers result in moisture loss and expose the flesh to invasion by rot-causing organisms. A key part of the storage process is the healing of cuts and bruises that occur during harvest and handling. The development of a waterproofing layer and then the formation of cells beneath that layer occurs most rapidly at temperatures near 70°F (21°C) and at a relative humidity of 95 percent. These conditions also favor decay-causing disease organisms. A compromise is to hold potato tubers at temperatures between 50 and 60°F (10–16°C) and a relative humidity of 95 percent for 10 to 14 days.

Adequate air movement is needed to provide oxygen for respiration and to dissipate field heat as well as the heat released by respiration. Air movement doesn't have to be vigorous and could simply be the airflow created by convection, if there is adequate air space around the tubers and an outside air source is provided. A sealed environment can lead to oxygen deficiency and black heart, an unsightly disorder where internal tissues suffocate and turn black.

Maintaining high relative humidity is critical throughout the storage period but is especially important during the curing period. Weight loss of sound potatoes is greatest during the first month of storage. Since potatoes are about 80 percent water, any movement of air containing less than 100 percent relative humidity will draw moisture from the tubers. But having free moisture on the tubers can increase rot and negatively impact respiration. Moisture on tuber surfaces in storage can be removed by air movement over the affected areas. Maintaining relative humidity near 95 percent during storage is an effective way to minimize water loss and allow for proper metabolism. Proper curing is critical to have a successful storage experience.

If rot potential is high due to disease, frost, wet conditions, or other reasons, tubers should be cooled rapidly and sold or consumed as soon as possible.

Holding Period

The goal in storing potatoes is to minimize weight loss and to maintain culinary quality. To accomplish this goal the moisture level in the storage should be as high as possible without having condensation on tuber surfaces or dripping from the ceiling, the respiration rate should be as low as possible, and sprouting should be delayed. Air circulation may be necessary to remove excess moisture from tuber surfaces and to maintain uniform temperature.

After the curing period, the temperature should be lowered to reduce respiration rate and to delay sprouting. For gardeners and small-scale producers of potatoes used for boiling or baking, long-term storage temperatures near 40°F (4°C) are desirable as sprout development is very slow and generally not visible at that temperature (Plate 163).

At temperatures below 50°F (10°C) some starch is converted to reducing sugars (glucose and fructose) in most cultivars. When potatoes with high-reducing sugars are fried, the fry color is dark and considered undesirable. Chilled tubers of cultivars bred for making potato chips or french fries can be reconditioned. Reconditioning converts sugars back to starch by storing at temperatures near 60°F (16°C) for three weeks or more. Sprout development and weight loss increase rapidly as temperatures increase above 40°F (4°C).

Potatoes should not be stored at temperatures near freezing as this increases respiration rates and sugar levels and may cause internal discoloration. Cold-stored tubers may have a sweet flavor when cooked and will definitely have dark color when fried.

Facilities

Storage facilities for gardeners and small-scale producers can be a challenge. Individuals who have access to root cellars or insulated sheds or garages have the potential to store potatoes for an extended period. Without access to such facilities storage is limited to the short term.

The storage of a small quantity of potatoes for a short time can be achieved in several ways. The storage units should be cool dark areas and can be in basements, garages, or insulated out-buildings. Tubers that have been cured can be stored in refrigerators in which the temperature has been adjusted to 40°F (4°C). Placing freshly harvested or uncured tubers in cold storage will result in significant shrinkage and loss of quality. In small quantities tubers can be stored in slotted plastic bags to minimize moisture loss while still allowing for air exchange. Plastic bags that don't have adequate openings can create conditions that result in oxygen deficiency or decay. Tubers that have been washed should be dry before they are placed in plastic bags.

The storage of intermediate quantities requires the physical space to accommodate the volume and provisions for environmental control, especially temperature and air exchange. Air exchange is most critical in the initial (curing) stage. Once temperatures are lowered to the holding temperature the amount of air exchange needed is diminished but still important. Storing in slotted bushel crates is an effective way of providing air space around tubers and facilitates stacking (Figure 10).

Large quantities of potatoes can be stored in bulk bins or pallet boxes. Slotted air ducts are required in bulk storage to allow for air movement through the pile. Air will move through the potatoes by convection currents or can be forced through by fans.

The principles of successful potato storage apply whether small or large quantities of potatoes are stored: store sound, mature tubers; cure at temperatures between 50 and 60°F (10–16°C) for 10 to 14 days; lower temperature gradually after curing to 40°F (4°C) for general table use and to 50°F (10°C) for frying; maintain high humidity throughout the storage period.

Figure 10. Slotted crates provide air circulation and can be stacked for long term storage.

CHAPTER 10

Uses of the Potato

EATING POTATOES IS, of course, the primary reason for which they are grown. The utilization of potatoes in developing countries and the expansion of processed forms of potatoes have propelled the potato into the world's third largest food crop (after rice and wheat) and the largest global root or tuber crop. Although food is the most common use of potatoes, it is not the only one. Several nonfood uses will also be discussed in this chapter.

Food Use and Nutritional Value

The nutritive value of potatoes was clearly demonstrated in Ireland prior to the potato famine in the mid-nineteenth century. A significant percentage of the population lived on a diet of potatoes that was supplemented periodically with cow's milk, eggs, or fish. The diet for an active healthy man amounted to a daily consumption of 5–10 pounds (2.3–4.5 kg) of potatoes. That level of consumption is, obviously, much higher than current potato consumption in developed countries. Even so, annual per capita consumption on a fresh weight basis is about 160 pounds (73 kg) in Canada and about 125 pounds (57 kg) in the United States.

About half of the potatoes consumed in Canada are fresh whereas in the United States fresh consumption is about 35 percent. Utilization of the remaining production is primarily as processed products, including frozen french fries, chips, and dehydrated products. A small percentage is used as seed and animal feed.

Potatoes provide a significant amount of nutrition (Figure 11). A medium-sized potato weighing about ⅓ pound (150 g) provides the following daily values: 45 percent of the recommended dietary allowance (RDA) of vitamin C, 18 percent of potassium, 10 percent vitamin B6, 8 percent dietary fiber, 8 percent thiamin, 8 percent niacin, 6 percent folate, 6 percent iron, and only 110 calories. Potatoes exceed bananas in their potassium-supplying power and are a good source of fiber.

Protein and Calories

The protein content of potatoes on a fresh weight basis is relatively low but on a dry weight basis the protein content is similar to that of cereals and very high in comparison with other roots and tubers. The protein in potatoes is of high quality. Potatoes do not contain fat or cholesterol. While the calorie content of fresh potatoes is low, it can be increased significantly when high fat ingredients are added in preparation. By modifying the type and quantity of the ingredients used in preparation, you can include potatoes in weight-reducing diets while still providing desirable nutrition.

Antioxidants and Pigments

Densely pigmented tubers add another dimension to the nutritional value of potatoes. Such tubers contain more antioxidants than their white-fleshed counterparts. The benefits of antioxidants include improved heart and eye health, and a reduction in the incidence of some cancers (Murphy 2004; Brown 2005). Yellow-fleshed cultivars, such as 'Island Sunshine', 'Yellow Finn', and 'Yukon Gold', are higher in carotenoids, such as lutein and zeaxanthin, than cultivars that produce white-fleshed tubers. Cultivars with blue- or red-pigmented flesh, such as 'Adirondack Blue', 'Adirondack Red', 'All Blue', and 'All Red', are rich in flavonoids such as anthocyanins and other phenolics (Plates 164 and 165).

Figure 11. Nutrition facts of the potato. Courtesy of the United States Potato Board.

Fresh Consumption

Before the advent of large-scale processing facilities, potatoes were primarily consumed as fresh product. Currently the use of fresh potatoes on a global basis is estimated to be less than half of potatoes produced. In the United States only about one third of consumed potatoes are typically eaten fresh.

Fresh potatoes can be used in a wide variety of ways. Recipes for exotic and simple dishes fill numerous cookbooks, a few of which are listed elsewhere in this book (see References). In the simplest form potatoes are boiled and served whole or mashed, baked or microwaved and used to complement the main entrée. In addition, they are used in soups, casseroles, salads and stews, as main dishes and many other ways. One of the authors (Joe) has a favorite potato soup recipe (see box).

Joe's No-Fat Potato Soup

3 celery stems (include leafy portions from center of stalk)
3 medium yellow onions
5 medium-sized, low dry matter potatoes (approximately 2 lbs. or 0.9 kg)
1 teaspoon fennel seed
1 teaspoon caraway seed
1–2 teaspoons salt (season to taste)
1–2 teaspoons ground black pepper (season to taste)

Cut celery, including leafy portions from center of stalk, into ½- to ½-in. (6- to 12-mm) pieces. Peel onions and dice into ½-in. (6-mm) pieces. Sauté onions and celery in a nonstick pan with a light coating of olive oil. Set aside. Peel and dice potatoes into ½-in. (12–mm) pieces. Place potatoes in a 3-qt (2.8-l) pot and cover with water. Bring to a boil. Add sautéed onions and celery, and fennel and caraway seeds. Reduce heat. Simmer for ½ hour. Makes 6 cups (1.4 liter) of soup. The recipe can be doubled with a portion frozen for later use.

Soup can be served as is, with chunks of potatoes intact. For a creamy soup blend, mash about ⅓ of the soup and then mix with the remainder of the unmashed soup. A variation of the above is to use a combination of low and high dry matter potatoes. The low dry matter potatoes will remain intact while the high dry matter potatoes will tend to fall apart. The combination of the two types of potatoes eliminates the need to blend or mash a portion of the potatoes to have a creamy soup.

Because humans can't digest the starch in uncooked potatoes, the potatoes have to be heated first. The best way to retain nutrients in preparing potatoes is to bake them in a conventional oven or a microwave. Some nutrients and minerals are leached when potatoes are boiled. Leaving the skins on potatoes when boiling will reduce the amount of nutrients leached (Woolfe 1987). Eating the skins with the flesh of potatoes increases the fiber and nutrient content. Baked potato skins are offered in some restaurants as snacks or appetizers.

Glycoalkaloids and Bitter Taste

Dark green skin tissue, sprouts, and fruits should not be consumed; although the green color itself (chlorophyll) will not hurt you, green potato tissue, sprouts, and fruits typically contain high levels of toxic glycoalkaloids.

Glycoalkaloids are naturally occurring compounds in potatoes and other plants that play a role in resistance to insects and diseases. There are a number of glycoalkaloids in potatoes that are usually grouped and referred to as total glycoalkaloids (TGA). They occur mostly in the sprouts, leaves, flowers, fruits, and "sunburned" portions of tubers.

In general the upper safety limit in the tubers is considered to be 20 mg TGA per 100 g fresh weight. TGA levels above 10 mg per 100 g fresh weight usually impart a bitter taste (Woolfe 1987).

Under normal conditions the tubers of most cultivars have TGA levels below 5 mg per 100 g fresh weight. However, under certain conditions the TGA level can increase. For example, when tubers are exposed to sunlight for extended periods, the exposed area will eventually turn green. Such green areas should be removed before preparation since they may have an elevated TGA level.

Dry Matter and Carbohydrates

As mentioned in chapter 11, the dry matter content of the tubers has a great influence on the culinary quality of the potatoes. Potatoes with low dry matter are best suited for serving whole or for use in soups, salads, or any form where the potatoes should be firm. Potatoes with high dry matter produce mealy, fluffy baked potatoes and are best suited for french fries. Potatoes with low dry matter may be marketed as "low carb." This is a relative term since these potatoes have less carbohydrates than potatoes with high dry matter. Nevertheless, if the amount of carbohydrates is a concern, then cultivars with low dry matter should be used.

Potatoes and Special Diets

Potatoes have recently been in the forefront of some widely advertised diets related to carbohydrates. Some these are the so-called low-carb diets. One of the most popular was the Atkins diet. Advocates of low-carb diets were recommending a low intake of carbohydrates (such as breads, pasta, and potatoes) for weight loss. While effective in the short term, this diet lacks the proper balance to be nutritionally sound. The low-carb diet was quite popular in the 1980s and 1990s, but its popularity appears to have waned in the 2000s.

Another major dietary movement which has affected the public perception of the nutrient value of potatoes is the glycemic index (GI). This is a measure of the effects of ingested carbohydrates on the level of glucose in the blood. Foods containing complex carbohydrates release glucose quickly into the bloodstream as they are digested. Those that lead to higher glucose, like potatoes, have a relatively high GI. This in turn can have implications for people with diabetes.

Recently much has been written about different foods and their relative GI. On the surface it would appear that foods with a high GI should be avoided. However such a conclusion is far too simplistic. The GI of foods is affected by the length of time the food is stored, the way the food is prepared, other foods eaten at the same time and other factors. Basing one's diet solely on the basis of the GI ignores the nutritional benefits of foods such as potatoes.

For a wholesome balanced diet consumers are advised to follow the U.S. Department of Agriculture's *Dietary Guide for Americans* and *My Pyramid* or Health Canada's *Eating Well with Canada's Food Guide*. The American Diabetes Association recommends that individuals with diabetes consult with a registered dietician or certified diabetes consultant.

Processed Products

Processing of potatoes began with the Incas, who produced the first freeze-dried potatoes (see chapter 12). Today the primary processed potato products are french fries, chips, and dehydrated products. Pre-prepared refrigerated whole, mashed, partially fried, salad, and other forms of potato are also available.

French Fries

While it appears obvious that french fries originated in France, that may not in fact be true. The Belgians claim to be the first to fry potatoes in the "french manner"; there is even a french fry museum in the city of Bruges, Belgium. In cooking terms "to french" is to cut in long slender strips. There lies the source of the confusion. Although the practice of deep frying slices of potatoes was quite common in Europe as early as the nineteenth century, it did not become so in North America until after World War I. North American soldiers who had landed in Belgium had become fond of the potatoes fried in the french manner and insisted on eating "french fries" at home as well.

The term *french fries* is not used in Europe. In France they are called *pommes de terre frites* or simply *pommes frites* and in the United Kingdom they are known as *chips*. Most french fries are produced in factories where tubers are peeled, pushed through cutting blades, parboiled (partially cooked), air dried, fried, frozen, and packaged. This segment of the potato industry has been growing faster than any other. Frozen french fries are a major export product of the North American and European potato industries.

Cultivars that produce elongated tubers with high dry matter and low reducing sugars (glucose, fructose) are best suited for french fry production. High dry matter tubers are desirable since the yield of fried product is greater and oil consumption is less than if low dry matter tubers are used. The quality of the finished product is higher as well. Tubers with low reducing sugars produce lighter color fries than those with high reducing sugars.

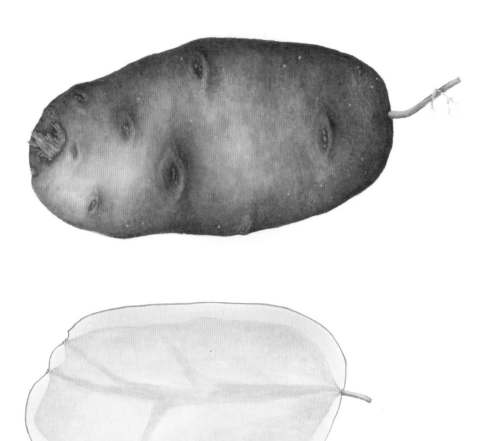

Plate 87. External and internal views of potatoes. © Jeanne Debons.

Plate 88. Potato plants in the foreground did not receive any fertilizer. Plants in the back were fertilized at recommended levels.

Plate 89. Seed furrow should be 3–4 in. (8–10 cm) deep.

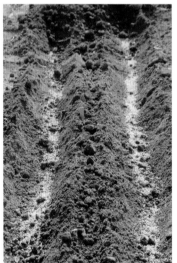

Plate 90. After potatoes are planted, furrows are made on each side of the seed furrow to partially cover the seed. These furrows should be slightly deeper than the seed furrow. Fertilizer is placed in the furrows.

Plate 91. Soil should be raked to cover both the fertilizer and the seed, leaving the planted area relatively flat. In areas prone to heavy rains, the row should be raised to allow for surface drainage.

Plate 92. Relatively young seed tubers are firm and free of sprouts or have only apical sprouts developing. High yield, late maturity, and relatively large tubers are associated with use of young seed.

Plate 93. Slightly aged seed tubers have short sprouts developing at apical and some lateral eyes. Such seed will produce earlier maturing plants and more tubers per plant than young seed.

Plate 94. Physiologically old seed tubers have multiple sprouts at multiple eyes. Poor emergence and low yield are associated with such seed.

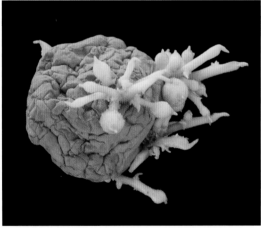

Plate 95. Very old seed tubers develop multiple sprouts that often form tubers. Seed in this condition may not form above ground plants and if plants develop yield will be low.

Plate 96. Whole seed tubers should weigh from 1½ to 2½ oz. (43–71g). Sprout development on the tubers shown is ideal for planting.

Plate 97. Short thick sprouts are formed on seed pieces exposed to light and warm temperatures. The light decreases the distance between nodes on sprouts. Green sprouting decreases the time between planting and emergence.

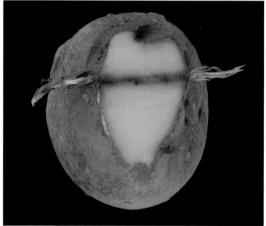

Plate 98. Rhizomes of quackgrass and nutsedge are especially troublesome since they are capable of penetrating potato tubers. Avoid planting in areas infested with these and other perennial weeds.

Plate 99. The development of hills should be a gradual process beginning when plants are 6–8 in. (15–20 cm) tall and terminating about the time plants are in bloom.

Plate 100. An ideal hill is broad and not pointed. The marker at the top of the hill is 12 in. (30 cm).

Plate 101. Wet soil conditions are responsible for enlarged and prominent lenticels (breathing pores). Enlarged lenticels can cork over and affect tuber appearance or be entry points for diseases that lead to decay.

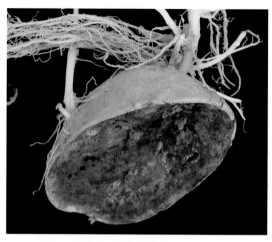

Plate 102. *Fusarium* seed piece decay is categorized by dark brown decay and is often a problem in wet soils on cut seed pieces.

Plate 103. The black slightly raised areas on these tubers are the resting bodies of *Rhizoctonia solani*. This stage of the disease is referred to as black scurf. © Thomas A. Zitter.

Plate 104. Late blight lesion showing the characteristic light green halo surrounding the brown dead tissue on the surface of the leaflets. White specks are residue from fungicide applied after infection was detected.

Plate 105. Sporulation in the halo area on the underside of a leaflet infected with late blight.

Plate 106. Late blight stem infection begins as a brown discoloration that quickly becomes slimy under moist conditions.

Plate 108. Mosaic patterns in foliage and stunted plants are symptoms of viruses. Photo courtesy of Stewart M. Gray.

Plate 107. Early blight lesions have irregular shapes and are characterized by concentric rings. © Thomas A. Zitter.

Plate 109. Plants infected with *Verticillium* often wilt on one side.

Plate 110. Dark discolored vascular tissue at the base of stems is an indication of *Verticillium* or *Fusarium* wilt.

Plate 111. Cupped leaflets in the upper portion of plants are symptoms of blackleg, *Rhizoctonia* stem canker, and various phytoplasmas.

Plate 112. Black slimy areas at the base of plants are characteristic of blackleg disease. © Thomas A. Zitter.

Plate 113. Aerial tubers are formed when the below ground vascular system is disrupted by diseases such as *Rhizoctonia* stem canker, blackleg and various phytoplasmas.

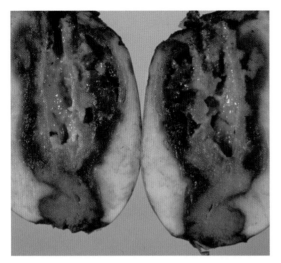

Plate 114. Decay starting at the stem end and extending to the center of tubers is typical of blackleg infected tubers.© Thomas A. Zitter.

Plate 115. Late blight tuber rot first appears as a tan to brown granular discoloration that quickly deteriorates in moist conditions. Photo courtesy of William E. Fry.

Plate 116. Corky potato scab lesions can be superficial or deeply pitted. Infected tubers lose moisture in storage and are hard to peel.

Plate 117. Growth cracks are primarily caused by irregular growing conditions. Some cultivars are prone to this disorder. *Rhizoctonia* may also cause growth cracks.

Plate 118. Misshapen tubers may be in the form of knobs or other distortions.

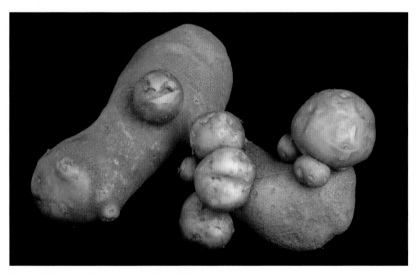

Plate 119. Some cultivars, such as 'Russet Burbank', are more susceptible to developing knobby tubers than others.

Plate 120. Dark green portions of tubers have been exposed to sunlight. Proper hilling will minimize greening.

Plate 121. Enlarged lenticels occur under wet conditions. They provide entry points for tuber decaying organisms. Lenticels that are not infected may become dry and corky.

Plate 122. Silver scurf on red-skinned tubers often appears as bleached out areas. On white-skinned tubers it appears blotchy tan. When the areas are moist the affected portions have a sheen.

Plate 123. Pinkeye is characterized by pinkish/tan discoloration at apical eyes and lenticels. The tissue may become infected with bacteria under wet conditions or become tan to brown under dry conditions. © Thomas A. Zitter.

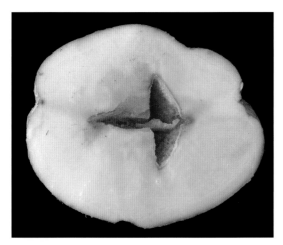

Plate 124. Hollow heart is primarily located in, but not restricted to, the center of tubers. Certain cultivars are prone to this disorder when plants are subjected to irregular growing conditions.

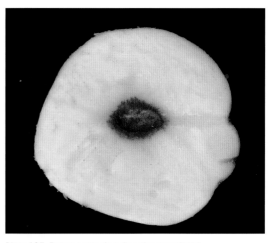

Plate 125. Brown center is a disorder associated with cool temperatures at tuber initiation. Cultivars differ in their susceptibility to this disorder.

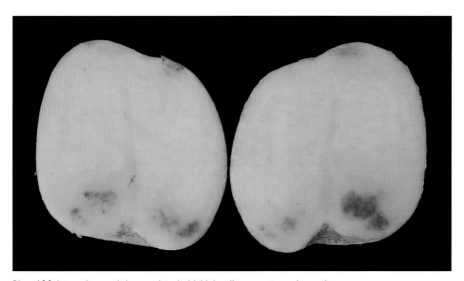

Plate 126. Internal necrosis is associated with high soil temperatures, low moisture level and calcium nutrition. The cultivar 'Atlantic' is especially susceptible.

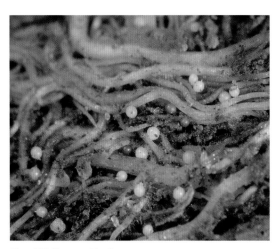

adult flea beetle

Plate 127. The round bodies on potato roots are potato cyst nematodes. Each cyst may contain as many as 200 eggs. As cysts of the golden nematode mature they turn golden brown. Photo courtesy of Xiaohong Wang.

Plate 128. Many small holes in leaflets are typical of flea beetle feeding. Flea beetle adults are the small black insects feeding on foliage. Tipburn on leaflets is to due leafhopper feeding. Photo courtesy of Ward M. Tingey.

Plate 129. Feeding by Colorado potato beetles can result in total defoliation of potato plants.

Plate 130. Colorado potato beetle egg masses are bright yellow-orange initially then darken as larvae begin to emerge.

Plate 131. Colorado potato beetle adults have distinct alternating yellow and black stripes on wing covers.

Plate 132. Colorado potato beetle larvae have reddish-orange hump-backed bodies. The larval stages of this insect have voracious appetites.

Plate 133. Potato aphids are relatively large aphids that feed primarily in the upper portion of plants. Photo courtesy of Ward M. Tingey.

Plate 134. Potato leaf hopper nymphs are small, wedge-shaped and pale green. The nymphs move rapidly sideways. Adults are winged and fly when plants are disturbed.

Plate 135. Scorching of leaves associated with high populations of leaf hoppers is referred to as hopperburn. The insects secrete a toxin when feeding that causes plant injury.

Plate 136. Just before emergence germinating annual weeds have the appearance of white threads. This is an excellent time for hoeing and/or cultivating.

Plate 137. Quackgrass plants are vigorous perennials that can reduce potato yield and quality.

Plate 138. Weedy plots are difficult to harvest.

Plate 139. Many species of lady beetle adults have domed shiny red to orange bodies with dark spots.

Plate 140. Lady beetle species vary in coloration and markings.

Plate 141. Lady beetle larvae have alligator shaped, dark gray to black bodies with yellow to orange markings.

Plate 142. Two-spotted stink bugs have very distinctive markings. These insects feed on beetle larvae and some caterpillars.

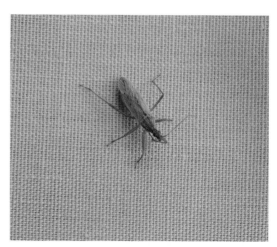

Plate 143. Damsel bug adults are slender, gray-brown and have long legs and bulging eyes. Adults and nymphs feed on a wide variety of insects.

Plate 144. Bodies of aphids parasitized by wasps become swollen and leathery.

Plate 145. Colorado beetles infected with the fungus *Beauveria bassiana* have white, cottony growth on their bodies.

Plate 146. Buckwheat is an effective weed suppressor in a noncrop year. Top growth should be incorporated into the soil prior to seed formation to prevent this species from becoming a weed in subsequent years.

Plate 147. Sorghum-sudangrass produces much biomass at warm temperatures. Mow periodically to keep it from becoming rank and fibrous. Incorporation as a green manure can reduce nematode levels in soil.

Plate 148. Soil covered with straw to conserve moisture. Photo courtesy of Arno Enss, Virgil, Ontario.

Plate 149. 'Yukon Gold' growing in a bed covered with black plastic mulch.

Plate 150. Potatoes growing in a compost bin. Photo courtesy of Tamara Thompson, Oakland, California.

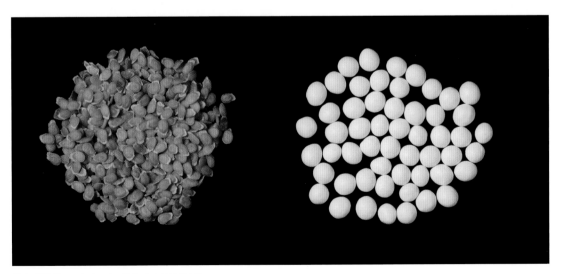

Plate 151. Uncoated and pelleted potato seeds.

Plate 152. Potato seedlings can be raised in a flower pot in early spring.

Plate 153. Potato seedlings transplanted to small containers such as plastic cells (one plant per cell).

Plate 154. Potato seedlings after they have been transplanted from the small containers to the field.

Plate 155. Tomato scion from 'Sub Arctic Maxi' grafted to rootstock of potato 'Kennebec'.

Plate 156. Grafted plants produce a good crop of tomatoes.

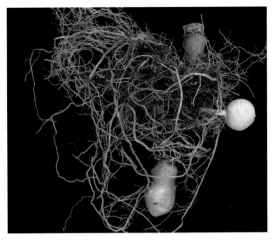

Plate 157. Grafted plants produce only a few very small tubers.

Plate 158. As plants mature leaves begin to yellow. Maturation of top growth is associated with skin set on tubers.

Plate 159. The use of a weed trimmer to shred some top growth of green vigorous vines as harvest approaches simulates natural maturity and aids in setting skin on tubers.

Plate 160. Hand harvest of small plots is often accomplished by using a spading fork. Begin digging at the edges of hills to minimize spearing tubers.

Plate 161. Use of a potato (silage) hook facilitates hand harvest.

Plate 162. One- or two-row potato diggers are useful in plantings larger than garden plots.

Plate 163. Sprouted tubers demonstrate the effect of temperature on sprout development. After being placed in 40°F (4°C) storage, tubers were moved to 60°F (16°C) storage for (from left to right) three, two, one, or zero weeks.

Plate 164. Potatoes with pigmented flesh are a good source of antioxidation.

Plate 165. Pigmented tubers can be used to produce processed products with interesting color patterns.

Plate 166. Bumblebee visiting a potato flower.

Plate 167. Collecting pollen on a watch glass by means of a battery-operated vibrator.

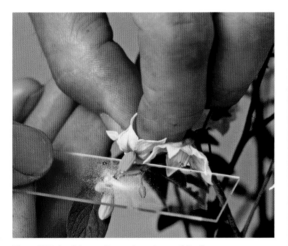

Plate 168. Applying pollen to the stigma of the flower of the female parent. Photo courtesy of Agriculture and Agri-Food Canada Potato Research Centre.

Plate 169. Female parent with labeled fruits.

Plate 170. Potato seedlings emerging in a seedling flat.

Plate 171. Potato seedlings transplanted to containers (one plant per cell).

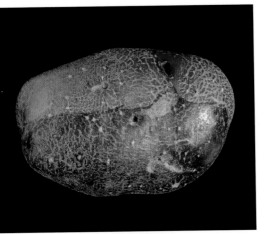

Plate 172. Mutants affecting tuber skin color can easily be detected even if they occur only rarely because they stand out among large numbers of "normal" tubers.

Plate 173. Genetic diversity for tuber shape and color among cultivated potatoes of the Andean highlands. © International Potato Center.

Plate 174. Wild potato species growing on a rocky hillside in the Andean highlands. © International Potato Center.

Plate 175. Potato plantlet growing *in vitro*.

Plate 176. *Solanum berthaultii*. Leaves and flower.

Plate 177. Close-up of *Solanum berthaultii* leaf showing the density of glandular hairs.

Plate 178. Green peach aphid entrapped by glandular hairs. Photo courtesy of Ward M. Tingey.

Plate 179. Typical tubers of 'King Harry' (left) and *Solanum berthaultii*.

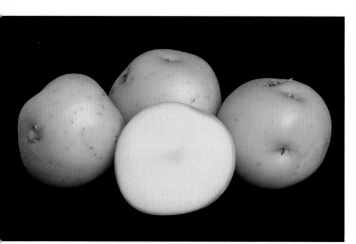

Plate 180. Andean cultivar 'Yema de huevo' ("egg yolk") contributed yellow flesh color to 'Yukon Gold', the standard for yellow-fleshed cultivars in North America.

Plate 181. Ceramic storage vessel. This Pre-Colombian ceramic storage vessel (A.D. 600–800) is modeled on the well-known native potato cultivar, 'Huayro', a traditional cultivar still grown throughout the Peruvian Andes. © International Potato Center.

Plate 182. Watercolor painting sent by de Sivry to Clusius in 1589. The inscription reads: "Taratoufli à Philip de Sivry acceptum Viennae 26 Januarii 1588 Papas Peruänum—Petri Ciecae." Photo courtesy of Museum Plantin Moretus, Antwerp.

Plate 183. 'Garnet Chili' features prominently in the pedigrees of most North American and many European cultivars.

Plate 184. In 1888 Elbert Carman offered a free tuber of 'Rural New Yorker No. 2' to any subscriber of his newspaper who asked for it.

Plate 185. Larva of the Colorado potato beetle.

Plate 186. Canada, 2000. Part of Canada's Millennium Series. French fries. Honoring the contribution of the McCain Foods Company to the potato industry in Canada and around the world. © Canada Post Corporation 2000. Reproduced with permission.

Plate 188. The Potato Museum in O'Leary, Prince Edward Island, one of several interesting potato museums around the world, is a favorite tourist stop. Photo courtesy of Gallery Charlene Williams, Prince Edward Island. Reproduced with permission.

Plate 187. United States, 1940. Honoring Luther Burbank, the great plant hybridizer and "patron saint" of American potato growers. Courtesy of U.S. Postal Service.

Plate 189. Monument in honor of 'Bintje' in Suameer, the Netherlands. This is the only potato cultivar in the world which has a monument dedicated to it. Jan van Loon explains that the smaller plant in front represents 'Bintje', and the two large stylized potato plants represent its parents. Photo courtesy of Robert Posthumus.

Chips

Potato chips (called *crisps* in the United Kingdom) are an American invention. In 1853 a chef by the name of George Crum in an upscale resort in Saratoga Springs, New York, was annoyed with a customer (claimed to have been Cornelius Vanderbilt) who repeatedly sent his french fried potatoes back to the kitchen because they were "too thick." Crum's response was to slice a potato so thin that it could not be speared by a fork and then fried the slices. This plan to aggravate the patron backfired when the patron was delighted with the new product. The invention was an instant success and became known initially as "Saratoga chips."

In today's chip factories potatoes are peeled, washed, sliced, deep-fried, dried, and packaged. Various flavors can be added to the chips. The shelf life of chips is much shorter than that of frozen french fries. Due to the bulky nature of chips they are not transported great distances from where they are produced. As with french fries, tubers with high dry matter and low reducing sugars are best suited for making chips. Typically tubers are sliced to a thickness of approximately $\frac{1}{16}$ inch (1.6 mm) thick and fried at 375°F (191°C) until moisture content is reduced to 1.3 to 1.5 percent (when chips stop bubbling).

Unlike for fries, desirable tuber shape for chips is round to oval. Chips made from cultivars with pigmented flesh are gaining popularity and can have an interesting array of color patterns. Most potato chips are produced by large processing companies. However, there are also numerous small scale "kettle" producers that fit local niche markets.

Dehydrated Potatoes

Dehydrated potato products include forms such as flour, flakes, granules, and diced. The need to feed armies during World Wars I and II was a great stimulus in the production of dehydrated potato products. The initial products left much to be desired in culinary quality. Texture and flavor improved dramatically as processing techniques advanced.

Potato flakes and granules are made by drying cooked mashed potatoes to a moisture level of 5 to 8 percent. Potato flour is ground from cooked, whole potatoes and retains a distinct potato taste. Dehydrated diced potatoes are primarily made by steaming and then drying potato pieces.

Dehydrated potatoes are primarily reconstituted as mashed potatoes. They are also used in extruded chips and other snacks, bakery products, pancakes, and as thickeners in processed soups and stews.

Nonfood Uses

The use of potatoes for purposes other than food is probably as old as the domestication of the crop. This is not surprising considering the way the potato is intertwined with the lives of people in many different cultures.

Expressions of Culture and Religion

Among the thousands of cultivars that were used by ancient civilizations in the Andes were those that had been selected for their red or blue internal flesh color. The juice of such pigmented tubers was used in the dyeing of textile fabrics and in religious ceremonies. These ceremonies sometimes involved pouring the blood of a llama over seed potatoes before planting. Potatoes with a blood red flesh were apparently also used in fertility ceremonies. In addition freeze-dried potatoes (chuño) were sometimes placed in tombs along with the bodies of the departed.

Alcoholic Beverages

In Europe and Russia in the late eighteenth century potatoes were used instead of expensive rye or wheat for the production of distilled alcoholic beverages. The Russian "vodka" and the German "schnapps" are often made from potatoes. The alcohol content of these drinks is usually quite high and often in the range of 35 to 40 percent.

Starch

The production of alcohol from potatoes eventually led to the development of the potato starch industry in Europe and elsewhere. Most potato starch is derived from potatoes specifically grown for that purpose. Cull potatoes and some waste products from processing plants are also used to manufacture starch. Potato starch is quite versatile and used by food, pharmaceutical, textile, wood, and paper industries as an adhesive, binder, texture agent, and filler, and by oil drilling firms to wash boreholes.

Bioplastics derived from potato starch have been recently developed and are fully biodegradable substitutes for polystyrene and other plastics used in disposable plates, dishes, and flatware. Adhesives derived from potato starch are being used in wallpaper paste and as glue on postage stamps. Such adhesives are also in demand for medical purposes where they are being used in plasters and dressings.

Biochemically, starch consists of polymers of glucose molecules. There are two basic types: amylose, which is essentially a linear arrangement of glucose molecules, and amylopectin, which is a highly branched arrangement of glucose molecules. Because of their different biochemical structures these two forms of starch have different physical properties important in industrial use. Generally potato starch consists of about 20 percent amylose and 80 percent amylopectin. Recently amylose-free potato cultivars (in which virtually all of the starch is in the form of amylopectin) have been developed for industrial use. Such cultivars have advantages in certain industrial processes. Although amylopectin and amylose can be separated industrially, this process is not economical. Pure amylopectin starch can be used to make yarn stronger, paper glossier, and can also be used to improve adhesives (by keeping the glue longer in liquid form).

Animal Feed

The use of potatoes as animal feed is still popular in eastern Europe. Around the world cattle are fed with waste products from potato processing plants. Ruminant animals such as cows, sheep, and goats can be fed raw potatoes. However, nonruminant animals such as pigs are unable to digest the raw starch. Potatoes need to be cooked or steamed before being fed to nonruminant animals.

Seed Potatoes

Statistically, on a global basis, approximately 10 percent of each year's crop is used to plant the next crop. Seed potatoes are discussed in chapter 4.

CHAPTER 11

Cultivar Development and Genetic Resources

THE DEVELOPMENT OF NEW CULTIVARS is an interesting and very time-consuming procedure that takes about 12 (or more) years. The process starts with the breeder gazing into a crystal ball and anticipating what will be needed 12 to 25 years in the future. The next step is the choice of the parents. Both parents should have traits which complement each other and which, ideally, will then be combined in a new cultivar.

Luther Burbank (1914), the famous American plant breeder, said this about potato breeding:

> Plant potato eyes and you get potatoes like the parents—improving, or retrograding, a little, according to the present environment in which they grow. But plant potato seeds and you tap a mine of heredity, infinite in its uncertainty, but infinite too, in its possibility.

Creating and Evaluating New Cultivars

In nature, hybridization (crossing) occurs when insects such as bumblebees visit potato flowers (Plate 166). In the process of searching for nectar the visiting insects brush small amounts of pollen onto the stigma of the flowers. The pollen tubes grow down the style and after fertilization has taken place in the ovary, the plant produces small green tomato-like fruits (Plate 2).

For breeding purposes it is necessary to make controlled pollinations. The breeder chooses which plant will serve as the female parent and which one will be the male parent. In such controlled pollinations the pollen is collected from the male parent and then transferred to the stigma of the flowers of the female plant (Plates 167 and 168). The pollinated flowers are then labeled (Plate 169). If the hybridization (cross pollination) is successful the female parent will produce small fruits, each of which will contain about 25 to 200 seeds. Breeders generally aim to obtain a dozen or more fruits from each cross combination. Genetically these tiny seeds are all different from each other, just like siblings in a human family.

The challenge then becomes the selection of a superior cultivar from among the thousands of siblings in such a potato family. On average breeders have to grow out at least 250,000 seedlings to find a successful major cultivar. This is a numbers game that requires skill, patience, selection of the right set of parents, and sometimes a bit of luck.

The seeds are sown in a greenhouse (Plate 170), and then transplanted into individual containers to produce small tubers (Plate 171).

These small tubers are planted in the field the following year, where the plants are evaluated under environmental conditions that are often harsh. Unlike a court of law where an accused is considered innocent until proven guilty, a potential new potato cultivar is considered inferior to existing ones unless its superiority can be proven. Recently, several new ways have been developed to produce new cultivars of potatoes by means other than traditional hybridization, for example, by genetic engineering of existing cultivars.

Regardless of how new cultivars are developed, it still takes many years to evaluate new potato selections to ensure that they are better than existing ones. The many rigorous tests include evaluating candidate cultivars for adaptation to different growing environments (such as hot and dry, cold and wet, hot and humid), resistance to many diseases (including common scab, late blight, and others) and, most importantly, consumer quality. Only those selections which pass the rigorous screening tests in any given year are tested in even broader and more rigid trials the subsequent year.

Potato trials invariably require a verdict by a large jury rather than a single judge. The entire testing process requires input from experts from a wide array of disciplines (growers, breeders, horticulturalists, plant pathologists, entomologists, and market specialists). Ultimately, consumers make the final decision. Cultivars usually achieve their highest potential in the geographical area where they were developed. However, some cultivars have a very wide adaptation and perform well over a much greater area.

The dry matter in potato tubers is primarily starch. Dry matter is an approximation of several quality traits. Tubers with high dry matter often tend to break apart (slough) more when boiled but when baked or fried they tend to have a mealy (granular) texture. French fry and potato chip manufacturers prefer high dry matter tubers because more finished product is produced per unit of raw potatoes and the finished product absorbs less cooking oil than when low dry matter potatoes are used. The lower the dry matter, the greater the oil absorption, which is costly to manufacturers. Low dry matter tubers tend to hold together well when boiled and therefore are preferred for salads and soups. In the North American potato industry dry matter is usually estimated by measuring specific gravity (density relative to water).

Spontaneous Mutations

Some major potato cultivars have arisen as result of spontaneous mutation (also known as sports). Mutations can affect many different traits, but many mutations are not easily recognized. Those affecting plant maturity, tuber skin texture, or color are easily recognized by the naked eye and have sometimes been used to develop selections with more desirable traits than the original cultivar. Mutations are often seen in commercial fields where large numbers of plants of one cultivar are grown. If one tuber or even a part of one tuber has a different skin color or skin texture than all the others, it stands out from the rest (Plate 172). Since potato is vegetatively propagated such mutants can easily be multiplied.

Sometimes the change is only to a deeper color hue. Several of the red-skinned cultivars carry mutations that confer deeper red color than the original parent cultivars. For example the red-skinned cultivars 'Norland', 'La Soda,' and 'Pontiac' gave rise to 'Red Norland' and 'Dark Red Norland', 'Red La Soda', and 'Red Pontiac' respectively. Sometimes mutations affect maturity. This often represents a reversion back to a shorter critical day length (see chapter 1). Such plants are easily identified because they are later maturing than other plants of the same cultivar; these plants are known as "bolters" or "giant hills." Some bolters have been selected and propagated to produce later-maturing, higher-yielding cultivars. Several strains of 'Russet Norkotah' originated this way. The most famous mutant potato cultivar is 'Russet Burbank', a russeted variant which arose from the smooth-skinned 'Burbank's Seedling'.

Genetically Modified Cultivars

Genetically modified potato cultivars have also been developed. In the 1990s the Monsanto company transformed 'Russet Burbank', 'Atlantic', 'Snowden', and 'Superior' with the *Bt* gene (obtained from the bacterium *Bacillus thuringiensis*), which confers a high degree of resistance to the Colorado potato beetle. These cultivars were respectively released as 'NewLeaf Russet Burbank', 'NewLeaf Atlantic', 'NewLeaf Snowden', and 'NewLeaf Superior'. Subsequently, resistance to potato virus Y and potato leafroll virus were added to several NewLeaf cultivars. The acreage planted to genetically engineered processing cultivars increased very rapidly in North America to more than 50,000 acres (approximately 20,000 ha) in the late 1990s. However, all New-Leaf cultivars were withdrawn from the market in the United States and Canada in 2001 due to controversy over the perceived safety of genetically altered food crops (Kaniewski et al. 2004). Although there is no evidence that genetically modified crops cause human health problems, no genetically modified potatoes are currently grown for human consumption in North America.

Genetic Resources and Narrow Genetic Foundation

Since the potato is one of the world's most important food crops, its genetic resources will undoubtedly play a very important role in future global food security. To feed the ever-increasing world population, agriculture has to produce more food on less land. Increasing awareness of the harmful environmental impact of various agricultural chemicals has led to a more judicious use of many chemical inputs. This has also resulted in a search for plants with the genetic potential to produce food more efficiently, for example, by more efficient use of nitrogen and water. Incorporating genetic resistance to pests and diseases will allow us to reduce the application of many pesticides. Global climate change is also placing demands for adaptation of all of our crop plants, including potatoes, for the ability to grow under environmental conditions that will be different from those of today. From a consumer standpoint the genetic resources of the potato have much to offer in terms of increased nutritional quality (see chapter 10).

There is a very great genetic diversity among cultivars in the Andes where the potato originated (Plate 173). This is partly the result of the selection and cultivation by local farmers in several different growing environments and for several different purposes. Only a very small sample of this diversity was introduced into Europe, however, and it was derivatives of these introductions that subsequently spread around the rest of the world. The diversity among the cultivated potatoes is not only for shape and skin color but also for many useful traits which are not visible to the naked eye.

For example, it is only recently that "modern" consumers have become aware of the health-enhancing qualities of antioxidants. These are substances which slow down the oxidation of oils and fats in the body; they are considered to have health benefits ranging from delaying eye degeneration to preventing heart and blood diseases, cancer and aging. Thus it is a rather humbling experience for consumers in the twenty-first century to learn that thousands of years ago Andean natives had already selected for these and possibly several other health-promoting substances in their "primitive" cultivars. Potatoes with deep yellow flesh color are high in the antioxidant lutein. Potatoes with red or blue flesh are high in anthocyanins, which are also antioxidants.

Potato scientists around the world are concerned about the dangers of a narrow genetic foundation for cultivated potatoes because it could potentially result in future catastrophes from perhaps yet unknown pests and diseases. The potato famine of the 1840s is an illustration of the vulnerability of the potato to a disease previously unknown in Europe.

The potato is not alone in having affected the life and death of large numbers of people. Wheat rust has plagued mankind for millennia. The Biblical seven years of famine in Egypt has been attributed to rust. Powdery mildew nearly destroyed the grape and wine industry of France in the mid-nineteenth century. Ergot of rye has created havoc since recorded history began. The fungus produces a toxin which throws consumers into violent convulsions. Ergotism was responsible for the death of tens of thousands of people in the Middle Ages and has affected the outcome of military battles. The coffee rust epidemic of the late nineteenth century virtually wiped out the coffee plantations of Ceylon (now Sri Lanka) and other Southeast Asian countries with disastrous economic results. Eventually the coffee plantations were replaced by tea and changed Great Britain from a nation of coffee drinkers to sippers of tea (Large 1940; Carefoot and Sprott 1967).

Potato Hunting

Many wild and primitive cultivated potato species are now losing their habitat. The factors leading to habitat loss include forest clearing, increased grazing, irrigation of dry lands, and changing farm practices such as the use of herbicides and destruction of field borders as the field sizes increase. When their natural habitat changes drastically, the wild species are often no longer able to compete with the (new) surrounding vegetation and, as a result, may become extinct. Also, the primitive cultivated species are gradually being replaced by modern cultivars. This "genetic erosion" means that we are in danger of losing extremely valuable potato genetic resources.

Wild potatoes grow in many different habitats including rock crevices, cactus deserts, open woodland, and forest borders (Plate 174). From the early twentieth century onward, when travel was often treacherous and time consuming, plant collectors sought representative samples of all potato species. Breeders, other scientists, and ultimately all potato growers and eaters owe a great debt of gratitude to the scientists who have collected samples of wild potato species.

Because potatoes are propagated in two different ways—sexually via botanical seed and asexually via tubers—scientists can collect wild species germplasm in the form of seed or tubers. Botanical seed is the preferred form as it is much easier to transport and maintain than tubers. While seed can be stored for decades under appropriate conditions, tubers must be planted once a year to maintain the specimen. Although collecting tubers allows for the maintenance of a specific combination of genes, in most cases collectors prefer to collect seeds because the primary interest is in preserving the genes themselves.

Collectors have to plan their expeditions to coincide with the time when (most) wild species have produced mature fruits. In addition to collecting fruits from a representative number of plants in a specific location, plant hunters also take herbarium specimens of the plants and record the exact location where each sample was taken. If specific cultivars are desired then the tubers must be collected, either from fields or local markets.

Even though the potato was first introduced into Europe during the latter part of the sixteenth century, it was several centuries before western governments became concerned about the need to collect and conserve potato germplasm to ensure future crops. Initially, introductions of germplasm resources from South America into Europe and North America were few and rather haphazard. Systematic germplasm collecting began with Russian expeditions in the late 1920s and early 1930s. This was followed by other large-scale expeditions from Germany, the United States, and Sweden.

Of particular interest is the contribution by the British pioneer Jack Hawkes. The description of his first British Empire Potato Collecting Expedition in South America in 1938–1939 (Hawkes 2004) makes for interesting reading. This expedition, which occurred on the eve of World War II, took Hawkes and two colleagues through Peru, Argentina, Bolivia, Ecuador, and Colombia. In Hawkes's own words:

> Starting from Lima, Peru, in January 1939 and ending in Panama at
> the end of August of the same year, the expedition traveled during
> these eight months some 9000 miles [14,500 km], exclusive, of course,
> of the journeys to and from South America. Travel was accomplished
> by air, steamship, rail, lorry, car, horse, mule and foot.

Hawkes went on to conduct many more potato expeditions and made major contributions to potato conservation. Since his first expedition many other botanists have followed in his footsteps. Seeds collected during these expeditions were deposited in genebanks for use by breeders and other scientists.

Germplasm Conservation

For future food security, as is the case for germplasm of all crop plants, it is very important that the great wealth of potato germplasm is being conserved in a systematic and secure way so that it is easily available for future use. There are several ways of doing this, each with its pros and cons. These different means are discussed here.

Off-site Germplasm Conservation

One way to preserve the valuable genes that endangered wild and primitive cultivated species may contain is to preserve them off-site, or *ex situ*, in genebanks. There are seven major potato genebanks around the world. They are seen as long-term public trusts, so are managed and funded by national

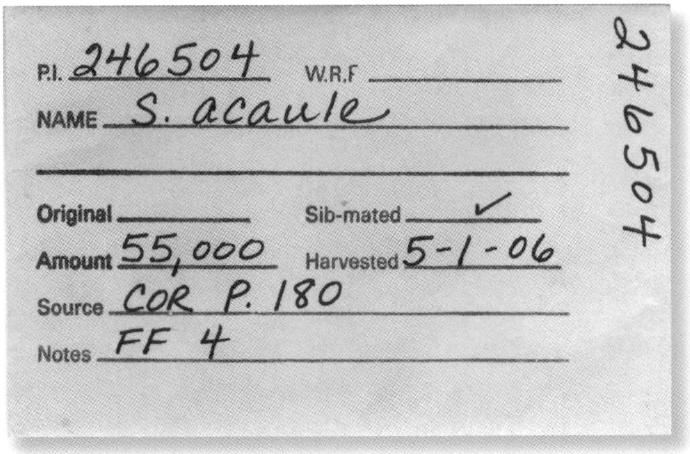

Figure 12. United States Potato Genebank. This particular envelope contains seed of *Solanum acaule*, a species that has proven useful, among other things, as a source of frost and virus resistance. This accession has Plant Introduction (P.I.) number 246504. Courtesy of John Bamberg.

governments. The principal North American potato genebank is managed by the U.S. Department of Agriculture and is located in Sturgeon Bay, Wisconsin. The curator is John Bamberg.

In 2009 this genebank had an inventory of 5704 accessions comprising 131 species (Bamberg 2009) (see Figure 12). Wild species, which represent the bulk of the holdings of most genebanks, are maintained as botanical seed and are distributed for research, breeding, and educational purposes. Most genebanks publish inventories of their holdings to enable scientists relatively easy access. Much of this data, which includes evaluation of useful traits, is now available on-line.

Of the approximately 5000 different native potato cultivars that are estimated to be grown in the Andes, about 4600 are currently maintained at the genebank of the International Potato Center (abbreviated as CIP, after its Spanish name) in Lima, Peru. To be useful to the scientific community it is important for genebanks to be able to share their germplasm. To meet plant quarantine regulations for moving plant material between countries, the material has to be free of virus and other diseases. For these reasons many of the cultivars in the CIP collection, as well as in other collections, have been freed of virus and disease and are maintained as plantlets, on an artificial substrate, *in vitro* (literally "in glass"). The maintenance of plantlets in sterile glass test tubes minimizes risk of re-contamination from infected plants (Plate 175).

An increasingly important issue related to germplasm is the question of ownership. In our economic system "plant breeders rights" allow breeding companies to claim a share of revenues for new cultivars (similar to patents for industrial products). If improved cultivars contain genes derived from wild germplasm, how should countries where the germplasm originated be compensated?

On-site Germplasm Conservation

There is growing interest in preserving wild species germplasm on-site, or *in situ*, where such germplasm is naturally found. Proponents of this approach have pointed out several disadvantages with preserving germplasm in genebanks. It is difficult and often expensive to capture and preserve the genetic diversity of wild relatives. If it is possible to leave species in their natural habitats, then the evolutionary processes that created them in the first place can continue. This cannot occur in genebanks.

The on-site approach is not yet used for the preservation of wild potato species. Considering the very large number of such species and their collective distribution in a wide range of habitats from sea level to 13,500 ft. (4100 m) in altitude and over a distance of some 8000 miles (13,000 km) in a north–south direction, systematic on-site preservation would be a major undertaking. It might be possible for species with relatively small geographic distribution, but it is not practical for many others (Maxted and Hawkes 1997).

Perhaps a stronger case for on-site preservation can be made for cultivated potatoes. It can be argued that the best way to preserve primitive cultivars is through their continued cultivation by the people whose cultures have selected them in the first place and in the locations where they were domesticated. This approach is not yet nearly as well implemented as off-site conservation of cultivated potatoes. In the area around Cuzco, Peru, farmers grow many different traditional cultivars in the same field. Traditional mixed cultivar planting provides stability; while yields may not be as high as with more modern cultivars, the cultivar mix guards against crop failures. Nevertheless, there is a concern that as farmers adopt more modern cultivars at least some of the more traditional ones may eventually be lost. The collection of native cultivars at the International Potato Center can be considered a compromise. Although these cultivars are not maintained by farmers, they are at least being maintained in the general region where they were initially selected.

Germplasm Conservation with Heritage or Heirloom Cultivars

It is not only wild and primitive cultivated potato species that disappear over time, "advanced," but still old cultivars, can also go extinct. Older cultivars are variously described as heritage, heirloom, traditional, vintage, antique, or classic cultivars. There is no clear definition for these terms; in general they are used synonymously. It has been suggested that, for a cultivar to be considered heirloom, it should be at least 50 years old (DeMuth 1998). In North America two national organizations, Seed Savers Exchange (SSE) in the United States, and Seeds of Diversity Canada (SDC), include potato in their respective agendas and serve as valuable sources of information and seed sources for heritage potato cultivars.

Since potato cultivars are maintained by vegetative propagation they tend to accumulate viruses and other diseases, which are readily passed on to the next generation through the tubers. The accumulation of such diseases may lead to the weakening and discontinued use of a cultivar. This is not a problem with vegetables that are seed-propagated because most viruses are not transmitted through seed. Diseases carried in potato tubers can be a problem when potato cultivars are exchanged on an informal basis, that is, without the benefit of a seed potato certification program.

To avoid this problem, and to assist the community-based effort to maintain and distribute healthy heirloom potato cultivars, Agriculture and Agri-Food Canada at the Potato Research Centre, Fredericton, New Brunswick, operates the Potato Gene Resources Repository, a node of Plant Gene Resources Canada. The annual *Potato Gene Resources Newsletter* includes an inventory of healthy potato cultivars which are available for distribution. The Centre's 2009 annual report shows an inventory of 159 accessions, of which 48 percent are heirloom cultivars. Nearly all of this material is maintained in disease-free condition *in vitro* and is available in small quantities for breeding, research, and evaluation purposes, as supplies allow.

Descriptions of many heritage cultivars, including pictures, can be found in the *Potato Gene Resources Newsletter*, catalogs of SSE and SDC, as well as catalogs of companies that sell heritage cultivars of many vegetable crops, including potatoes (see appendix 1 for addresses of these resources). In the *Seed Savers 2009 Yearbook* the SSE members offered 657 potato cultivars. Regardless of which cultivar is being planted, you can avoid a lot of trouble later if you first ensure that the seed potatoes were produced by bona fide certified seed potato growers (see chapter 4).

Germplasm Utilization

The traditional transfer of desirable traits from primitive cultivated and wild species to cultivated potato is a long-term process that usually takes several decades. The reason is that from the standpoint of a potato grower or consumer wild species also carry a lot of undesirable baggage. Hybrids between wild species and well-adapted cultivars are almost invariably not well adapted to growing in the potato fields of North America or Europe. Many wild species, and their offspring, also have traits that are undesirable from a horticultural standpoint, such as extremely deep eyes, very small tubers, and extremely long stolons.

Thus several cycles of crossing, initially between the wild species and a cultivar, followed by several backcrosses to cultivars, and selection at each stage for adaptation among the progeny, is usually necessary to obtain the desirable wild species genes in a genetic background that is acceptable to farmers and consumers. Even so, breeders around the world have made great progress in utilizing potato germplasm resources.

Many important traits, including disease resistance and processing quality, have already been incorporated into cultivated potato. In fact, the potato was probably the first crop plant in which breeding for disease resistance was done. This was primarily the result of the potato famine caused by the late blight outbreak of the 1840s. Scientists in many countries introduced foreign germplasm that was presumed resistant to late blight. An example of this is the introduction of 'Rough Purple Chili' by Chauncey Goodrich in New York in 1851. Although this cultivar did not turn out to be resistant to late blight, its descendants feature very prominently in very many North American and European cultivars.

Disease Resistances Derived from Species

There is now a very long list of cases where germplasm has been successfully used in developing improved cultivars. For example, from *Solanum tuberosum* subsp. *andigena* breeders have transferred genes for resistance to potato cyst nematodes and potato viruses X and Y. These genes are now present in many modern cultivars.

In addition to contributing specific traits, *Solanum tuberosum* subsp. *andigena* has been widely used in broadening the genetic base of the cultivated potato. The Potato Research Centre in Fredericton, New Brunswick, Canada, has developed several selections with multiple disease resistances. One pre-breeding project there involved the development of a population of long-day adapted clones of *S. tuberosum* subsp. *andigena* with disease resistances to late blight, common scab, potato virus Y, and wart (Tarn et al. 2003).

Another project at the same Research Centre involved the development of a parent with varying degrees of resistances to late blight, *Verticillium*, early blight, wart, potato cyst nematode, and potato viruses X and Y. In this case the species contributing to this disease-resistance package include *Solanum tuberosum* subsp. *andigena*, *S. tuberosum* subsp. *tuberosum* from Chile, *S. demissum*, *S. stoloniferum*, and several European cultivars of unknown ancestry (De Jong et al. 2001). Materials such as those described above will be very useful in further genetic enhancement of the cultivated potato.

A search of the pedigrees of modern cultivars shows many wild species in the backgrounds. For example, *Solanum acaule*, a species of the Altiplano of Peru and Bolivia, has contributed genes for a high degree of resistance to potato viruses X and Y. The frost-resistant cultivar 'Alaska Frostless', now in very limited supply, is only three crossing generations removed from *S. acaule*. *Solanum chacoense*, another wild species, occurs in the pedigrees of many modern cultivars, including 'Atlantic', where it has contributed to high dry matter (or specific gravity), which is important in potato processing.

A number of nematode pests represent serious threats to potatoes worldwide. The most serious are potato cyst nematodes, soil-borne pests that can remain dormant in the soil for decades and can be spread from field to field by infested soil clinging to seed tubers. *Solanum tuberosum* subsp. *andigena* contains a major gene for resistance that has already been incorporated in many cultivars. Several wild diploid species from the eastern slopes of the Andes in Bolivia and northern Argentina also have a high degree of resistance to the potato cyst nematode. It appears that in this general area various *Solanum* species evolved in the presence of potato cyst nematodes, and thus over many thousands of years clones with resistance were the primary survivors.

Insect Resistance Derived from a Wild Species

The development of the insect-resistant 'King Harry' at Cornell University is an interesting case study in the utilization of exotic potato germplasm. This involved the utilization of the wild species *Solanum berthaultii* (Plates 176 and 177).

For several decades it had been known that this species is resistant to many different insects. The mechanism of resistance is complex but resides in the presence of specialized hairs on the lower surface of the leaves. These hairs have glands at their tips. When an insect rubs against a hair the gland ruptures and exudes a gluelike substance that entraps small insects (Plate 178), impeding their movement so that they eventually starve. The glandular hairs also deter feeding and egg-laying by larger insects. Most *Solanum berthaultii* accessions have two types of glandular hairs, short ones (Type A) and longer ones (Type B). Both types are important in conferring resistance to various types of insects.

Solanum berthaultii was first described by the late Jack Hawkes on his first collecting expedition in Bolivia in 1939. In his memoirs (2004) he described the location and surroundings of this species. Someone had told him that there was a wild potato growing on a little rocky hill southeast of Cochabamba. In Hawkes's own words:

> The hill was called Cerro San Pedro and when we got there we found an abundance of wild potato plants with glandular pubescence and a pleasant aroma. The tubers were quite large and some plants had green berries. This was certainly a new species, which I later named S. *berthaultii* in honor of the well-known French Solanaceae expert Pierre Berthault. It later became quite famous, showing resistance to potato blight, wart, common scab, *Fusarium* wilt, potato viruses X and Y, various insects and spider mites, and some races of potato cyst nematode. Consequently, Cerro San Pedro later became a kind of pilgrimage site for potato germplasm collectors! Why this one species possesses so much resistance to all sorts of pests and diseases nobody knows. Finding it was just an extraordinary example of chance, or some would say, serendipity.

In 1980 the first hybridization between *Solanum berthaultii* and a commercial cultivar was made by Robert Plaisted and Ward Tingey at Cornell

University. After six backcrosses and subsequent selections during the following decade, the selection NYL 235-4 was released in 1992. This was the first selection from this project with resistance to the Colorado potato beetle, aphids, flea beetles, potato leafhoppers, and the potato tuber moth as well as reasonable agronomic characteristics (Plaisted et al. 1992). It was named 'Prince Hairy' by Jim Gerritsen of Wood Prairie Farm in Bridgewater, Maine.

Plaisted's successor at Cornell, Walter De Jong, released a second selection in 2007. 'King Harry' (also named by Jim Gerritsen) represents a considerable agronomic improvement over 'Prince Hairy' because, in addition to its insect resistance, it has earlier maturity and higher yield. Cultivation of the wild species *Solanum berthaultii* under long-day conditions in North America is impractical because of the production of very small tubers. A comparison between the tubers of 'King Harry' and *S. berthaultii* demonstrates how plant breeders have been able to combine some of the favorable traits of this wild species with the ability to produce a good yielding cultivar (Plate 179). In 2007 'King Harry' won a Green Thumb Award from the Mailorder Gardening Association.

Both 'Prince Hairy' and 'King Harry' have the short (Type A) glandular hairs but not the longer (Type B) hairs. This in turn means that they do not have resistance to mites, which can be a problem if potatoes are growing where dusty conditions may occur (such as proximity to an unpaved road).

Yellow Flesh Color Derived from a Cultivated Species

'Yukon Gold' is another example of the utilization of Andean cultivars. It was developed by the late Gary Johnston at the Agriculture and Agri-Food Canada potato breeding program in Guelph, Ontario, Canada. Until the mid-twentieth century nearly all potato cultivars in North America had white flesh, whereas the European cultivars were (and still are) predominantly yellow-fleshed. In response to the consumer demands from the immigrant communities of European descent in southern Ontario, Johnston started searching for potential yellow-fleshed parents. He obtained several candidates from the U.S. Potato Genebank in Sturgeon Bay, Wisconsin. One of these was a hybrid from *Solanum phureja* 'Yema de huevo' ("egg yolk") (Plate 180). This unnamed hybrid had rather small, unattractive tubers but deep yellow flesh. In 1966 Johnston crossed it with 'Norgleam'. After growing hundreds of progeny seedlings he eventually selected a clone, which after many years of evaluation in different locations, was released as 'Yukon Gold' in Canada in 1980. Since then it has become the standard for yellow-fleshed cultivars in North America.

Above we have described several examples of important traits that were transferred to cultivated potato from germplasm collections. In each case these traits were used to solve known problems. Potentially much more important is the possibility that potato germplasm can solve future problems that have not yet been encountered. If, for example, a hitherto unknown disease similar to the late blight epidemic of the 1840s were to threaten a major world food crop such as potato, then a large part of the world population might face starvation. Maintaining germplasm with as much genetic diversity as possible helps ensure that we have the means to tackle such threats as they arise.

CHAPTER 12

Distribution, Domestication, and Classification

THE POTATO HAS MORE WILD RELATIVES than any other major crop. Its classification has been the subject of a lengthy ongoing debate. This is no surprise considering its importance as a major world food crop. The wild relatives are very widely distributed throughout much of the Americas. Slowly but surely scientists are unraveling the events leading to the domestication of the potato. It is hoped that a better understanding of the classification, distribution, and domestication of the potato will lead to its further improvement and use.

Geographic Distribution

Most wild potato species occur in the Americas between latitudes 38 degrees North and 41 degrees South, at altitudes between 6,600 and 13,000 ft. (2000–4000 m), although some are also found at sea level. There are two geographic centers of diversity (areas with a high degree of genetic variation) of wild potato species: one in the southwestern United States, Mexico, and Guatemala and another in South America.

The largest concentrations of wild species are in Peru and Bolivia. Argentina and Mexico also have a relatively large number of potato species. Several species grow in relatively small geographical areas; many occupy considerably less than 40 square miles (about 100 square kilometers), confined, for example, to a specific valley. This is no surprise considering how quickly growing environments can change over short distances in the area where these species are found.

Differences in altitude alone can contribute to vast differences in growing environment. Some species are rare and in danger of extinction, as their habitats are destroyed by human development. Other species occupy a large geographical area. For example, *Solanum chacoense* grows in five countries (south Bolivia, north and central Argentina, Paraguay, Uruguay, and south Brazil) and is often found as a weed in cultivated fields.

It is thought that the wild tuber-bearing species originated in Mexico because the most "primitive" wild species are found here. Some of these species then migrated to South America about 3.5 million years ago after the Panama isthmus was formed. Arguably the most primitive living tuber-bearing species is *Solanum morelliforme*. This is an epiphyte (growing on another plant for support but not parasitic) that grows on mossy branches of oak trees in cloud forest environments in the mountains of central and southern Mexico (Hawkes 1990, 1994).

Evolution and Domestication

Domestication can be defined as the human creation of a new form of a plant or animal—one that is clearly different from its wild ancestors and wild relatives. Considering the amount of time humans have been on earth, agriculture is a very recent development. The oldest forms of agriculture (which involved domestication of plants and animals) we know of began roughly 10,000 years ago. Domestication is similar to the natural process of evolution, except that, instead of nature, humans determine the selective pressures, and can choose offspring that exhibit desirable traits such as rapid growth, ease-of-harvest, yield, and food quality.

When humans place different values on biological traits than nature does, they intervene in key aspects of the life cycle of a species, creating new rules for survival and reproductive success. Only those plants (or animals) able to survive and produce offspring under the new man-made rules contribute genetic information to the next generation. Then, after several hundreds or thousands of years, a new or modified form of plant or animal arises. Thus it can be said that domestication and subsequent plant and animal breeding are part of "human-guided evolution."

Domestication not only results in changes in the plants and animals being domesticated, but also changes the people who carried out the domestication. Eventually, after several millennia, relationships of increasing mutual dependence arise to the point where neither party can easily survive without the other. Highly domesticated crop plants may not be able to survive in the wild since selection may reduce fitness to survive and reproduce in the wild, and by the same token modern major civilizations are dependent on the production of modern crop plants (agriculture).

It is agriculture that enabled humans to settle in permanent communities. Agriculture released a substantial segment of the population from the requirement to hunt or gather food, permitting them to produce various crafts and ply new trades (which eventually led to modern manufacture and commerce). Only a relatively small number of people are now needed to produce food, not only for themselves but also for those involved in nonagricultural pursuits.

Potato, along with other crops and animals that had previously been domesticated by Andean natives, contributed greatly to many Andean cultures, culminating in the Inca Empire. The Incas ruled over 10 million people for about 300 years and their empire stretched for about 3000 miles (4800 km) from Colombia to central Chile. They were able to do so largely due to their advanced agricultural system and the growing of potato, a high-yield, high-energy crop.

The potato is not the only crop with origins in the Andes. At the time of the Spanish conquest, the Incas cultivated a wide array of root and tuber crops such as oca, mashua, and olluco, as well as grains such as quinoa, legumes such as beans and lupins, vegetables such as peppers and squashes, and many fruits and nuts. Many other Andean crops have thus far been overlooked as potential world food crops (Lyon 1989). Along with plants, several animals were also domesticated in the Andes, including llama, alpaca, and guinea pig.

The First Cultivated Potato

The technical definition of a wild species is *an organism captive or living in the wild that has not been subject to breeding to alter it from its native state.* In the potato world the distinction between wild and cultivated occasionally breaks down. Sometimes the wild species most closely related to cultivated species grow in the same environments as cultivated ones. Even today, the tubers of these wild potatoes may be gathered by indigenous peoples from the woods and hillsides to supplement their ordinary food supplies.

On a morphological basis it can be difficult to distinguish between wild and cultivated potatoes. Some "wild" species may originally have been cultivated but then reverted to the wild (Spooner et al. 1999). Sometimes tubers of wild species are "harvested" from a field but enough tubers are left behind to keep the crop from dying out (Hawkes 2004).

Andean farmers often grow mixtures of cultivars and even mixtures of different species in the same field (although *Solanum tuberosum* subsp. *andigena* is generally the most abundant species). In addition there can be an ongoing natural hybridization between cultivated and wild potatoes which results in exchanges of genes between them. For example, this is known to occur quite frequently between the primitive cultivated species *S. stenotomum* and the wild species *S. sparsipilum*.

There is general agreement among potato scientists that *Solanum stenotomum* was the first domesticated species. Most authors also agree that this species is at least one of the parents of *S. tuberosum* subsp. *andigena*, which in turn led to the selection of *S. tuberosum* subsp. *tuberosum*.

For many crop plants there is a debate whether there has been a single origin (after which the plant would have diffused over a wider area) or several origins at different locations and times. This is also the case in potatoes. Sukhotu and Hosaka (2006) have proposed multiple origins of both *Solanum stenotomum* and *S. tuberosum* subsp. *andigena*, whereas Spooner et al. (2005) have presented evidence that primitive indigenous cultivated potatoes (landraces) have a single origin.

The growing environments in the Andean region are highly variable and range from subtropical conditions at low elevations to a cool, temperate climate at higher altitudes. Thus it is unsurprising that different potato species for different growing environments were domesticated locally. For example, *Solanum ajanhuiri*, *S. curtilobum*, and *S. jucepczukii*, all of which have considerable frost tolerance, are cultivated in the highlands of Peru and Bolivia at altitudes of 12,500–13,500 ft. (3800–4100 m), where most other cultivated species would not thrive. They were probably selected by the Aymará Indians in the harsh climate and poor soils of the Andes of southern Peru and northern Bolivia. Regionally adapted species were so important to communities that they became embedded in the culture; there is even a local folksong dedicated to *S. ajanhuiri* (Huamán et al. 1980). In contrast to these three species, *S. phureja* is grown in mountain valleys at the much lower altitudes of 2600–3300 ft. (800–1000 m), in environments unsuitable for other potato species. Its area of cultivation stretches all the way from western Venezuela to central Bolivia (Hawkes 1990). It is early maturing and, because of its exceptionally short dormancy, can be grown twice in the same year.

Whatever the wild species ancestry may have been, the scientific consensus is that domestication of the potato probably started some eight thousand years ago around Lake Titicaca on the border between Bolivia and Peru. Pictures of potato plants and tubers on ancient pottery demonstrate that the potato was cultivated for thousands of years before the Spanish conquistadors reached South America. Plate 181 shows a Pre-Colombian ceramic storage vessel (A.D. 600–800) modeled on 'Huayro', a well-known traditional cultivar that is still grown throughout the Peruvian Andes.

Bitter Potatoes

Many wild potato species contain natural compounds called *glycoalkaloids* which confer resistance to insects and diseases. While useful to the plant, glycoalkaloids also have a serious drawback: they impart a bitter taste and, at high enough levels, are toxic to humans. Glycoalkaloids are heat-stable, thus cooking does not eliminate the toxicity or bitterness.

A major step in the domestication of wild potato species was discovering ways to circumvent glycoalkaloids. One straightforward, albeit unappealing approach is still practiced in some regions of the Altiplano (a high plateau in the Andes). Here people knowingly eat toxic potatoes, but also eat a special clay which binds to glycoalkaloids, thus neutralizing them (Reader 2008).

A more intricate system to eliminate glycoalkaloids, involving freeze-drying, was also developed in the Andes. Bitter tubers are exposed to freezing temperatures for three or four nights. During the day the potatoes are trampled by foot to remove moisture and potato skins. The trampled potatoes are then transferred to a stream of water to allow the glycoalkaloids to leach out. The final product is called *chuño*. There are two basic types of chuño: white (chuño blanco) and black (chuño negro).

In her book, *The Potato in the Human Diet*, Jennifer Woolfe (1987) describes in considerable detail how the different forms are produced. Chuño is almost free of glycoalkaloids and can be stored for a year or longer. It is usually used to make soups and stews. This freeze-dried product essentially represents the oldest known form of potato processing. Chuño was used by populations from higher altitudes to barter for products from lower elevations. It could be stored by the central-controlled Inca government and distributed to areas where there had been crop failures. Chuño was also used to feed the workers in the silver mines of Potosí (in current south central Bolivia).

Origin of the European Potato

In addition to the debate about the domestication of potato *per se*, there is a related debate about the origin of the European potato. In particular, how did the potato get to Europe, and from which part of South America did it come? There are two competing theories about the nature of the first material brought to Europe. These theories have been at the root of much scientific and historical research and have also led to political controversy.

One hypothesis is that the first potatoes taken to Europe were *Solanum tuberosum* subsp. *andigena*. These potatoes would have come from the Andes and were then perhaps shipped from present-day Colombia. Ocean transport from northern Colombia was much easier than from the Pacific coast of South America. In the Andes these potatoes would have been adapted to areas relatively close to the equator, where the length of day is similar to the length of night. In other words, they were selected for their ability to form tubers under short days.

In Europe, however, day length during the growing season is much longer. Short days in Europe do not occur until late in the fall. This means that any plants brought from the Andes would only start to tuberize in fall, and consequently would not produce much of a crop before winter. Adaptation to photoperiod (the scientific word for day length) is under genetic control, so that after several cycles of growing and selecting in Europe, it would have been possible for long-day adapted *Solanum tuberosum* subsp. *tuberosum* to arise from short-day adapted *S. tuberosum* subsp. *andigena*.

A second hypothesis contends that the first potatoes taken to Europe came from places in southern Chile, such as Chiloé, where the day length during the growing season is comparable to that of southern Europe. Figure 13 shows that the day length of Chiloé Island is similar to that of Rome, Italy. Potatoes traveling this route would thus not have required extensive selection for ability to tuberize in Europe. Analysis of potato chloroplast DNA has shown that most European potatoes are descendents of Chilean *tuberosum* (Rios et al. 2007).

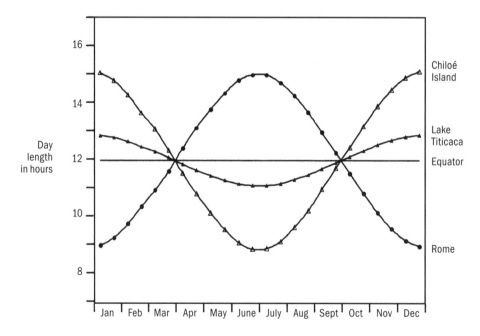

Figure 13. Day length at four different latitudes. Compiled from Baker and Baker (2008).

Even though modern potatoes appear to be primarily of Chilean origin, there is still debate about when Chilean germplasm first reached Europe. Many of the early introductions into Europe (and their descendants) were wiped out by the late blight epidemic of the 1840s. For a long time it had been thought that original Andean germplasm introductions were replaced by Chilean germplasm—but only after the late blight epidemic.

Recent evidence from the Canary Islands, one of the first European regions where potatoes were introduced from South America, hinted that Chilean material reached Europe before the late blight epidemic. The earliest known record of potato cultivation in the Canary Islands is from 1567. Analysis of landraces growing there showed that while some had been derived from highland Andean material, most others could be traced back to Chile.

Even more compelling is molecular genetic analysis of old European herbarium specimens. The results clearly demonstrate that Chilean potatoes were introduced into Europe as early as 1811, thus Chilean potatoes were already cultivated in Europe before the 1840s (Rios et al. 2007; Ames et al. 2008).

These scientific findings have subsequently created some political tension between Chile and Peru. Because most of today's modern cultivars can be traced back to parents of Chilean origin, the Chilean government has asserted that Chile, rather than Peru, is the home of the potato. This in turn is disputed by Peru, because both the Andean and the Chilean cultivars have a common Peruvian origin. The argument is unnecessary because both countries are correct (Figure 14). Modern potatoes did descend, most recently, from long-day adapted Chilean potatoes. Long-day adapted Chilean potatoes, in turn, descended from the potatoes first domesticated around Lake Titicaca on the border of Bolivia and Peru. Potato domestication is an ongoing process; it doesn't have a single defined endpoint.

Unsurprisingly, perhaps, there is even disagreement about the evolution of Chilean *tuberosum* itself. Hawkes (1990) originally postulated that the selection for adaptation to long days that purportedly led from *S. tuberosum* subsp. *andigena* to *S. tuberosum* subsp. *tuberosum* in Europe also took place in southern Chile, where potatoes have been grown for several thousand years. But analysis of chloroplast DNA suggests a different path.

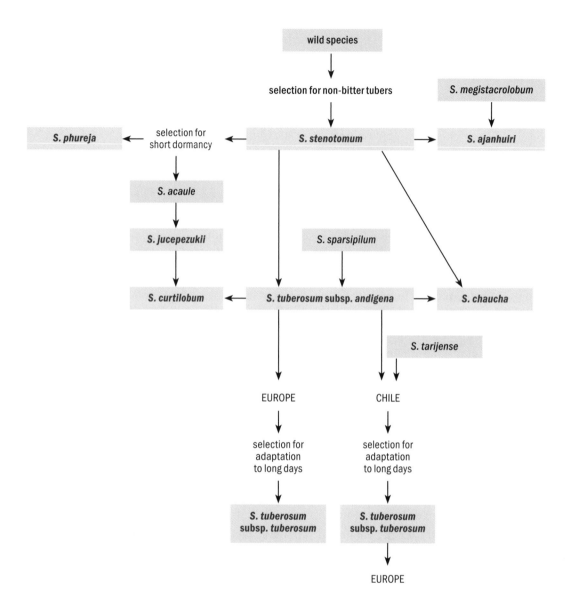

Figure 14. Postulated evolution of cultivated potatoes. Cultivated species are purple.

Chloroplast DNA is separate from the chromosomes of the cell nucleus, and has an interesting property that makes it suitable for tracing history of female (maternal) parents. During reproduction nuclear DNA is transmitted to the progeny via both the female (egg cells) and male (pollen) germ cells. Chloroplast DNA, however, is transmitted to the progeny only through egg cells. This feature of chloroplast DNA enables scientists to study the female origin of species. The chloroplast DNA present in Chilean cultivated potatoes is most easily explained by natural hybridization between the wild species *Solanum tarijense* as the female parent and *S. tuberosum* subsp. *andigena* as the male (Hosaka 2004).

The story of 'Rough Purple Chili' is interesting in light of the above. This potato was introduced into the United States by Chauncey Goodrich of New York in 1851. He had obtained this clone, along with several others, through the courtesy of the American consulate in Panama. He believed that these clones had come from Chile (which he spelled "Chili"). Subsequent research results, including chloroplast DNA analysis, agree with Goodrich's opinion. 'Rough Purple Chili' was indeed Chilean *tuberosum*. It was already adapted to long days and this may explain its success as a parent: 'Rough Purple Chili' is in the pedigree of most modern North American as well as many European cultivars. It is an ancestor of 'Russet Burbank' which, in terms of area grown, is still the top ranking cultivar in North America. Considering the economic impact that its descendants have had, 'Rough Purple Chili' is one of the most important plant importations that has been made into the United States (Hougas and Ross 1956).

Classification

The science that describes, classifies, identifies, and names plants is known as plant taxonomy, or classification. Modern classification of plants originated with the Swedish scientist Carl von Linné (1707–1778), also known as Carl (or Carolus) Linnaeus. Prior to his time the described species often had common or long and complex names that were difficult to use and were often different in different places. Linnaeus introduced the binomial Latin system where the first name indicates the genus and the second one the species. Today there are international standards for the naming of plants of wild origin that are governed by the International Code of Botanical Nomenclature.

The name *Solanum tuberosum* ("swollen underground stem," referring to the tuber which functions both as a storage as well as a reproductive organ) was first applied to the potato by the Swiss botanist Gaspard Bauhin (1560–1624) in his *Phytopinax* in 1596. A quarter of a century later Bauhin, in his *Prodromos Theatrici Botanici* (1620), extended the name to *Solanum tuberosum esculentum* (*esculent* means "edible, fit for eating"). This last term was omitted by Linnaeus in his *Species Plantarum* (1753) in order to fit the name for potato into his binomial system.

The potato belongs to the family Solanaceae which can be further subdivided as follows:

Family: *Solanaceae*
  Genus: *Solanum*
    Subgenus: *Potatoe*
      Section *Petota*, containing the tuber-bearing species

The Solanaceae comprises about 90 genera and 2800 species, including eggplant, pepper, petunia, tobacco, tomato, and tomatillo. Because there are so many species in the genus *Solanum*, botanists have established various subgenera, of which *Potatoe* is one. Subgenus *Potatoe* has been further subdivided into sections, where *Petota* includes the tuber-bearing species. Although sweet potato is often assumed to be part of the Solanaceae, it is not. Sweet potato (*Ipomoea batatas*) belongs, instead, to the morning glory family (Convolvulaceae).

Because of their great value as genetic resources, potato species have attracted considerable attention from botanists. Those who study potatoes do not always agree on how to classify the many species. It should be no surprise that with so many species there has been much debate about how best to classify them and that the classification of both wild and cultivated potato species is frequently under revision. The availability of more and better quality information (such as DNA sequence data) has also contributed to several recent revisions of potato taxonomy.

Just as with the classification of other plants, there are potato botanists who are "lumpers" whereas others are "splitters." The lumper school advocates the similarities between species or groups of species; the splitters tend to divide species based on relatively small differences. The early classifications were primarily based on physical features such as plant habit and many different characters of the stem, leaf, flower, fruit, and tuber. Later other features such as interspecific crossability (the ability to hybridize different species with each other), chromosome number, and biochemical markers have also been used.

British taxonomist John Gregory Hawkes (1990, 1994) divided section *Petota* into 19 series of tuber-bearing *Solanum* species and an additional 2 series of nontuber-bearing species. The series *Tuberosa* consists of all the cultivated as well as many wild species. Hawkes recognized a total of 235 species, of which 7 (S. *ajanhuiri*, S. *chaucha*, S. *curtilobum*, S. *jucepczukii*, S. *phureja*, S. *stenotomum*, and S. *tuberosum*) are cultivated. In this system S. *tuberosum* was further subdivided into subspecies (subsp.) *tuberosum* and subsp. *andigena*.

More recently, and using new molecular marker data that was not available to Hawkes, other botanists have revised Hawkes's classification. Spooner and Salas (2006), using several DNA-based and other modern tools, proposed a revised list and reduced Hawkes's list of 235 species to considerably less than 200. A contemporary of Hawkes, the Russian botanist Vadim Lechnovitch (1971) proposed a list of 21 different cultivated species. Others felt that Hawkes's list of seven cultivated species was too long and that several species could be considered as subgroups of *Solanum tuberosum* (Dodds 1962; Spooner et al. 2007).

The International Code of Nomenclature for Cultivated Plants (ICNCP) has devised a classification system for cultivated plants where cultivars are placed in groups. The cultivar groups are not based on morphological or biochemical differences but rather on traits which are of use to agriculturalists. In lay terminology cultivars are often referred to as varieties. Using the criteria of the ICNCP, all landrace populations of cultivated potatoes (primitive indigenous cultivars) were recently recognized as a single species, *Solanum tuberosum*, with the following eight cultivar groups: Ajanhuiri, Andigenum,

Chaucha, Chilotanum, Curtilobum, Jucepczukii, Phureja, and Stenotomum (Huamán and Spooner 2002).

Spooner and his coworkers (2007) have proposed a reclassification of Hawkes's list of seven cultivated species into four. To maintain the names that are still most common in the literature for cultivated species, we have used Hawkes's (1990, 1994) nomenclature in this book, even though many compelling recent publications by David Spooner (at the University of Wisconsin-Madison) and his colleagues will almost certainly lead to substantial changes in potato names in the future.

 **CHAPTER 13**

History of the Potato in Europe and North America

Now a staple food in Europe and North America, the potato was originally grown at high altitudes in the Andes. How it made the journey from South America to Europe, and then eventually to North America, is the subject of this chapter.

Europe

There is no specific document which records the introduction of the potato to Europe. Jean-Henri Fabre's well-known quote from the nineteenth century about the origin of wheat is equally applicable to potatoes:

> History celebrates the battlefields whereon we meet our death, but scorns to speak of the plowed fields whereby we thrive; it knows the names of kings' bastards but cannot tell us the origin of wheat. This is the way of human folly.

Several legends and myths surround the introduction and subsequent early history of the potato in Europe. This is partly the result of the early confusion between the potato and the sweet potato and other tuber- and root-forming plants. One legend has it that the potato was introduced into Europe by Sir Walter Raleigh who in turn had obtained it from his colony which he called

"Virginia" (now North Carolina). This is incorrect because Raleigh never visited Virginia.

Another story has it that the potato was introduced into England by Sir Francis Drake. On a trip in 1586 Drake had stopped in Virginia and picked up survivors of Raleigh's colony on Roanoke Island. Thomas Hariot, a famous mathematician and one of the colonists Drake brought back to England, later became farm manager of an estate in Ireland owned by Raleigh. It has been suggested that Drake took potatoes from Virginia to England. However, there is no evidence that potatoes were growing in Virginia at that time. In his description of the Virginia settlement, Hariot described several roots but not potatoes. If Drake did have potatoes on board on the return from his 1585–86 trip then they might have come from Cartagena, Colombia, which he had plundered that winter. Nevertheless, it is possible that Raleigh and Hariot were involved in taking the potato from England to Ireland, but not taking the potato from Virginia to England (Hawkes 1990).

The confusion about the potato having been introduced from Virginia to England was exacerbated by the English botanist John Gerard (1545–1612). In his famous *Herball, or Generall Historie of Plantes* published in 1597, Gerard stated that the potato had come from Virginia where it was growing naturally. This in turn created a misconception which still lives on today. There are several cloak-and-dagger stories surrounding Gerard and his methods and possible motives; Gerard may have been one of several people who invested in Raleigh's Virginia. His scientific ability was questioned by his peers who also accused him of plagiarism and inaccuracy (Reader 2008).

Canary Islands as a Gateway to the European Continent

The first known written record of potatoes in Europe was in 1567 when potatoes were sent from Grand Canary Island to Antwerp. They may have been introduced to the Canary Islands a few years earlier to develop an export crop but there is no record of that. The first record of potatoes on the continent is from 1573 when they were recorded on a list of purchases by a hospital in Seville, Spain (Hawkes et al. 1993).

As discussed in chapter 12, there are two theories about where in South America the European potato originated. One hypothesis is that it came from the Andean highlands, possibly Colombia, and was of a short-day adapted, Andigena type. Evidence in support of this theory includes the earliest illustrations of potato plants in herbals which show plants with much foliage and flowers but with small tubers and many stolons. This is typical when short-day adapted plants are being grown in long-day environments. The above-mentioned records of the hospital in Spain also suggest that the potatoes which were purchased by the Hospital de la Sangre were of the short-day type. Most of the purchases were made in December of 1573 and continued into January of the following year. This suggests that the potatoes were not harvested until that time, again consistent with the idea that these were short-day potatoes which matured very late in the long-day environment of Spain (Hawkes et al. 1992).

The other theory argues for a Chilean source, where the potatoes were already long-day adapted before they reached Europe. Evidence from the Canary Islands suggests that there were several introductions of both Andean and Chilean sources. It appears that the Andean germplasm may have been the first to be introduced there and subsequently into Spain, but because the Chilean sources were so much better adapted, they became the dominant germplasm for the early European cultivars (Rios et al. 2007).

Botanical Curiosity for Nearly Two Centuries

It is surprising that it took so long for the potato to become accepted as a food crop in Europe because the Spanish conquistadors who first encountered the potato immediately realized its importance and used it as food for their slaves in the gold and silver mines (Salaman 1949; Reader 2008). Nevertheless, for nearly two centuries the potato was not much more than a botanical curiosity which was maintained primarily in botanical gardens and described in herbals.

A major figure in the study of the potato in Europe was the French botanist Charles de l'Écluse (1526–1609), also known as Carolus Clusius. He was both a court physician and an eminent botanist and is probably best known for having introduced the tulip to the Netherlands. But he is also known as "the potato propagator of the 16th century" (Roze 1899). Clusius had influential friends in many places which enabled him to travel widely and to disburse and promote the potato.

In his monumental herbal *Rarorium plantarum historia* published in 1601, Clusius mentioned that, while he was the court botanist for the Holy Roman Emperor in Vienna in 1588, he received two potato tubers and a fruit from Philippe de Sivry, Prefect of Mons, in Belgium, who in turn had received them under the name of "taratouffli" from a friend of the Papal Legate in Belgium in 1587. In 1589 de Sivry followed this up by sending Clusius a watercolor painting of part of a potato plant and tubers (Plate 182). This is the first pictorial representation of the potato in Europe. Clusius subsequently provided a botanical description and two woodcut illustrations in *Rarorium* (Figure 15).

The name "taratouffli," which implies that the new tubers were grown like truffles, suggests that the potato had come to Belgium from Italy. "Taratouffli" eventually became "Kartoffel" in German. Clusius did not seem to have a very high opinion of potatoes; he found them rather crude, rough, and flatulent. He indicated that he did not know how the potato came to Italy.

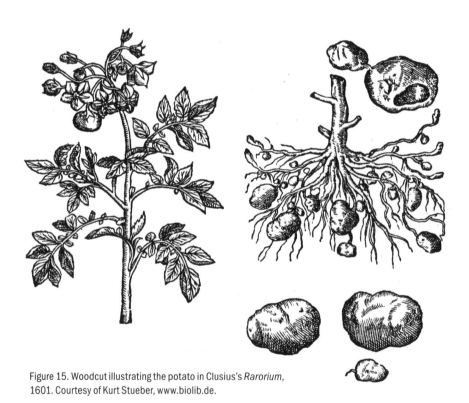

Figure 15. Woodcut illustrating the potato in Clusius's *Rarorium*, 1601. Courtesy of Kurt Stueber, www.biolib.de.

There is now evidence that in Seville, Spain, the potato was being grown in the garden of the "barefooted" Carmelites in the late 1570s. In 1584 the same order founded a monastery in Genova, Tuscany, Italy. In *Storia della patata in Italia* the author (Biadene 1996) described the history of the potato in Italy in great detail and reported that it was these barefooted Carmelites who brought the potato to Italy.

Clusius found it surprising that the knowledge of the potato reached him so late. He reported that the potato was frequently grown in some places in Italy where the tubers were boiled with mutton and eaten like turnips and carrots, and even fed to swine. It was still more surprising to him that the potato was unknown at the prestigious university of Padua since it was already common in many gardens in Germany. This suggests that there was a major disconnect between the circles of academics on the one hand and of practical farmers and gardeners on the other. Although the academics of the day did excellent scientific work in their botanical gardens and herbals, they were apparently out of touch with the local farming communities and had failed to notice the cultivation of a new staple crop.

Potatoes, Politics, and Persecution

The potato appeared on the European scene shortly after the beginning of the Reformation. Thus it should be no surprise that it got caught up in several of those turbulent events. This has been described in detail in the Dutch book of which the translated title is "The Bread of the Poor: The History of the Potato Among Heretics, Monks and Church Princes" (Oliemans 1988). The author of this book suggests that the areas in Italy which Clusius reported to be producing potatoes were the valleys in the Piedmont region of northern Italy where the religious group known as Waldensians had already been farming since shortly after the Reformation. This group was founded in the Middle Ages and was severely persecuted because they displeased the Roman Catholic Church authorities. In their search for religious freedom these refugees naturally took their technology, including the growing of potatoes, with them to their respective new homelands, which included the Netherlands and Switzerland.

A similar situation developed in France where the potato had been grown by progressive Protestant farmers, including Huguenots and Anabaptists. They were protected by the Edict of Nantes which was issued in 1598. This was a major milestone in granting these Protestant groups tolerance in a predominantly Roman Catholic country. However, under the slogan "one king, one law, one faith," the Edict of Nantes was eventually revoked in 1685 and the subsequent persecution of these religious groups resulted in a mass emigration of some of the best French farmers and their agricultural know-how to other countries. The tolerant countries they moved to benefited at the expense of France. It would take another century and the promotional efforts of Antoine Parmentier (see below) before the potato was again recognized for its value in France.

More Hurdles

One of the reasons for the slow acceptance of the potato was, as already mentioned, its initial poor adaptation to the long days during the European growing season, but there were also other reasons. The potato was, at various times, considered to be poisonous and considered to cause various diseases. This was at least in part due to the widespread Doctrine of Signatures, a philosophy promulgated by herbalists for centuries, which held that God marked objects with a sign, or signature, for their purpose. For example, since walnuts resemble brains, they were prescribed as a cure for problems with the brain.

But in the case of the potato this doctrine seems to have been invoked to claim the reverse. Potatoes were at one time thought to cause leprosy, presumably because the rough and irregular shapes of the tubers in those days reminded people of the deformed hands and feet of leprosy patients. Since the fruits of the potato plants resemble the fruits of the poisonous nightshades, it was speculated that the tubers of the potato plant must also be poisonous. Others frowned upon the potato because it was not mentioned in the Bible.

One of the agricultural obstacles standing in the way of widespread potato cultivation was the three-year crop rotation system which was practiced over much of Europe. This system had been introduced by the Romans and lasted until about the end of the eighteenth century. The basic pattern was in the first year to plant winter cereal such as wheat or rye, in the second spring to plant oats or beans and to fallow the land in year three. One advantage of this system was that if the first winter cereal crop failed, possibly as result of unfavorable weather conditions, then another crop could still be planted the following spring.

The one year of fallow gave the land rest and a chance to recuperate. In many countries the village land was divided into three parts with each farmer having a share in each of the three parcels. This meant that an individual farmer was unable to change the crop rotation of his allotment even if he wanted to. Since potatoes did not fit into this system, they could not be cultivated widely until the crop rotation system itself was eventually changed. That occurred when the farming system switched from allowing the cattle to graze on community pastures to keeping them in stables or barns. The resulting production of manure at the stable was then available to fertilize the cropland. The manuring eliminated, at least in part, the need for a year of fallow and thus allowed for the insertion of potatoes and other crops in the rotation system.

Another hurdle was the fact that the potato required a new method of handling. It was the first crop which grew from tubers rather than from seed. Instead of the familiar pattern of scattering handfuls of seed across a seedbed farmers had to plant each seed tuber individually by hand. When food is scarce, why risk experimenting with something as drastically new as potato?

War, Public Relations, and Trickery

Eventually the potato received help from several governments of the day. In Prussia in 1744 Frederick the Great ordered his subjects to grow and eat potatoes. When one town refused—the inhabitants complained that not even the dogs would eat potatoes—he threatened to cut off their ears and noses. There is no evidence that the threat was ever carried out. It was during the Seven Years War (1756–1763) which pitted Prussia against France that the advantages of potato became more apparent. Unlike cereal crops which could be burned or trampled by marauding armies, the potato crop remained in the ground to be harvested after the armies had left.

This benefit was not lost on the French pharmacist Antoine-Augustin Parmentier who had been a prisoner of war in Prussia for several years during the Seven Years War. Parmentier credited the potato for his survival and upon his return to France in 1763 used every opportunity to promote it. He wrote several articles and tracts, including a prize-winning essay in which he extolled the virtues of the potato which, in times of need, could be substituted for the more usual foods, such as grains. In 1763 Parmentier expanded this essay in his *Examen chimique des pommes de terre.*

In the turbulent years leading up to the French revolution Parmentier was an influential figure at the court of Louis XVI and Marie Antoinette. Potatoes were on the royal menu and Marie Antoinette has been said to wear potato flowers in her hair. Benjamin Franklin, the American ambassador to France, attended Parmentier's potato feast in 1767. Parmentier also obtained the king's permission to plant a field on the western edge of Paris with potatoes. As harvest time approached he shrewdly had the field guarded by soldiers during the day. This predictably raised the profile of this crop in the minds of the local population. The curiosity created during the day led to the intended thievery at night!

In 1778, Prussia, still under Frederick the Great, was again at war, this time with Austria (War of the Bavarian Succession, 1778–1779, also known as the Potato War). The opposing generals limited their strategic measures to preventing the enemy from access to their food supply. The war ended when all the locally available potatoes had been consumed!

England and Ireland

The potato probably reached England around 1590. It is not clear when the potato reached Ireland but it was likely around the same time. We have already considered why Sir Walter Raleigh could not have introduced the potato into Europe from Virginia. However, Raleigh may have had a hand in taking the potato from England to Ireland. It is equally possible that the same order of barefooted Carmelites who took the potato from Spain to Italy, may also have taken the potato from Spain to Ireland (Oliemans 1988). The climatic conditions of Ireland were very well suited for its cultivation.

A result of high population density and scarcity of suitable land available to peasants was that the Irish started growing potatoes on marginal land which could not be worked with horse-drawn equipment, typically because it was either too steep or too stony. The system which they developed was known as the "Lazy Bed" system, very much a misnomer because lazy beds were extremely hard to work. The approach involved growing the potatoes on ridges: manure or seaweed was spread on the ground and the seed potatoes were laid on top. Then a foot-wide (30-cm) strip of sod or soil on either side of the line of seed potatoes was cut free and placed over the seed potatoes. During the growing season the trenches might be dug deeper and the new soil added to the ridges. This system was particularly suitable in areas where the layer of top soil was very shallow. It also provided drainage in wet soils and enabled the soil to warm up faster. Although this system was abandoned long ago, in some places in Ireland and Scotland traces of the ridges can still be seen today.

The practice of growing potatoes (and other vegetables) on raised beds is still in use by home gardeners in many places around the world. The lazy bed system has been particularly popular in some areas of the Atlantic provinces in Canada, especially Newfoundland (Omohundro 2006). It is of interest to note that a similar system of growing potatoes on raised beds was used around Lake Titicaca (Peru and Bolivia) thousands of years ago. It appears that Andean and Irish farmers were confronted with similar problems regarding soil and weather conditions. Both groups faced the same need to produce food by the safest, easiest, and quickest means possible (Salaman 1949).

Irish Potato Famine

In addition to the favorable climatic conditions, the socio-economic conditions in Ireland were also favorable for the cultivation of the potato. Much of the best Irish agricultural land was owned by predominantly Protestant absentee landowners, many of whom lived in England. Their agents rented out small parcels of land at high prices to local predominantly Catholic peasants. With the decisions about what to grow in Ireland being made in England, Ireland was, in effect, an agricultural colony of England. The primary crop grown in Ireland was grain which was exported to England, even during the famine years. It is therefore no surprise that the potato quickly became the main food for the large Irish farm families who only had a very small amount of land from which to extract a living. Thus, by necessity, the potato was adopted much faster there than elsewhere in Europe.

The second half of the eighteenth century was the golden age of the potato in Ireland. The expansion of potato production coincided with, and may have contributed to, a population explosion in Ireland. Between 1760 and 1840 the population of Ireland increased from 1.5 to 9 million, an increase of 600 percent in 80 years (Hobhouse 1987). Very quickly the potato became so interwoven with the lives of the Irish that around the world it became known as the "Irish potato."

The Irish population was so dependent on the potato that when the late blight disease attacked the crop for several successive years in the 1840s, the result was the catastrophic Irish potato famine—*An Gorta Mór*, "The Great Hunger." At the time British economic policy was dominated by a laissez-faire philosophy which in turn delayed relief efforts. The famine resulted in the death of more than one million from starvation and associated diseases such as cholera and typhus. At least another million Irish refugees emigrated, mostly to North America (Woodham-Smith 1962).

The Birth of Modern Plant Pathology

If there is a silver lining in this disastrous famine then it was the debate among scientists about the cause of this plant disease, which eventually led to the birth of modern plant pathology. At that time diseases were thought to be caused by spontaneous generation rather than by microorganisms. Regarding late blight there were several different views about its cause. Some opined that the disease was caused by the devil; others that it was a punishment by God. Yet others thought that the disease was caused by the "puffing, hooting locomotives that thundered up and down the countryside at the unholy speeds of 20 miles per hour" which were "discharging electricity into the air."

One of the major debaters was John Lindley, professor of botany and the editor of the prestigious *The Gardeners' Chronicle and Agricultural Gazette*. He maintained that the "Potato Murrain" was caused by environmental factors such as rain. This position was quite common at the time; the germ theory of disease had not yet been proposed. It was not until the early 1860s that the French scientist Louis Pasteur proved germs are the cause rather than the consequence of disease.

Lindley was opposed by Miles Berkeley, a clergyman and amateur biologist who had observed the fungus microscopically on potato leaves and named it *Botrytis infestans*. Berkeley made the at-the-time amazing suggestion that this might be the cause of the disease. This was revolutionary thinking. Both Lindley and Berkeley published their heated arguments in *The Gardeners' Chronicle*, but Berkeley was unable to provide further proof of his ideas.

The matter was eventually settled in 1861 by the German scientist Anton de Bary, the father of modern plant pathology. De Bary grew two groups of potato plants. One of these groups he infected with spores of diseased plants while maintaining the other group healthy. The answer was very clear; only the infected group became diseased. De Bary renamed the fungus *Phytophthora infestans*, the terrible plant destroyer. We now know that Lindley was wrong in his views that the late blight fungus was a consequence rather than the cause of the disease. But we now also recognize that the spread of this disease is greatly enhanced by environmental factors such as humidity and temperature.

Copper as a Fungicide

In the middle of the nineteenth century the Welsh town of Swansea had several copper smelters. In the summer of 1846 someone reported to *The Gardeners' Chronicle* that the copper smoke from the smelter in his neighborhood seemed to have an inhibiting effect on the late blight disease. Potatoes growing within 200 yards (180 m) of the smelter were free from the disease. Lindley did not recognize this for what it was and interpreted it as simply one environmental factor suppressing another one. Nevertheless, it is somewhat of a mystery that it would take another forty years until it was finally realized that copper can control plant diseases such as late blight. This happened in 1885 in the Bordeaux region of France when it was discovered that a mixture of copper sulfate and lime could be used to control downy mildew on grapes. Several more years went by until the now famous Bordeaux mixture was applied to control late blight on potatoes (Reader 2008). It is still in use today, sometimes spelled as Bordo, especially in organic potato production.

"Curl"

Long before the outbreak of late blight it became apparent in several countries by the middle of the eighteenth century that potatoes degenerated from one year to the next. The reasons for this were not clear but initially it was given the name of "curl" because the leaves tended to curl, or roll. Subsequent crops planted with tubers harvested from infected crops produced increasingly lower yields, hence the idea that potato cultivars would degenerate over time. The problem became so severe that by the 1770s it was feared that potato cultivation would have to cease at several locations in western Europe.

As was the case with late blight, a debate ensued in the learned societies about the cause of the degeneration. Some held to the idea that the disease had something to do with poor climatic or soil conditions at the location where the potatoes were grown. Others were convinced that the problem was due to stress and weakness from old age or fatigue. This led to the development of many new cultivars to replace the old ones. Indeed new cultivars initially had very little curl but after a few years they also would degenerate.

It would take one and a half centuries after the serious problems in the 1770s before the mystery of curl was finally solved. In 1905 a German scientist coined the term *leafroll disease*. Later the English acronym PLRV (potato leafroll virus) was applied but, of course, giving it a name did not solve the problem. In 1916 Dutch researchers discovered that curl was an infectious disease. Since they could not find any microscopic organism which might cause this disease they suggested it was caused by a virus. Yet, it was rather hard to convince others that it existed since it could not be seen with a light microscope. Also, it remained unclear how such a virus could be transmitted from one plant to another.

It took another four years until the loop was finally closed: PLRV is transmitted from sick to healthy plants by certain aphids feeding on the plants. This finding also explained why potatoes grown in some areas "degenerated" much faster than those grown in other locations. Seed potatoes derived from crops grown in areas at higher elevations or in cooler, more northern locations were much healthier than those grown in warmer or more southern regions. The reason for this difference now became clear: the higher elevations and cooler northern regions had fewer aphids. Nevertheless, it took several more decades before the "virus theory" was generally accepted. This is no surprise. Since the electron microscope did not come on to the scene until the 1930s, the existence of a virus could not be proven.

We now recognize that, since potato is vegetatively propagated, it is prone to virus diseases that can be spread from the mother tuber to daughter tubers. PLRV is the most important potato virus disease worldwide. The discoveries about the cause and transmission of PLRV and other potato viruses subsequently led to effective control measures which basically are twofold: the control of the aphid carrier of the virus and the removal of the source of infection, namely, plants that are already infected. These principles are now embedded in the seed potato certification systems of virtually all seed potato producing countries.

North America

The potato was probably introduced into North America on several occasions. An unconfirmed report has it that in 1623 the captain of an English trading ship gave a barrel of potatoes to the early settlers in Port Royal in Nova Scotia. In 1685 William Penn, describing Pennsylvania for potential immigrants, included potatoes in a long list of crops which did well there (Zuckerman 1998). In 1719 a group of Scottish Presbyterian immigrants from Northern Ireland settled in Londonderry, New Hampshire, and among the goods they brought with them was the potato. Although this group of settlers is often credited with the introduction of the potato to general use in North America, it appears from the above that they may not have been the first.

By 1750 the potato had become a prominent food in the colonies. George Washington had potatoes planted on his estate in 1767; Thomas Jefferson ate potatoes as early as 1772 and listed them in his farm journal for 1794 (Zuckerman 1998). By 1939 the New England states, New York, Pennsylvania, and New Jersey, were the leading potato-growing states; New York alone raised 30 million bushels—about 1600 tons (Bidwell et al. 1925). In 1837 Henry Spalding was the first to grow potatoes in Idaho. The initial crop was so poor that he had to save virtually all of it for seed potatoes the following year. But soon things turned around and the next year he had a bountiful crop (Davis 1992).

If there was an introduction of the potato into Nova Scotia in 1623, then it did not result in cultivation of the crop. There is no record of potato cultivation there until 1725. The first record of potato production in Prince Edward

Island comes from a 1771 report sent by the first colonial governor to England in which he described the potato crop as a "phenomenal success."

Peter Kalm, a student of Linnaeus, the founder of modern taxonomy, traveled across North America from 1748 to 1751. His diaries include some interesting observations about potatoes. While visiting Albany, New York, in 1749 he observed that potatoes were planted there "by almost everyone" (Wilson 1959). In the same year, while visiting the St. Lawrence settlements in Canada, Kalm noted (Sulte 1893; Laufer 1938):

> Few people took notice of potatoes, and neither the common nor the Bermuda ones [by this he meant sweet potatoes] were planted in Canada. When the French here are asked why they do not plant potatoes, they answer that they cannot find any relish in them, and they laugh at the English who are so fond of them.

Potato Mania

The late blight also attacked the potato crop on this side of the Atlantic. In the decades following the famine in Ireland there was a flurry of activity to find new cultivars which would be resistant to this disease. As new cultivars came to the market they were accompanied by unrealistic expectations that they would deliver great results to the farming community. This in turn drove up the price of seed potatoes of new cultivars to the point that by 1868–69 one new cultivar ('King of the Earlies') fetched $50 per tuber! Henry Ward Beecher (1870), who described this potato mania, mused: "Prospectors, with pick and pan, may do very well in the Rocky Mountains, but the true way to dig for gold in New York State, is to let your potatoes do it for you." However, not all potato breeders became wealthy.

Chauncey Goodrich of New York, whom Beecher called "the pioneer and patriarch of the New Kingdom of Potatoes," died a pauper. He was completely devoted to finding a cure for the late blight disease and spared no effort or expense towards this end. During his twenty years of breeding activity (1843–1863) Goodrich raised sixteen thousand seedlings. One of these, 'Garnet Chili', a daughter of 'Rough Purple Chili', features prominently in the pedigrees of most North American and many European cultivars. For example,

'Early Rose', an offspring from 'Garnet Chili' (Plate 183), is the female parent of 'Russet Burbank', and 'Irish Cobbler' is a reputed mutant of 'Early Rose'.

Potato Contests

In the fall of 1868 W. T. Wylie of Bellefonte, Pennsylvania, offered "The $100 Prize Essay on the Cultivation of the Potato." The prize was awarded in 1870 to D. H. Compton of Hawley, Pennsylvania. His 28-page essay contains many comments which are still applicable today. When he published this essay Wylie also published an article by Pierre Blot on "How to Cook the Potato." Both are delightful reads (Compton et al. 1870).

Another promoter of potatoes was Elbert Carman, editor of *The Rural New Yorker*. Among his achievements on the potato scene are his book *The New Potato Culture* (1891) and the creation of the 'Rural New Yorker No. 2' cultivar (Plate 184). Carman also carried out his own private experiments on acreage he referred to as the "Rural Experiment Grounds." In North America, just as in Europe in the latter part of the nineteenth century, the expectation was that potatoes would degenerate over time. To counteract this Carman raised large numbers of seedlings from true potato seed. He wondered why farmers rarely ever tried this and gave advice on how to do it. In 1888, after selecting among thousands of seedlings for 12 years, he decided to release 'Rural New Yorker No. 2' and offered a tuber free of charge to any subscriber of his newspaper who asked for it (Plaisted et al. 1987).

Carman also experimented with several crop management techniques and was not shy about reporting his negative results along with the positive ones. He was a strong advocate of the trench system where potatoes were planted in a shallow trench and subsequently hilled similar to today's practice but a new method of growing potatoes in his day. So confident was Carman of this new trench method that in 1888 he wagered $50 that he would be able to harvest 700 bushels per acre (about 15 tons per hectare). The money was to go for a benevolent purpose. A committee of judges was appointed who determined that the yield was only 583 bushels per acre (about 13 tons per hectare). So Carman lost his $50, but this initial failure did not deter him from proposing a second contest in the following year. This time he wagered $200. Fortunately for him there were no takers, because his yield again fell well short.

In 1888 Carman offered through his magazine the Women's National Potato Contest. The total amount of prize money was $1000 which went in sums of $150 and less to wives of American farmers for the largest yields of potatoes to be produced on not less than one-fortieth of an acre (about 100 square meters). There were over one thousand entries. He must have been elated when the trench system finally yielded over 700 bushels per acre. This happened in another competition, organized by *American Agriculturalist*; in this contest the prescribed area was not less than one acre (0.4 hectare). The first prize of $1100 went to a farmer from Presque Island, now Presque Isle, Maine. As time went on, Carman became well aware of the danger of extrapolating yield data from small plots, an issue today's experimenters also have to heed.

Colorado Potato Beetle

The potato beetle occupies an interesting place in North American potato history. It was first discovered in 1811 in the Rocky Mountains where it was feeding on buffalo-bur (*Solanum rostratum*), a wild relative of the potato. The 10 stripes across the back of the adult are responsible for it receiving the scientific name of *Leptinotarsa decemlineata*. The common name Colorado potato beetle is really a misnomer because it did not originate in Colorado. Instead it is believed to have come from Mexico. For a while it was known by different names such as potato bug, ten-lined beetle, and ten-striped spearman. The entomologist C. V. Riley was the first in 1867 to coin the term Colorado potato beetle.

The beetle's appetite for potato was not known until 1859 when it started devouring potatoes 100 miles (160 km) west of Omaha, Nebraska, planted there by early settlers. It then started its march eastwards, often hitchhiking along the newly built railroads. On average it moved about 85 miles (136 km) per year. By 1874 it had reached the East Coast. In 1870 it crossed the Detroit River into Canada and by 1883 it had reached Prince Edward Island.

The rather photogenic adult beetles have been featured in some of the most unusual places (Plate 185). In the 1870s the adult beetle had such a high profile in society that for a few years black-and-yellow-striped evening gowns were fashionable. A picture of the beetle has also been featured on the postage stamps of many countries.

During or immediately after World War I the beetle became established around American military bases near Bordeaux, France. By World War II it had spread across much of Europe. During World War II the German government claimed that American planes were dropping potato beetles over Germany. After the war, the East German government, under Soviet occupation, also blamed the Americans for dropping potato beetles. The propaganda was reinforced by the publication of a large number of posters and tracts (Alyokhin 2008).

Return to Europe via Acadian Expulsion

As stated earlier, the potato sometimes spread across Europe as a stowaway in the luggage of (religious) refugees. For similar reasons, the potato was reintroduced into France from North America. The reintroduction is attributed to Acadians, the inhabitants of a French colony in the region now occupied by the Canadian Maritime Provinces of Nova Scotia, New Brunswick, and Prince Edward Island. The Acadians had migrated to this area from France in the seventeenth century. They were a very industrious group and were noted for their diking of salt marshes. At the Treaty of Utrecht in 1713 Acadia was granted to Britain. The British suspected that the Acadians remained loyal to France and considered them a security risk because they refused to swear an oath of allegiance to the British crown. This came to a head in 1755 when Britain ordered the expulsion of Acadians from their homeland. Thousands of Acadians were uprooted; many ended up in Louisiana, others returned to France. Those who returned to France introduced the potato to their new settlements in Bretagne (Sulte 1983), well before Parmentier got the credit for "introducing" it into that country.

Garden Crop in Fur Trading Posts and Mission Stations

The garden plots of fur traders and early missionaries often contained potatoes. In 1779 Peter Pond, one of the founders of the Northwest Company, later absorbed by the Hudson Bay Company, grew potatoes and other vegetables at the now-abandoned Pond's Fort, 30 miles (48 km) up the Athabasca River from Lake Athabasca. This was probably the first attempt by a person of European descent at agriculture in Alberta. The Methodist mission post in Victoria, Alberta, was one of many mission stations where potatoes were being grown. They were often traded and used as relief food for indigenous peoples when the large buffalo herds disappeared. In the middle of the nineteenth century the potato already occupied an important place in the culture of several First Nations along the West Coast (Suttles 1951).

Spanish Explorers, Russian Fur Traders, and First Nations on the West Coast

There is evidence that not all potatoes cultivated in North America are derived from those grown in Europe. Some were directly imported from South America. After conquering South America the Spanish were seeking to reinforce their position on the West Coast. In the summer of 1792 they established a fort at what is now known as Neah Bay in northwest Washington; however, they abandoned it within a few months. It appears that the Spanish explorers had established a garden, presumably including potatoes, which the native Makah people found after the Spanish left and have grown ever since. The Makah named the potato 'Ozette' after one of their villages. Although the Makah have been growing 'Ozette' for more than two centuries, it was relatively unknown until it was "discovered" by the "outside world" in the 1980s.

It had been assumed that the Spanish had brought 'Ozette' directly from Peru. Recent molecular fingerprinting indicates that this is probably not the case but that it likely originated in Chile and came to Neah Bay via Mexico (Zhang et al. 2009). A cultivar grown by the Tlingit ('Maria's Potato') and one grown by the Haida ('Kasaan') in southeast Alaska are genetically closely related to 'Ozette' and may have a similar background.

Another source of potatoes on the West Coast may have been Russian fur traders. It has been suggested that the cultivar 'Banana' (synonym 'Russian Banana') may have been introduced in British Columbia (where it has been grown for a very long time) by Russian fur traders who traded with local peoples and early settlers (Coffin et al. 1993).

APPENDIX 1

Sources for Seed Potatoes

The various seed potato certification agencies can provide information where seed potatoes of specific cultivars may be available.

Seed Potato Certification Agencies in the United States

In the United States seed potato certification is a state jurisdiction. Although there are some differences between the systems used in the various states, they are highly similar in nature.

Alaska Plant Materials Center
5310 South Bodenberg Loop Road
Palmer, Alaska 99634
(907) 745-8724
www.dnr.state.ak.us/ag/ag_pmc.htm

California Crop Improvement Association
Parsons Seed Certification Center
One Shields Avenue
University of California
Davis, California 95616
(530) 754-9649, fax (530) 752-4735
www.ccia.ucdavis.edu

Colorado Potato Certification Service
San Luis Valley Research Center
0249 East Road 9 North
Center, Colorado 81125
(719) 754-3496, fax (719) 754-2619
www.colostate.edu/Depts/PCS

Idaho Crop Improvement Association
1680 Foote Drive
Idaho Falls, Idaho 83402
(208) 522-9198, fax (208) 529-4358
www.idahocrop.com

Maine Department of Agriculture
28 State House Station
Augusta, Maine 04333
(207) 287-3891, fax (207) 287-7548
www.state.me.us/agriculture/pi/
    mspb/#Sliverskip

Michigan Seed Potato Association
4355 Whitehouse Trail
P.O. Box 1865
Gaylord, Michigan 49734
(989) 732-4433, fax (989) 732-4770
www.mipotato.com/mspa

Minnesota Department of Agriculture
312 4th Avenue NE
East Grand Forks, Minnesota 56721
(218) 773-4956, fax (218) 773-4959
www.mnseedpotato.org

Montana State University Seed Potato Certification Program
223 Plant Growth Center
Montana State University
P.O. Box 172060
Bozeman, Montana 59717
(406) 994-3150, fax (406) 994-6042
www.montanaspud.org

Nebraska Potato Certification Association
190 Brayton Road
P.O. Box 339
Alliance, Nebraska 69301
(308) 762-1674, fax (308) 762-1674
www.nebraskapotatoes.com

New York State Foundation Seed Potato Program
Cornell University
334 Plant Science Building
Ithaca, New York 14853
(607) 254-8243, fax (607) 255-4471

North Dakota State Seed Department
P.O. Box 5257
Fargo, North Dakota 58105
(701) 231-5435, fax (701) 231-5401
www.nd.gov/seed/potato/
    potatoseedcertification.aspx

Oregon Seed Certification Service
Oregon State University
31 Crop Science Building
Corvallis, Oregon 97331
(541) 737-4513, fax (541) 737-2624
www.seedcert.oregonstate.edu

Utah Crop Improvement Association
4855 Old Main Hill
Logan, Utah 84322
(435) 797-2082, fax (435) 797-3376
www.utahcrop.org

Washington State Department of Agriculture
Plant Services Program
1111 Washington Street
P.O. Box 42560
Olympia, Washington 98504
(360) 902-1984, fax (360) 902-2094
www.agr.wa.gov/PlantsInsects/default.htm

Wisconsin Seed Potato Certification Program
2960 Neva Road
P.O. Box 328
Antigo, Wisconsin 54409
(715) 623-4039, fax (715) 623-6970
www.potatoseed.org/contact.cfm

University of Wyoming
Department of Plant Sciences
Box 3354
University Station
Laramie, Wyoming 82071
(307) 766-2397, fax (307) 766-5549

Seed Potato Certification in Canada

Canada has one nationwide system for seed potato certification conducted by the Canadian Food Inspection Agency (CFIA), with several regional offices.

CFIA Headquarters
59 Camelot Drive
Ottawa, Ontario K1A OY9
(613) 773-7162; (800) 442-2342

CFIA Ontario Area
Guelph District Office
259 Woodlawn Road W, Suite A
Guelph, Ontario N1H 8J1
(519) 837-9400

CFIA Quebec Area
Plant Health and Biosecurity Directorate
Room 671-D
2001 University Street
Montreal, Quebec H3A 3N2
(514) 283-8888

CFIA Atlantic Area—New Brunswick,
    Nova Scotia, Prince Edward Island,
    Newfoundland and Labrador
Federal Building
1081 Main Street
PO Box 6088
Moncton, New Brunswick E1C 8R2
(506) 851-7400

CFIA Western Area—British Columbia,
    Alberta, Saskatchewan, Manitoba
1115 57 Avenue NE
Calgary, Alberta T2E 9B2
(403) 292-4301

Selected Sources for Home Garden Seed Potatoes in North America

In addition to the sources listed here, many local garden centers carry seed potatoes.

American Seed Company
6051 Carlton Avenue
Spring Grove, Pennsylvania 17362
www.americanseedco.com

Dick Bedlington Farms
8497 Guide Meridian
Lynden, Washington 98264
www.bedlingtonfarms.com

Eagle Creek Seed Potatoes
Range Road 14
Bowden, Alberta
Canada T0M 0K0
www.seedpotatoes.ca

Fedco Seeds
P.O. Box 520
Waterville, Maine 04903
www.fedcoseeds.com

Garden City Seeds
5045 Robinson Canyon Road
Ellensburg, Washington 98926
www.gardencityseeds.net

Hope Seeds
P.O. Box 130
Glassville, New Brunswick
Canada E7L 4T4
www.hopeseed.com

Johnny's Selected Seeds
955 Benton Avenue
Winslow, Maine 04901
www.johnnyseeds.com

Maine Potato Lady
P.O. Box 65
Guilford, Maine 04443
www.mainepotatolady.com

Ronniger Potato Farm
12101 2135 Road
Austin, Colorado 81410
www.ronnigers.com

Seed Savers Exchange
3094 North Winn Road
Decorah, Iowa 52101
www.seedsavers.org

Seeds of Change
3209 Richards Lane
Santa Fe, New Mexico 87507
www.seedsofchange.com

Seeds of Diversity Canada
P.O. Box 36, Stn Q
Toronto, ON M4T 2L7
www.seeds.ca

Territorial Seed Company
20 Palmer Avenue
Cottage Grove, Oregon 97424
www.territorialseed.com

Tucker Farms
Hobart Road
Gabriels, New York 12939
www.tuckertaters.com

Veseys
P.O. Box 9000
Charlottetown, Prince Edward Island
Canada C1A 8K6
www.veseys.com

Wood Prairie Farm
49 Kinney Road
Bridgewater, Maine 04735
www.woodprairie.com

Selected Sources for True Potato Seed in North America

Amazon
www.amazon.com

ECHO (Educational Concerns for Hunger
   Organization) Book and Seed Store
www.echobooks.org/

Nichols Garden Nursery
Albany, Oregon 97321
www.nicholsgardennursery.com.

Territorial Seed Company
20 Palmer Avenue
Cottage Grove, Oregon 97424
www.territorialseed.com

APPENDIX 2

Organizations and Newsletters

Canadian Horticultural Council (CHC)
www.hortcouncil.ca

A voluntary national association representing various sectors of Canadian horticulture, including potatoes.

Global Potato News
www.potatonews.com

A free monthly electronic newsletter.

International Potato Center
www.cipotato.org

An international agricultural research center which seeks to reduce poverty and achieve food security on a sustained basis in developing countries through scientific research and related activities on potato, sweet potato, and other root and tuber crops.

National Potato Council (NPC)
www.nationalpotatocouncil.org

Advocates for the economic well-being of United States potato growers on federal legislative, regulatory, environmental, and trade issues.

Potato Association of America (PAA)
http://potatoassociation.org

A professional society for those interested in advancing the potato industry. The website includes information on most topics discussed in this book, including cultivars, soils, seed potatoes, crop management, pest management, organic production, and storage. Publications include *North American Potato Variety Inventory*, *Variety Images and Descriptions*, *American Journal for Potato Research*, and *Insider: Newsletter of the PAA*.

PotatoNet
http://lists.oregonstate.edu/mailman/listinfo/potatonet

An e-mail forum to discuss and share potato-related issues. Sponsored by the Oregon State University Potato Program and the Potato Association of America.

United States Potato Board (USPB)
www.uspotatoes.com

A marketing organization for United States potatoes and potato products. Publications include nutritional information and recipes.

APPENDIX 3

Potato Names

The etymology (study of origins and development of words) of potato names can be of great help in understanding the history and spread of the potato. The most ancient names for potato come from the Aymará and Quechua languages. Aymará is spoken primarily around Lake Titicaca; Quechua was the official language of the Inca Empire.

Papa The most common word for potato in South America is the Quechua word *papa*. Originally used in the Inca Empire, this word was later adopted by the Spanish conquistadors who spread it further throughout South America and also took it to Europe. *Papa* is the name that was used by early European botanists, but this name did not stick in Europe, presumably because in Italian and Spanish the name is also used to refer to the Pope.

Potato The name *potato* is derived from *batata* which was (and still is) the Spanish name for sweet potato. The relationship between the names *batata* and *potato* has been the principal cause of a great amount of confusion regarding the origin and spread of the potato. Batatas were already grown in the West Indies when the Europeans first arrived there. From there the sweet potato was taken by British colonial merchants (and pirates!) to Virginia and eventually to Britain. It was for a long time erroneously believed that the potato was taken by Sir Francis Drake from Virginia to Britain when, in reality, as described in chapter 13, the potato was first introduced into Spain and subsequently spread to the rest of Europe.

Spud There is some controversy around the origin of the name *spud*. Some believe that, in an effort to warn the Irish not to eat too many potatoes, the Society for the Prevention of Unwholesome Diet was formed and that the word *spud* came from the first letters in the Society's name.

Another, and perhaps more likely explanation is that the term *spud* originally meant some kind of spade or digging fork, especially the kind used for digging potatoes (Salaman 1949).

Truffle In Italy potatoes were harvested the same way as truffles, an edible underground fungus, and hence they became known as *tartuffoli*. From this evolved the German *Tartuffel* and eventually *Kartoffel*. The Russian and Polish *kartofel* was, in turn, derived from *Kartoffel*.

Earth Apple and Earth Pear In some countries the potato became known as *earth apple* or *earth pear*. Examples of *earth apple* are the French *pomme de terre* and the Dutch *aardappel*. The *earth pear* concept can be traced via the German *Grundbirne* to *krumpir* in several Slavic languages, the Pennsylvania-Dutch *krumbeer* and similar names in many other languages. The Polish *ziemniaki* means "from the earth."

Bulb Several Slavonic peoples in Eastern Europe seem to have obtained one of their names for potato from the Greek and/or Latin word for *bulb* (Latin: bulbus), a term used in both languages for any swollen root or tuber, especially vegetables. This can be explained by the fact that throughout the Turkish Empire trade was carried on by Greek and Jewish merchants. The Ukrainian word for potato is *bulba*. The Russian *gulba*, the Czech *barabol*, and the Yiddish *boulbé* are also derived from the same root word (Salaman 1949).

Horse Bell, Earth Bean, and Foreign Taro There are several names for potato in China. This is not surprising considering the size of the country, its population, and the fact that China now produces more potatoes than any other country in the world. Some of the most common names are *malingshu* which means horse bell, *tudou* (earth bean), and *yangyu* (foreign taro).

Colorful Indian Cultivar Names

Both the Quechua and Aymará languages have many names for potatoes. For wild potatoes alone there are 15 names in Quechua and 10 in Aymará, each describing a different kind of potato. For cultivated potatoes there are many more names, often referring to specific cultivars, and they can be quite descriptive. In addition to color, shape and taste, these names may also invoke gender, animal and human body parts, tools, and other concepts.

The Aymará 'Huila Imilla' means "Red Girl" and 'Saq'ampaya' means "Long Male Potato." The former has a red and the latter a white skin. Red potatoes are usually considered female while white ones are associated with maleness. 'Saq'ampaya' is one of four different cultivars featured on a set of Bolivian postage stamps issued in 2008 commemorating the International Year of the Potato.

An example of invoking an animal name is the Quechua 'Katari Papa' which means "Snake Potato"; the shape resembles a snake. A rather amusing name is the Quechua 'Cachan huacachi' which means "Potato Which Makes the Daughter-in-Law Cry." It is apparently so named because it has very deep eyes that makes it difficult to peel (Hawkes 1947).

Colorful European and North American Cultivar Names

Potato salespeople have often been creative in choosing cultivar names to facilitate marketing. Colorful old North American cultivar names include 'Beauty of Hebron', 'Earliest of All', 'Flower of Eden', 'King of the Roses', 'Member of Parliament', 'Mortgage Lifter', 'Pride of the Table', 'Rot Proof', 'Silver Dollar', 'Wonder of the World' and so on (Johnston n.d.).

As can be expected, evocative cultivar names are not restricted to the English language. In French we can find 'Géant Sans Pareille' ("Unequalled Giant"), 'Belle de Fontenay' ("Beauty of Fontenay"), 'Incomparable', and 'Bonne Wilhelmine'.

The Dutch have invoked female beauties in potato cultivar names such as 'Cleopatra' and 'Monalisa'. The current list of North American cultivars includes names such as 'Cupids', 'Dakota Rose', 'Mirton Pearl' and 'Goldrush'.

The German cultivar 'Ackersegen' ("Acres' Blessing") has a religious connotation. No doubt the linguistic wealth of names for the potato reflects some measure of the esteem in which it is held by farmers, gardeners, and consumers around the world.

Synonyms and Homonyms

Occasionally a single cultivar is known by many names (synonyms); less often the same name (homonym) is used for different cultivars. This problem is not new. In the early part of the twentieth century synonyms presented a major problem to the potato industry; it was very easy to simply rename an old cultivar and make it appear like a new one. This was especially the case with popular cultivars. So, in a sense, one could measure a cultivar's success by the number of synonyms it had!

In the United Kingdom the problem of synonyms was so bad that in 1919 the National Institute of Agricultural Botany appointed a Potato Synonym Committee to sort out the mess. In 1920 Dr. Salaman became the chairman of this committee. In his well-known history book (1949) he mentions some of the struggles against seed potato trade organizations which his committee had to endure before the problem of synonyms was finally solved.

Today the seed potato certification and cultivar registration systems in Europe and North America have, to a large extent, cut problems with cultivar names to a minimum. The registration systems typically require proof that a particular cultivar is unique, which in turn prevents the proliferation of synonyms. Certification systems also ensure that cultivars are "true to type" and that only "healthy" seed potatoes are marketed. Unfortunately, potato cultivars produced in limited volumes are often produced outside of these regulatory systems. This in turn can lead to situations where enterprising merchants may promote old cultivars under a new name. As mentioned in chapter 2, 'All Blue' is the current "prize-winner" when it comes to the number of synonyms. It has at least 17 synonyms or purported synonyms.

Fortunately homonyms are not as widespread, although they do occur. For example, several other (yellow-fleshed) cultivars are sometimes marketed as "Yukon Gold." In this case the problem seems to be primarily with potatoes offered for consumption rather than with seed potatoes.

APPENDIX 4

Stamps, Museums, and Monuments

Many countries have featured the potato on one or more of their postage stamps, another indication of the potato's global esteem. These stamps illustrate various aspects of the history, cultivation, rural economy, research, utilization and art of the potato. Canada issued a stamp in 2000 (Plate 186) recognizing the McCain Food Company, reportedly the world's largest producer of frozen french-fried potatoes, while an older (1940) U.S. stamp (Plate 187) honored Luther Burbank.

With the rich history and culture of the potato it is no surprise that there are several potato museums around the world. Four of these are in North America, including one on Prince Edward Island (Plate 188). Of the five potato museums in Europe, one is devoted exclusively to french fries, and in the Netherlands a monument is dedicated to the Dutch cultivar 'Bintje' (Plate 189).

The Potato Museum
Albuquerque, New Mexico, United States
www.potatomuseum.com

Idaho Potato Museum
Blackfoot, Idaho, United States
www.potatoexpo.com

Potato World Museum
Centreville, New Brunswick, Canada
www.potatoworld.ca

Prince Edward Island Potato Museum
O'Leary, Prince Edward Island, Canada
www.peipotatomuseum.com

Erdaepfelmuseum
Prinzendorf a.d. Zaya, Austria

Frietmuseum
Brugge (Bruges), Belgium
www.frietmuseum.be/en/

Petit musée de la pomme de terre
Troussey/Lorraine, France
http://www.balado.fr/balades/
    petit-musée-pomme-terre

Kartoffelmuseum
Munich, Germany
www.kartoffelmuseum.de

Vorpommersches Kartoffelmuseum
Tribsees, Mecklenburg-Vorpommern,
    Germany
www.m-vp.de/2730/museum_1.htm

Glossary

amylopectin: A type of starch having a highly branched arrangement of glucose molecules. Generally potato starch consists of about 80 percent amylopectin and 20 percent amylose. For certain industrial processes pure amylopectin starch is preferred. For this purpose some amylose-free (amf) cultivars have been developed.

amylose: A type of starch having a linear arrangement of glucose molecules.

anthocyanin: Water-soluble red, blue, and purple pigments which occur in the flowers, tubers, and other tissues of some potato cultivars. Anthocyanins are potent antioxidants.

antioxidant: A substance that slows down the oxidation of oils and fats in the body; considered to have health benefits ranging from delaying eye degeneration to the prevention of heart and blood diseases, cancer, and aging.

apical dominance: Inhibition of the growth of lateral buds by the terminal (apical) bud of a stem. In the case of potatoes (which are really stems) the eyes (buds) at the apical end of the seed tuber possess dominance over the other eyes and will normally sprout first. As the tubers age the apical dominance gradually diminishes.

backcross: A cross of a hybrid with one of its parents.

bolter: A potato mutant which affects response to day length. This is usually a reversion back to a shorter critical day length (CDL). Such plants are easily identified in large fields because they are later maturing than the other plants of the same cultivar. Also known as "giant hills."

cambium: A cylindrical layer of tissue in the stems and roots, consisting of cells that divide rapidly to form new layers of tissue.

carotenoids: Organic pigments imparting yellow to orange color. Most carotenoids have antioxidant activity.

CDL: See *Critical Day Length*.

chitting: See *green sprouting*.

chloroplast: A chlorophyll-containing subunit in plants that is the site of photosynthesis. Also contains a very small amount of DNA that can be useful in genetic studies.

chromosome: A structural unit in the nucleus of a cell which carries the genes in a linear array. The number of chromosomes in a cell is constant in any species.

chuño: A freeze-dried potato product traditionally made by Quechua and Aymará civilizations in the Andean highlands of South America. The resulting product can be stored for a year or longer.

cleft: V-shaped cut in the rootstock portion of a graft.

clone: A group of plants originating by vegetative propagation from a single plant. In potatoes all cultivars are clones (except those rare cultivars that are grown from true potato seed).

corolla: The flower petals as a unit.

cortex: In potato tubers a narrow band of storage tissue between the skin (periderm) and the outer medulla or storage parenchyma.

Critical Day Length (CDL): For potatoes this is the day length which triggers tuber initiation. Cultivars have different critical day lengths. Tuber initiation begins when the day length is shorter than a cultivar's CDL.

cultivar: A cultivated plant that has been selected and given a name because of its useful characteristics. The word is a contraction of the term *cultivated variety* and in a general sense it is synonymous with variety.

determinate growth: Development of new potato foliage terminates at tuberization. In other plants, such as tomatoes, termination of growth is associated with flower/fruit formation. Some cultivars are determinate, others indeterminate, and many somewhere in between.

dormancy: A physiological stage during which there is no measurable sprout growth. Several factors control dormancy: genetics, storage temperature, and previous growing conditions. True potato seed is usually dormant for several months.

dry matter content: A measure of solid content. Potato tubers contain approximately 80 percent water; the remainder, mainly starch, is referred to as dry matter.

epidermis: The outermost layer of cells. Usually colorless. In potato tubers the skin consists of the epidermis and the underlying periderm.

epiphyte: A plant growing on another non parasitically.

ex situ: Off-site. The term is used in relation to the preservation of potato germplasm in genebanks which are located outside of the area where the germplasm was initially found. The opposite is preservation *in-situ* (on-site).

flavonoid: A naturally occurring plant compound with antioxidant properties.

gamete: A reproductive cell that unites with another gamete during sexual reproduction. In plants male gametes are pollen and female gametes are egg cells.

genebank: A collection of potentially useful potato species which contain genes of significance to potato breeding. Genebanks represent a treasure chest of potentially useful traits that may someday be bred into new cultivars.

genetic erosion: Loss of wild and primitive cultivated species. In the case of wild species this is primarily a result of a change in their natural habitat and, in the case of primitive cultivars, replacement by modern cultivars.

germplasm: Collective term for genetic stocks.

giant hill: See *bolter*.

Glycemic Index (GI): A ranking of carbohydrates according to their effect on blood glucose levels.

glycoalkaloids: Naturally occurring compounds in potatoes and other plants that play a role in resistance to insects and diseases. Glycoalkaloids are bitter compounds that in high concentrations may be toxic. They are present in potato foliage, flowers, fruits, sprouts, and green portions of tubers exposed to sunlight.

green sprouting: A practice of storing seed potatoes at warm temperatures and light exposure to produce short stubby sprouts. Also referred to as chitting, and pipping.

heirloom cultivar: Old cultivar. In general, for a cultivar to be considered heirloom, it should be at least 50 years old. Synonym for heritage cultivar.

heritage cultivar: See *heirloom cultivar*.

homonym: Same name used for different cultivars.

interspecific crossability: Ability of different species to produce viable progeny when crossed with each other. This is one measure of relatedness between different species.

in situ: On-site. The term is used in relation to the preservation of potato germplasm in areas where the germplasm was initially found. The opposite is preservation *ex-situ* (off-site).

in vitro: Literally "in glass." In the meristem culture method of producing seed tubers, disease-free microplants are grown in glass test tubes.

indeterminate growth: Growth that continues indefinitely. Opposite of determinate growth.

landrace: Early cultivated clones, usually evolved from wild species. See also primitive cultivar.

leaf hairs: Virtually all potatoes have leaf hairs (trichomes) but some have many more than others. Of particular interest are glandular leaf hairs (such as in the wild species *S. berthaultii*). At the tip of these hairs are glands which contain a sticky substance that can "glue" small insects coming in contact with them.

lenticels: Breathing pores on the surface of the tuber skin. They serve the same function as stomates on the leaves.

medulla: Storage tissue. Potato tubers have an outer and an inner medulla. The outer medulla, also called storage parenchyma, is the principal storage tissue of the tuber. The inner medulla, or pith, extends toward each eye, forming continuous tissue that connects all the eyes of the tuber.

mutation: Sudden change in the hereditary material of a cell. Many mutations are difficult to detect with the naked eye. In potato the exceptions are changes in tuber skin color or texture and response to day length because they are easily detected in commercial fields.

narrow genetic foundation: Only a very small sample of the great genetic diversity among potato cultivars in the Andes was introduced into Europe. The derivatives of these introductions subsequently spread around the rest of the world and are the genetic basis upon which most of our cultivated potatoes are "built."

organelles: Subcellular structures (e.g., chloroplasts in plants) carrying out various functions in plants and animals.

parasitic: Plant or animal living in or on a host and obtaining nutrition from it.

pathogen: A disease-causing organism.

periderm: Several layers of corky cells immediately below the epidermis. Anthocyanin pigment that colors red and blue potatoes, if present, is in the periderm.

photosynthesis: The process of converting sunlight, carbon dioxide and water into plant sugars and oxygen.

physiological age: Primarily a measure of sprout development in the seed tuber. After genetic control of sprouting has taken its course, factors such as temperature determine how fast tubers age. As storage temperatures increase above 40°F (4°C) the physiological age of tubers increases proportionally. Physiological age also affects internal quality of tubers.

pistil: The female reproductive organ of flowers.

pith: Central part of the tuber which branches out to the eyes. See *medulla* (inner).

polymer: A compound consisting of a chain of repeating units. Amylose and amylopectin are polymers of the simple sugar glucose.

photoperiod: Often referred to as day-length effect. In fact it is more commonly a response of flowering or tuberization to length of darkness.

primitive cultivar: Indigenous cultivar derived from and more refined than landrace.

prostrate: A plant growth habit in which the plant growth is close to the ground (not erect).

respiration: The process of taking in oxygen and converting carbohydrates into energy, carbon dioxide, and water.

rhizome: Stem that grows horizontally below ground and sends out roots and shoots from its nodes. See also stolon.

rootstock: The lower portion of a graft.

russet: Coarse-textured, usually brownish skin.

scion: The upper portion of a graft.

selective herbicide: A chemical that will kill certain plants but not affect others.

skin set: The firming and hardening of the tuber periderm (skin) which provides a barrier that reduces moisture loss and mechanical damage.

slough: Tubers break apart upon cooking

specific gravity: Estimate of dry matter content. There are several methods for determining the specific gravity of tubers. The most common one is using a scale and weighing the same tuber sample in air and in water. The formula is: [weight in air] divided by [(weight in air) minus (weight in water)].

stamen: The male reproductive organ of flowers.

stolon: In a strict botanical sense a stolon is a stem that grows horizontally above ground and which produces new plants from buds at its tips. However in potato under ground stems are referred to as stolons. Tubers are formed at the tips of stolons. A stolon not covered by soil develops into a normal stem with leaves. See rhizome.

stomate: Breathing pore. Mostly located on the underside of leaves but also present on stems.

storage parenchyma: The principal storage tissue in a potato tuber. See medulla (outer).

synonym: Different name for the same object, such as a different name for the same cultivar.

suberin: Waxy substance formed on cut surfaces of tubers. Part of the wound healing process.

systemic herbicide: A chemical that enters the plant and kills it by affecting some normal processes within the plant.

taxonomy: The science of classification of plants.

TPS: See *True Potato Seed*.

transpiration: Evaporation from plant tissue, such as from leaves or tubers.

True Potato Seed (TPS): Botanical seed is the means of sexual propagation of potatoes as compared to the standard way of propagation by way of seed tubers. TPS is similar to tomato seed in size and shape.

variety: Synonymous with cultivar.

vascular ring: The vascular ring of the tuber is located between the cortex and the storage parenchyma and consists of phloem and xylem. The vascular system transports carbohydrates, nutrients, and water within the plant.

vegetative propagation: The reproduction of plants without the production of sexually developed seeds. Planting tubers is a form of vegetative propagation also known as asexual propagation.

References

Introduction

Graves, C., ed. 2000. *The Potato, Treasure of the Andes. From Agriculture to Culture.* Lima, Peru: International Potato Center.

Chapter 1: Plant Structure and Function

Huamán, Z. 1986. Systematic botany and morphology of the potato. International Potato Center. Technical Information Bulletin 6. *http://www.cipotato.org/library/pdfdocs/TIBen21132.pdf.* Accessed 01 February 2009.

Nemose. 2008–09. *Solanum tuberosum,* potato. *http://www.geochembio.com/biology/organisms/potato/potato-geochembio-pdf.pdf.* Accessed 06 November 2009.

Chapter 2: Cultivar Descriptions A to Z

Canadian Food Inspection Agency. n.d. Canadian potato varieties descriptions. *http://www.inspection.gc.ca/english/plaveg/potpom/var/indexe.shtml#a.* Accessed 06 November 2009.

Davis, J. W. 1992. *Aristocrat in Burlap. A History of the Potato in Idaho.* Eagle, Idaho: Idaho Potato Commission.

Potato Association of America. 2009. Varieties. *http://potatoassociation.org.* Accessed 06 November 2009.

Washington State University. 2009. Potato varieties and seed potatoes—Catalogs, lists and databases. *http://potatoes.wsu.edu/links/vars.html.* Accessed 25 January 2009.

Chapter 3: Soils and Fertility

Brady, N. C., and R. R. Weil. 2008. *The Nature and Properties of Soils.* New Jersey: Pearson Education.

Clark, A. 2007. Managing cover crops profitably. Handbook Series Book 9. Third edition. Beltsville, Maryland: Sustainable Agriculture Network. *http://www.sare.org/publications/covercrops/covercrops.pdf.* Accessed 15 May 2009.

Gaskell, M., R. Smith, J. Mitchell, S. T. Koike, C. Fouche, T. Hartz, W. Horwath, and L. Jackson. 2007. Soil fertility management for organic crops. Vegetable Research Information Center. Organic Vegetable Production in California Series. University of California, Davis. *http://anrcatalog.ucdavis.edu/pdf/7249.pdf.* Accessed 06 April 2009.

Halseth, D., J. Sieczka, and S. Klausner. 1996. Potato nutrition guidelines. Cornell University Department of Fruit and Vegetable Science Report 57.

Hue, N. V. n.d. Organic fertilizers in sustainable agriculture. College of Tropical Agriculture and Human Resources (CTAHR), University of Hawaii. *http://www.ctahr. hawaii.edu/huen/hue_organic.htm*. Accessed 10 February 2009.

North Carolina Department of Agriculture. n.d. A homeowner's guide to fertilizer. *http://www.agr.state.nc.us/cyber/kidswrld/ plant/label.htm*. Accessed 08 June 2009.

Schonbeck, M., and R. Morse. 2004. Choosing the best cover crops for your organic no-till vegetable system. Rodale Institute. *http://newfarm.rodaleinstitute.org/ features/0104/no-till/chart.shtml*. Accessed 29 May 2009.

Sullivan, P. 2001. Alternative soil amendments. Appropriate Technology Transfer for Rural Areas (ATTRA). *http://attra.ncat. org/attra-pub/PDF/altsoil.pdf*. Accessed 28 March 2009.

Zublena, J. P., V. Baird, and J. P. Lilly. 1997. Nutrient content of fertilizer and organic materials. North Carolina Cooperative Extension Service. Publication AG-439-18. *http://www.soil.ncsu.edu/publications/ Soilfacts/AG-439-18/*. Accessed 18 May 2009.

Chapter 4: Seed Potatoes

Struik, P.C., and S. G. Wiersema. 1999. *Seed Potato Technology*. Wageningen: Wageningen Pers.

Wiersema, S. G. 1985. Physiological development of potato seed tubers. International Potato Center. Technical Information Bulletin 20. *http://www.cipotato.org/ training/Materials/cipp5w5.pdf*. Accessed 29 November 2008.

Chapter 5: Establishing and Maintaining Plants

Andersen, C. R. n.d. Irish potatoes. Home Gardening Series. FSA6016-PD-2-03RV. Cooperative Extension Service. University of Arkansas. *http://www.uaex.edu/Other_ Areas/publications/pdf/FSA-6016.pdf*. Accessed 10 January 2009.

Burton, W. G. 1989. *The Potato*. New York: John Wiley.

Churchill, J., and K. Witthaus. 2004. Growing potatoes in the home garden. Master Gardeners Santa Clara County California. *http://www.mastergardeners.org/ publications/growing_potatoes.html*. Accessed 13 January 2009.

Dean, B. B. 1993. *Managing the Potato Production System*. New York: The Hawthorn Press.

Dwelle, R. B., and S. L. Love. 2003. Potato growth and development. In *Potato Production Systems*. Eds. J. C. Stark and S. L. Love. Moscow, Idaho: University of Idaho. *http://www.ag.uidaho.edu/ potato/PotatoProductionSystems/Topics/ Growth&Development.pdf*. Accessed 24 October 2009.

Farm Extension Services. 2007. Potatoes for the garden. Prince Edward Island Department of Agriculture, Fisheries and Aquaculture. Agdex 208/25. *http://www.governmentofpei. ca/af/agweb/index.php3?number=71617*. Accessed 23 February 2009.

Garden Helper, The. 2000. Growing potatoes in the home vegetable garden. *http://www.*

thegardenhelper.com/potato.html. Accessed 08 April 2009.

Harris, P. M. 1982. *The Potato Crop: The Scientific Basis for Improvement.* New York: Chapman and Hall.

Jauron, R. 2002. Growing potatoes in the home garden. Iowa State University. University Extension. Horticulture and Home Pest News. *http://www.ipm.iastate.edu/ipm/hortnews/2002/3-8-2002/potatoes.html.* Accessed 13 October 2009.

Johnson, S. B. 2009. Growing potatoes in the home garden. University of Maine Cooperative Extension Bulletin 2077: Potato Facts. *http://www.umext.maine.edu/onlinepubs/htmpubs/2077.htm.* Accessed 02 October 2009.

Lamont, W. J. 2008. Growing potatoes: Culture and cultivars. Pennsylvania State University. College of Agricultural Sciences. Agricultural Research and Cooperative Extension. *http://pubs.cas.psu.edu/FreePubs/pdfs/uj245.pdf.* Accessed 09 January 2009.

Lerner, B. R., and M. N. Dana. 2000. Potatoes. Purdue University Cooperative Extension Service. Vegetables HO-62W. *http://www.hort.purdue.edu/ext/HO-62W.pdf.* Accessed 26 March 2009.

Manitoba Agriculture, Food and Rural Initiatives. n.d. Growing potatoes in the home garden. *http://food.cimnet.ca/cim/dbf/growing_potatoesfeb_2007_final_copy.pdf?im_id=448&si_id=43.* Accessed 27 September 2009.

Martin, O. 2008. Potatoes in the home garden. University of California, Santa Cruz. Center for Agroecology and Sustainable Food Systems. *http://repositories.cdlib.org/casfs/fg/potatoes_handout/.* Accessed 25 August 2009.

McLaurin, W. J., D. Adams, and T. Eaker. 2009. Potato production in the home garden. University of Georgia Cooperative Extension Circular 849. *http://pubs.caes.uga.edu/caespubs/pubcd/C849/C849.htm.* Accessed 21 March 2009.

Mississippi State University Extension Service. 2009. Vegetable gardening in Mississippi. Irish potatoes. *http://msucares.com/lawn/garden/vegetables/list/potato.html.* Accessed 25 October 2009.

Mosley, A., O. Gutbrod, S. James, K. Locke, J. McMorran, L. Jensen, and P. Hamm. 1995. Grow your own potatoes. Oregon State University Extension Service. EC 1004. *http://ir.library.oregonstate.edu/jspui/bitstream/1957/13855/1/ec1004.pdf.* Accessed 12 August 2008.

Pack, J. E., J. M. White, and C. M. Hutchinson. 2009. Growing potatoes in the Florida home garden. University of Florida IFAS Extension Publication HS933. *http://edis.ifas.ufl.edu/HS183.* Accessed 25 October 2009.

Polomski, B., D. Bradshaw, and D. Shaughnessy. 2009. Potato. Clemson University. Clemson Extension. HGIC 1317. *http://www.clemson.edu/extension/hgic/plants/vegetables/crops/hgic1317.html.* Accessed 23 October 2009.

Potato Growers of Alberta. n.d. Grow your own potatoes. *http://www.albertapotatoes.ca/files/Grow+your+own+potatoes.pdf.* Accessed 15 January 2009.

Reiners, S., and C. H. Petzoldt, eds. 2004. Integrated crop and pest management guidelines for commercial vegetable production. Chapter 24, Potatoes. Cornell Cooperative Extension. *http://www.nysaes. cornell.edu/recommends*. Accessed 03 October 2009.

Rhodes, D. 2009. Potatoes—HORT410—Vegetable Crops. Department of Horticulture and Landscape Architecture. Purdue University. *http://www.hort.purdue.edu/rhodcv/ hort410/potat/potat.htm*. Accessed 03 October 2009.

Sieczka, J. B., and R. E. Thornton, eds. 1992. *Commercial Potato Production in North America*. Potato Association of America Handbook.

Smith, O. 1969. *Potatoes: Production, Storing, Processing*. Westport, Connecticut: Avi Publishing.

Thompson-Johns, A., S. L. Love, M. K. Thornton, P. Nolte, and W. H. Bohl. 2002. Potato production in the home garden. University of Idaho. College of Agricultural and Life Sciences. CIS 1000. *http:// info.ag.uidaho.edu/pdf/CIS/CIS1000.pdf*. Accessed 14 September 2009.

University of Arizona. 1998. The vegetable garden. In *Arizona Master Gardener Manual: Potatoes*. Arizona Cooperative Extension, College of Agriculture, University of Arizona. *http://ag.arizona.edu/pubs/garden/ mg/vegetable/potatoes.html*. Accessed 20 January 2009.

University of Hawaii at Manoa. n.d. Potato. Farmer's Bookshelf. University of Hawaii at Manoa. Department of Tropical and Plant Sciences. *http://www.ctahr.hawaii.edu/fb/ home.htm*. Accessed 12 December 2008.

University of Illinois. 2009. Potato. Watch your garden grow. University of Illinois Extension. *http://www.urbanext.uiuc.edu/veggies/ potato1.html*. Accessed 19 August 2009.

Wittmeyer, E. C., M. Riofrio, and M. Bennett. 1992. Growing potatoes in the home garden. Ohio State University Extension Fact Sheet HYG-1619-92. *http://ohioline. osu.edu/hyg-fact/1000/1619.html*. Accessed 24 March 2009.

Chapter 6: Pests and Other Problems

Banks, E. 2004. *Potato Field Guide: Insects, Diseases and Defects*. Publication 823. Toronto: Ministry of Agriculture and Food.

Cornell University. 2009. Vegetable MD online. Cornell University Department of Plant Pathology. *http://vegetablemdonline. ppath.cornell.edu/cropindex.htm*. Accessed 26 September 2009.

Draper, M. A., G. A. Secor, and H. A. Lamey. 1994. Management of potato diseases in the home garden, PP-756 (Revised). North Dakota State University. *http://www. ag.ndsu.edu/pubs/plantsci/hortcrop/pp756w. htm*. Accessed 05 September 2009.

Harrison, J. 2009. Potatoes blight. *http://www. allotment.org.uk/vegetable/potato/potato- blight.php*. Accessed 08 May 2010.

Kelly, C. B. 2003. Potato scab in home gardens. University of Guelph Pest Diagnostic Clinic. *http://www.uoguelph.ca/ pdc/Factsheets/Diseases/PotatoScabHome- Gardens.htm*. Accessed 08 June 2009.

Lajeunesse, S. 1997. Potato diseases. Montana State University Extension Service. *http:// diagnostics.montana.edu/PlantDisease/ Topics/DISEA019.htm*. Accessed 27 August 2009.

Lewis, D. 2008. Colorado potato beetle control in the home garden. Iowa State University, University Extension. IC-499(10). *http://www.ipm.iastate.edu/*

ipm/hortnews/2008/6-4/potatobeetle.html. Accessed 26 April 2009.

New Brunswick Department of Agriculture, Fisheries and Aquaculture. 2005. Late blight of potato and tomato in the home garden. *http://www.gnb.ca/0029/00290048-e. pdf.* Accessed 08 May 2010.

Ohlendorf, B., ed. 2008. Pest management guidelines: Potato. University of California. Integrated Pest Management. *http://www. ipm.ucdavis.edu/PDF/PMG/pmgpotato.pdf.* Accessed 23 July 2009.

Strand, L. L., and P. A. Rude, eds. 2006. *Integrated Pest Management for Potatoes in the Western United States.* University of California Publication 3316.

Traunfeld, J. 2003. Late blight of potato and tomato. Home and Garden Mimeo HG38, Maryland Cooperative Extension, University of Maryland. *http://www.hgic.umd.edu/_ media/documents/LateBlightofPotatoand TomatoHG38pfv.pdf.* Accessed 13 June 2009.

Welty, C., and C. W. Hoy. 2009. Colorado potato beetle in the home garden. Ohio State University Extension Fact Sheet HYG-2204-09. *http://ohioline.osu.edu/hyg-fact/2000/pdf/2204.pdf.* Accessed 11 October 2009.

Chapter 7: Growing Potatoes the Organic Way

Berry, R. E. 1998. Damsel bugs. Oregon State University Fact Sheet. *http://uspest.org/ mint/damselid.htm.* Accessed 15 January 2009.

Bostock, M. 2008. *Growing Potatoes Organically from Market Garden to Field Crop.* Ottawa: Canadian Organic Growers.

Diver, S. 2002. Flame weeding for vegetable crops. National Sustainable Agriculture Information Service CT165. *http://attra. ncat.org/attra-pub/flameweedveg.html.* Accessed 09 February 2009.

Grubinger, V. 1997. Ten steps toward organic weed control. University of Vermont Extension. *http://www.uvm.edu/vtvegandberry/ factsheets/orgweedconrtol.html.* Accessed 10 October 2009.

Kuepper, G. 2003a. Colorado potato beetle: Organic control options. National Sustainable Agriculture Information Service CT107. *http://attra.ncat.org/attra-pub/coloradopotato. html.* Accessed 13 August 2009.

Kuepper, G. 2003b. Manures for organic crop production. National Sustainable Agriculture Information Service IP127. *http:// attra.ncat.org/new_pubs/attra-pub/manures. html?id=NewYork.* Accessed 09 March 2009.

Kuepper, G., and P. Sullivan. 2004. Organic alternatives for late blight control in potatoes. National Sustainable Agriculture Information Service. *http://attra.ncat.org/ attra-pub/PDF/lateblight.pdf.* Accessed 19 May 2009.

McCaskill, K. 2006. Producing potatoes organically in Maine. University of Maine Cooperative Extension, Bulletin 2419. *http://www.umaine.edu/umext/ potatoprogram/Fact%20Sheets/organic%20 potatoes.pdf.* Accessed 22 August 2009.

Newton, B. 2004. Damsel bugs. University of Kentucky Department of Entomology. *http://www.uky.edu/Ag/CritterFiles/casefile/ insects/bugs/damsel/damsel.htm#damsel.* Accessed 18 June 2009.

Reiners, S., C. H. Petzoldt, and M. P. Hoffmann, eds. 2004. Resource guide for organic insect and disease management.

http://www.nysaes.cornell.edu/pp/
resourceguide/cmp/solanaceous.php#i6.
Accessed 09 July 2009.

Schonbeck, M. 2009. Plant and manage cover
crops for maximum weed suppression.
Virginia Association for Biological Farming. http://www.extension.org/article/18525.
Accessed 19 September 2009.

Stone, A. 2009. Organic management of late
blight of potato and tomato (*Phytophthora
infestans*). Oregon State University Cooperative Extension. http://www.extension.org/
article/18361. Accessed 05 August 2009.

University of California. 2004. Natural ene-
mies gallery: Minute pirate bugs. University
of California. Integrated Pest Management
Online. http://www.ipm.ucdavis.edu/PMG/
NE/minute_pirate_bug.html. Accessed 20
July 2009.

U.S. Department of Agriculture. 2007. The
national list of allowed and prohibited substances. USDA, National Organic Program.
http://www.ams.usda.gov/AMSv1.0/getfile?d
DocName=STELPRDC5068682&acct=no
pgeninfo. Accessed 14 April 2009.

Weeden, C. R., A. M. Shelton, and M. P.
Hoffman. 2007. Biological control: A guide
to natural enemies in North America. Cornell University. http://www.nysaes.cornell.
edu/ent/biocontrol/. Accessed 04 January
2009.

Chapter 8: Special Techniques for Growing Potatoes

Burbank, L. 1914. The tomato and an interesting experiment: A plant which bore
potatoes below and tomatoes above. In
*Luther Burbank: His Methods and Discov-
eries and Their Practical Application*. Eds.
J. Whitson, R. John, and H. S. Williams. 7:
109–144. http://digital.library.wisc.edu/1711.
dl/HistSciTech.Burbank07. Accessed 03
October 2009.

Healy, S. 2009. Growing potatoes in straw.
Colorado State University Extension Master
Gardener. http://www.colostate.edu/Dept/
CoopExt/4DMG/VegFruit/potatoes.htm.
Accessed 23 July 2009.

McGee, R. M. N., and M. Stuckey. 2002. *The
Bountiful Container*. New York: Workman
Publishing.

Quist, T. 2009. Potato/tomato grafting. Purdue University. Hort 201. Plant Propagation Laboratory Exercise 9. http://www.
hort.purdue.edu/hort/courses/HORT201/
LabHandouts/Lab09_WillowTomato
Potato09.pdf. Accessed 19 October 2009.

Chapter 9: Harvesting and Storing

Bubel, M., and N. Bubel. 1991. *Root
Cellaring: Cold Storage of Fruits and Vege-
tables*. North Adams, Massachusetts: Storey
Publishing.

Kleinhenz, M. 2000. Potato storage management tips. Ohio State University Extension.
http://www.ag.ohio-state.edu/~vegnet/news/
tt200.htm. Accessed 13 June 2009.

Suslow, T. V., and R. Voss. 2009. Potato
(immature early crop). Recommendations
for maintaining postharvest quality. Produce Facts. http://postharvest.ucdavis.edu/
produce/producefacts/veg/potato-early.shtml.
Accessed 24 August 2009.

Woodell, L., N. Olsen, and J. Wilson. 2009.
Options for storing potatoes at home.
University of Idaho Extension. http://
info.ag.uidaho.edu/pdf/CIS/CIS1153.pdf.
Accessed 15 October 2009.

Chapter 10: Uses of the Potato

American Chemical Society. 2007. Two cooks and a bath. *http://acswebcontent.acs.org/landmarks/landmarks/dehydration/cooks.html*. Accessed 12 May 2009.

Beals, K. A. 2005. The glycemic index: Research meets reality. U.S. Potato Board. *http://www.healthypotato.com/Content/pdf/WhitePages/GlycemicIndex-WhitePaper.pdf*. Accessed 14 August 2009.

Brown, C. R. 2005. Antioxidants in potato. *American Journal of Potato Research* 82: 163–172.

Diabetes Network. 2007. Glycemic index. *http://www.diabetesnet.com/diabetes_food_diet/glycemic_index.php*. Accessed 08 June 2009.

Food Innovation Online. 2009. Dehydrated potato products (potato flakes, granules, flour) in the United States. PotatoPro Newsletter. *http://www.potatopro.com/Newsletters/20090420.htm*. Accessed 23 June 2009.

Health Canada. 2007. Eating well. Canada's food guide. *http://www.hc-sc.gc.ca/fn-an/food-guide-aliment/context/index-eng.php*. Accessed 25 September 2009.

Murphy, A. M. 2004. Potatoes with coloured flesh may promote health. Agriculture and Agri-Food Canada. *http://www4.agr.gc.ca/resources/prod/doc/pfra-arap/PDF/rainbow-coloured_potatoes-e.pdf*. Accessed 12 September 2008.

Prokop, S., and J. Alber. 2008. Potato, nutrition and diet. International Year of the Potato 2008. *http://www.potato2008.org/en/potato/factsheets.html*. Accessed 14 July 2009.

Sonnino, A. 2008. Potato and biotechnology. International Year of the Potato 2008. *http://www.potato2008.org/en/potato/biotechnology.html*. Accessed 15 July 2009.

Talburt, W. F., and O. Smith. 1967. *Potato Processing*. Westport, Connecticut: Avi Publishing.

U.S. Department of Health and Human Services. 2005. Dietary guidelines for Americans 2005. *http://www.health.gov/DietaryGuidelines/dga2005/document/default.htm*. Accessed 21 September 2009.

Vodopivec, J., S. Grkman, M. Cernic Letnar, and M. Berovic. 2004. Effect of starch coating during the leaf casting technique. ICOM-CC graphic documents meeting, Ljubljana. *http://www.infosrvr.nuk.uni-lj.si/jana/ICOMd/14JVodopivec.pdf*. Accessed 18 May 2009.

Woolfe, J. A. 1987. *The Potato in the Human Diet*. Cambridge: Cambridge University Press.

Chapter 11: Cultivar Development and Genetic Resources

Bamberg, J. 2009. NRSP-6—United States potato genebank. *http://www.ars-grin.gov/nr6/*. Accessed 16 November 2009.

Burbank, L. 1914. The potato itself—Who will improve it further? In *Luther Burbank: His Methods and Discoveries and Their Practical Application*. Eds. J. Whitson, R. John, and H. S. Williams. 7: 267–302. *http://digicoll.library.wisc.edu/cgi-bin/HistSciTech/HistSciTech-idx?type=turn&entity=HistSciTech001100340016&isize=M*. Accessed 15 March 2009.

Carefoot, G. L., and E. R. Sprott. 1967. *Famine on the Wind: Plant Diseases and Human History*. London: Angus and Robertson.

De Jong, H., K. G. Proudfoot, and A. M.

Murphy. 2001. The germplasm release of F87084, a fertile, adapted clone with multiple disease resistances. *American Journal of Potato Research* 78: 141–149.

DeMuth, S. P. 1998. Vegetables and fruits: A guide to heirloom varieties and community-based stewardship. *http://www.nal.usda.gov/afsic/AFSIC_pubs/heirloom/heirloom.htm.* Accessed 26 February 2009.

Hawkes, J. G. 1947. On the origin and meaning of South American Indian names. *Journal of the Linnean Society of London. Botany* 50: 205–250.

Hawkes, J. G. 2004. *Hunting the Wild Potato in the South American Andes: Memories of the British Empire Potato Collecting Expedition to South America 1938–1939.* Nijmegen, Netherlands: Botanical and Experimental Garden, University of Nijmegen.

Hils, U., and L. Pieterse, eds. 2009. *World Catalogue of Potato Varieties.* Clenze, Germany: Agrimedia GmbH.

Johnston, G. n.d. History of potato varieties in Ontario. Unpublished manuscript.

Kaniewski, W. K., and P. E. Thomas. 2004. The potato story. *http://www.agbioforum.org/v7n12/v7n12a08-kaniewski.htm.* Accessed 10 October 2009.

Large, E. C. 1940. *The Advance of the Fungi.* New York: Henry Holt.

Maxted, N., and J. G. Hawkes. 1997. Selection of target taxa. In *Plant Genetic Conservation: The In Situ Approach.* Eds. N. Maxted, B. V. Ford-Lloyd, and J. G. Hawkes. London: Chapman and Hall.

Plaisted, R. L., W. M. Tingey, and J. C. Steffens. 1992. The germplasm release of NYL 235-4, a clone with resistance to the Colorado potato beetle. *American Potato Journal* 69: 843–846.

Salaman, R. N. 1949. *The History and Social Influence of the Potato.* Cambridge: Cambridge University Press.

Seed Savers Exchange. 2009. Catalog of heirloom seeds, books, and gifts. *http://www.seedsavers.org/pdf/SSE2009.pdf.* Accessed 25 February 2009.

Tarn, T. R., A. M. Murphy, D. H. Wilson, V. J. Burns, and K. G. Proudfoot. 2003. Multiple resistance to diseases in a population of long-day adapted Andigena potatoes. *Acta Horticulturae* 619: 189–194.

Chapter 12: Distribution, Domestication, and Classification

Ames, M., and D. M. Spooner. 2008. DNA from herbarium specimens settles a controversy about origins of the European potato. *American Journal of Botany* 95: 252–257.

Baker, C., and M. Baker. 2008. Day length for various latitudes. *http://www.orchidculture.com/COD/daylength.html.* Accessed 19 August 2009.

Dodds, K. S. 1962. Classification of cultivated potatoes. In *The Potato and Its Wild Relatives.* Ed. D. S. Correll. Renner, Texas: Texas Research Foundation. 517–539.

Flores, H. E., T. S. Walker, R. J. Guimaraes, H. P. Bais, and J. M. Vivanco. 2003. Andean root and tuber crops: Underground rainbows. *HortScience* 38: 161–167.

Foster, N., and L. S. Cordell, eds. 1992. *Chilies to Chocolate: Food the Americas Gave the World.* Tucson, Arizona: University of Arizona Press.

Hawkes, J. G. 1990. *The Potato. Evolution, Biodiversity, and Genetic Resources.* Washington, DC: Smithsonian Institute Press.

Hawkes, J. G. 1994. Origins of cultivated potatoes and species relationships. In *Potato*

Genetics. Eds. J. E. Bradshaw and G. R. Mackay. Wallingford, United Kingdom: CAB International. 3–42.

Hawkes, J. G. 2004. *Hunting the Wild Potato in the South American Andes: Memories of the British Empire Potato Collecting Expedition to South America 1938–1939.* Nijmegen, Netherlands: Botanical and Experimental Garden, University of Nijmegen.

Hijmans, R. J., and D. M. Spooner. 2001. Geographic distribution of wild potato species. *American Journal of Botany* 88: 2101–2112.

Hosaka, K. 2004. Evolutionary pathway of T-type chloroplast DNA in potato. *American Journal of Potato Research* 81: 153–158.

Hougas, R. W., and R. W. Ross. 1956. The use of foreign introductions in breeding American potato varieties. *American Potato Journal* 33: 328–339.

Huamán, Z., J. G. Hawkes, and P. R. Rowe. 1980. *Solanum ajanhuiri*: An important diploid potato cultivated in the Andean Altiplano. *Economic Botany* 34: 335–343.

Huamán, Z., and D. M. Spooner. 2002. Reclassification of landrace populations of cultivated potatoes (*Solanum* Sect. *Petota*). *American Journal of Botany* 89: 947–965.

Incas, The. n.d. Inca agriculture. *http://incas. homestead.com/inca_agriculture.html.* Accessed 09 November 2009.

Lechnovitch, V. S. 1971. Cultivated potato species. In *Flora of Cultivated Plants.* Ed. S. M. Bukasov. Leningrad: Kolos. 9: 41–302.

Lyon, P. J. 1989. *Lost Crops of the Incas: Little-known Plants of the Andes With Promise for Worldwide Cultivation.* Washington, DC: National Academies Press.

Reader, J. 2008. *Propitious Esculent: The Potato in World History.* London: William Heinemann.

Rios, D., M. Ghislain, F. Rodriguez, and D. M Spooner. 2007. What is the origin of the European potato? Evidence from Canary Island landraces. *Crop Science* 47: 1271–1280.

Simmonds, N. W. 1976. Distribution of the tuber-bearing species of *Solanum.* In *Evolution of Crop Plants.* Ed. N. W. Simmonds. London: Longman. 279–283.

Spooner, D. M., K. McLean, G. Ramsay, R. Waugh, and G. J. Bryan. 2005. A single domestication for potato based on multilocus amplified fragment length polymorphism genotyping. *Proceedings of the National Academy of Sciences* 102: 14694–14699.

Spooner, D. M., J. Nunez, G. Trujillo, M. del Rosario Herrera, F. Guzman, and M. Ghislain. 2007. Extensive simple sequence repeat genotyping of potato landraces supports a major reevaluation of their gene pool structure and classification. *Proceedings of the National Academy of Sciences* 104: 19398–19403.

Spooner, D. M., and A. Salas. 2006. Structure, biosystematics, and genetic resources. In *Handbook of Potato Production, Improvement, and Postharvest Management.* Eds. J. Gopal and S. M. P. Khurana. New York: Haworth Press.

Spooner, D. M., A. Salas Lopez, Z. Huamán, and R. J. Hijmans. 1999. Wild potato collecting expedition in Southern Peru Departments of Apurimac, Arequipa, Cusco, Moquega, Puno, Tacna in 1998: Taxonomy and new genetic resources. *American Journal of Potato Research* 76: 103–119.

Sukhotu, T., and K. Hosaka. 2006. Origin and evolution of Andigena potatoes revealed by chloroplast and nuclear DNA markers. *Genome* 49: 636–647.

Woolfe, J. A. 1987. *The Potato in the Human Diet*. Cambridge: Cambridge University Press.

Chapter 13: History of the Potato in Europe and North America

Alyokhin, A. 2008. History. *http://www.potato-beetle.org*. Accessed 27 February 2009.

Beecher, H. W. 1870. The potato mania. In *Best's Potato Book*. Ed. G. W. Best. Utica, New York: G. W. Best. 5–23.

Biadene, G. 1996. *Storia della Patata in Italia*. Bologna: Avenue Media.

Bidwell, P. W., and J. I. Falconer. 1925. *History of Agriculture in the Northern United States*. Washington, DC: Carnegie Institution.

Carman, E. S. 1891. *The New Potato Culture: As Developed by the Trench System*. New York: The Rural Publishing Company. Reprinted in 2008 by BiblioBazaar.

Coffin, R., M. K. Keenan, D. Lynch, A. McKeown, J. Wilson, G. A. Nelson, and R. Yada. 1993. Banana: a yellow-fleshed fingerling type potato for home garden production. *American Potato Journal* 70: 1–5.

Compton, D. H., and P. Blot. 1870. The $100 prize essay on the culture of the potato; and how to cook the potato. *http://www.gutenberg.org*. Accessed 10 February 2009.

Davis, J. W. 1992. *Aristocrat in Burlap. A History of the Potato in Idaho*. Eagle, Idaho: Idaho Potato Commission.

Hawkes, J. G. 1990. *The Potato. Evolution, Biodiversity, and Genetic Resources*. Washington, DC: Smithsonian Institute Press.

Hawkes, J. G., and J. Francisco-Ortega. 1992.
The potato in Spain during the late 16th century. *Economic Botany* 46: 86–97.

Hawkes, J. G., and J. Francisco-Ortega. 1993. The early history of the potato in Europe. *Euphytica* 70: 1–7.

Hobhouse, H. 1987. *Seeds of Change: Five Plants That Transformed the World*. New York: Harper and Row.

Laufer, B. 1938. *The American Plant Migration. Part I: The Potato*. Chicago: Field Museum of Natural History.

Oliemans, W. H. 1988. *Het Brood van de Armen: De Geschiedenis van de Aardappel Temidden van Ketters, Kloosterlingen en Kerkvorsten* [The Bread of the Poor: The History of the Potato Among Heretics, Monks, and Church Princes]. The Hague: SDU Publisher.

Omohundro, J. 2006. An appreciation of lazy beds. *www.newfoundlandquarterly.ca/issue420/lazy_beds.php*. Accessed 20 February 2009.

Plaisted, R. L., and R. W. Hoopes. 1987. The origin of Rural New Yorker No. 2. *American Potato Journal* 64: 41–46.

Reader, J. 2008. *Propitious Esculent: The Potato in World History*. London: William Heinemann.

Rios, D., M. Ghislain, F. Rodriguez, and D. M Spooner. 2007. What is the origin of the European potato? Evidence from Canary Island landraces. *Crop Science* 47: 1271–1280.

Roze, E. 1899. *Charles de l'Escluse d'Arras. Le Propagateur de la Pomme de Terre au XVIe siècle. Sa Biographie et sa Correspondance* (Charles de l'Escluse of Arras. The potato propagator of the 16th century. His biography and his correspondence). Paris:

J. Rothschild and J. Lechevallier. Reprinted in 1976 by Landré et Meesters b.v. and Kew Books.

Salaman, R. N. 1949. *The History and Social Influence of the Potato.* Cambridge: Cambridge University Press.

Sulte, B. 1893. La pomme de terre. *Revue Canadienne* 29: 84–92.

Suttles, W. 1951. The early diffusion of the potato among the coast Salish. *Southwestern Journal of Anthropology* 7: 272–288.

Wilson, M. T. 1959. Americans learn to grow the Irish potato. *The New England Quarterly* 32: 333–350.

Woodham-Smith, C. 1962. *The Great Hunger.* New York: Old Town Books.

Zhang, L., C-P. Yang, D. Andrade, C. Smith, H. Denney, N. Ward, D. Culley, and C. R. Brown. 2009. A study of the origin of the Ozette potato from the Makah nation in the Pacific Northwest using SSR markers. *http://www.ars.usda.gov/research/publications/publications.htm?SEQ_NO_115=_ 173191.* Accessed 11 December 2009.

Zuckerman, L. 1998. *The Potato: How the Humble Spud Rescued the Western World.* Boston: Faber and Faber.

Statistics

U.S. Department of Agriculture. 2008. U.S. potato statistics. USDA, Economic Research Service. *http://usda.mannlib.cornell.edu/MannUsda/viewDocumentInfo.do?documentID=1235.* Accessed 01 September 2009.

U.S. Department of Agriculture. 2009. Food availability (per capita) data system: Food availability spreadsheets. USDA, Economic Research Service. *http://www.ers.usda.gov/ Data/FoodConsumption/ FoodAvailSpreadsheets.htm#potatoes.* Accessed 05 October 2009.

Potato Cookbooks

Ashcraft, S. 2004. *101 Things to Do With a Potato.* Salt Lake City: Gibbs Smith.

Australian Women's Weekly. 2003. Potatoes. *Australian Women's Weekly.* Sydney: ACP Publishing.

Barker, A. 2008. *Potato—150 Fabulous Recipes: A Definitive Cook's Identifier to Potatoes.* London: Lorenz Books.

Brown, S. 2002. *The Williams-Sonoma Collection: Potato.* New York: Free Press.

Cordon Bleu Chefs, Le. 1998. *Potatoes.* Berkeley, California: Periplus Editions.

Coyle, E. 2001. *Irish Potato Cookbook.* Dublin: Gill & Macmillan.

Finamore, R. 2001. *One Potato, Two Potato: 300 Recipes from Simple to Elegant.* Boston: Houghton Mifflin.

Gayler, P. 2001. *A Passion for Potatoes: 150 Culinary Treats, from Classic to Contemporary.* London: Kyle Cathie.

Hogan, J., ed. 1982. *The All-American Potato Cookbook.* Elmsford, New York: Benjamin Company.

Lauterbach, B. 2002. *Potato Salad: Fifty Favorite Recipes.* San Francisco: Chronicle Books.

Mansfield, S. 2000. *Potato.* London: Lorenz Books.

Marshall, L. 1992. *A Passion for Potatoes.* London: Harper Perennial.

McNair, J. 1989. *James McNair's Potato Cookbook.* San Francisco: Chronicle Books.

Nichols, A. 2003. *Potatoes.* London: Ryland Peters & Small.

Paré, J. 2001. *The Potato Book.* Edmonton: Company's Coming Publishing.

Parragon Publishing. 2002. *Quick and Easy Potatoes.* Bath, United Kingdom: Parragon Publishing.

Patil, M. 2005. *The Ultimate Potato Cookbook.* New York: Penguin Group.

Reeves, J. 1997. *The Potato Cookbook.* Gretna, Louisiana: Pelican Publishing.

Reynolds, S. 1997. *50 Best Mashed Potatoes.* New York: Broadway.

Siegel, H. 2000. *The Totally Potato Cookbook.* Berkeley, California: Celestial Arts.

Toews-Andrews, A. 1985. *The Incredible Potato. A Cookbook and History.* Trenton, Ontario: Toews Andrews Publishing.

Weinstein, B., and M. Scarbrough. 2003. *The Ultimate Potato Book: Hundreds of Ways to Turn America's Favorite Side Dish into a Meal.* New York: Harpercollins.

Index